Death of an Assassin

TRUE CRIME HISTORY SERIES

DEATH OF AN ASSASSIN

The True Story of the German Murderer
Who Died Defending Robert E. Lee

Ann Marie Ackermann

THE KENT STATE UNIVERSITY PRESS
Kent, Ohio

To the city of Bönnigheim

and three of my favorite inhabitants,

Dieter, Alexander, and Dennis

What atonement is there for blood spilt upon the earth?

—Aeschylus

Contents

Preface: The Murder Case That Broke All the Rules

After a murder, the investigative clock starts ticking.

Back in the early nineteenth century, if detectives couldn't solve a murder case within the first few weeks following the crime, they weren't going to solve it at all. They were forced by both the rules of evidence and the lack of modern forensic techniques to rely primarily on witness statements and confessions. And if suspects or witnesses didn't talk during the early phases of the investigation, they were unlikely to talk at all. With modern DNA analysis, it is now possible to solve cases that are decades old. But two centuries ago, solving a case that old was unprecedented. When cases went cold, they stayed cold.

Two hundred years ago, investigators found their solutions in the town or region in which the victim or offender lived. And it was usually a law enforcement officer who solved the case.

But there was one nineteenth-century murder case that broke all those rules. The murder occurred in Germany, but it was solved in Washington, D.C. It was Germany's only nineteenth-century murder case to be solved in America apart from a confession. It wasn't an investigator who solved it, but a civilian—nearly four decades after the murder.[1]

If you dig deeper, you will find that the case left its fingerprints on history. This murder mystery is set against the backdrop of the antebellum United States and the first battle of one of the most beloved Civil War heroes of U.S. history, Robert E. Lee.

It is also the story of the birth of forensic ballistics. In his zeal to identify the murder weapon, the German investigator assigned to this case stumbled upon an investigative technique fifty years before it was supposedly invented. He may have been the first man in history to employ ballistic finger-printing in a murder case.

It was birds that led me to this case. Bird-watching has been my hobby since childhood; as an adult, I have published a handful of academic articles based on my observations and private research. In 2013, I offered to write an article about the history of local birdlife in my German town for the local historical society journal, based on archival material referencing birds within the town limits and in our municipal forest, orchards, and vineyards. Kurt Sartorius, the society's chairman, handed me a transcript of an unpublished forester's diary from the nineteenth century. "Surely," he said, "the forester mentioned birds somewhere in here."

There, between his sightings of kingfishers on the brook behind the palace and his hunting excursions for woodcock and hazel grouse in the surrounding woodland, the forester detailed a murder investigation. He had found, in the forestry department archives, evidence to corroborate the solution to an assassination of a mayor, committed almost forty years prior. The assassin had fled to America and the solution had come from Washington, D.C.

That diary entry spurred the former American prosecutor in me to further research. Who in my German town would be better qualified to tackle this case than I would, as an American with a background in criminal law and as a German-to-English legal translator? With an eye toward a second article for the historical society, I located the original German investigative file in the Baden-Württemberg state archives in Ludwigsburg and began tracking the assassin through the American archives. My research took me on two trips to Philadelphia's archives; I also hired several researchers to assist me with archival research in other parts of the country. Their names are in the acknowledgments.

This nineteenth-century true crime investigation pulls back the curtains on two of the least explored chapters of American history. One is covert immigrant criminals. "My" assassin did what many German criminals of the time did when faced with the prospects of capture and the death penalty in the country of his birth. He fled to the United States. It was a risk; criminals often fled illegally, without papers, with falsified ones, or possibly with assumed names. A dark wave of unreported immigration statistics, they nevertheless became part of the American heritage. Once in the United States, they sought to blend in, hoping their past would cease to haunt them from across the vast expanse of the Atlantic. They certainly didn't admit their deeds to the American authorities. For that reason, we know little about them today. Only rarely did the true reasons for their immigration find their way into government files and statistics.[2] In this case, it is the interlocking puzzle pieces of both German and American archives that finally haul the assassin's secret, spitting and baring its claws, into the light and set it squarely into the United States' antebellum legacy. His story offers us a rare glimpse into the life of a nineteenth-century immigrant criminal, self-exiled in the United States.

This murder case also illuminates one of the least explored aspects of the Mexican-American War in 1846–48: the role of German soldiers. It was a multicultural American army that fought that war, a war in which the United States acquired almost a third of its current territory.[3] Thousands of immigrants enlisted; so many, in fact, that without their participation it is questionable whether the American army would have been able to accomplish what it did. About 40 percent of the recruits for the regular army consisted of immigrants, mostly Irish and German.[4] Although the volunteer militia contained higher percentages of native-born participants, it boasted all-German companies from Missouri[5] and Ohio.[6] The assassin enlisted in a company from Pennsylvania considered exclusively German.[7]

Although Irish soldiers in the Mexican-American War have received scholarly attention, very little has been published about the role of German soldiers in the war. What has appeared consists primarily of three diaries by German participants and one set of letters. None of those authors were in Pennsylvania's all-German company. Of those publications, only one diary and the set of letters have been translated into English.[8] The assassin, to my knowledge, didn't leave behind any diary or letters that survived. But his story, reconstructed from the archives, other soldiers' diaries, and even Robert E. Lee's letters, adds to the historical literature on German soldiers. This is the second book-length account of a German participant to appear in English.[9]

I did not expect the assassin to lead me to Robert E. Lee. But when he did, it became clear that this is more than just a German murder mystery. This is American history. And it's my highest pleasure to share this story with you.[10]

Acknowledgments

It is impossible to conduct research of this sort without assistance from a number of people, who in one sense are the real heroes of this book because they helped bring this story to light.

In Germany, the following people and institutions offered help and advice without which this book would have never seen fruition: Kurt Sartorius (Historische Gesellschaft Bönnigheim), Dr. Hermann Stierle (Archiv des ev. Pfarramts Bönnigheim), Helga Engster-Möck (Stadtarchiv Bönnigheim), Kornelius Bamberger (mayor of Bönnigheim), Albrecht Hartmann (Stadtarchiv Schwaigern, Gemeinde Stetten am Heuchelberg), Annette Schuhkraft and Pfarrer Martin Bulmann (ev. Pfarramt Stetten am Heuchelberg), Dr. Martin Häußermann and Wolfgang Schneider (Landesarchiv Ludwigsburg), Wolfram Berner, M.A. (Kreisarchiv Ludwigsburg), Hans-Peter Rosenberger (ev. Pfarramt Kirchheim am Neckar), Volker Schäfer (Landeskriminalamt Baden-Württemberg), Joachim Stark (Polizeiposten Bönnigheim), Sandy Krüger (Stadtarchiv Besigheim), Elisabeth Biechl, Axel Pantermühl, Adalbert Schmezer, Markus Beck, Horst Seizinger, and Larissa Leibrock-Plehn, as well as the employees of the Hauptstaatsarchiv Stuttgart, Staatsarchiv Ludwigsburg, Stadtarchiv Heilbronn, Stadtarchiv Ludwigsburg, and the Württembergische Landesbibliothek in Stuttgart.

The images of the crime scene sketch and the Frederick Rupp letter are reprinted with permission of the Landesarchiv Baden-Württemberg, Staatsarchiv Ludwigsburg; the photograph of Christoph Ulrich Hahn with permission of the Württembergische Landesbibliothek Stuttgart, Graphische Sammlungen; the images of pellets and rifling with permission of

Volker Schäfer, Landeskriminalamt Baden-Württemberg; the photograph of Mayor Rieber's grave with permission of Jochen Richter; the topographical map with the permission of the Landesamt für Geoinformation und Landentwicklung Baden-Württemberg; and the photograph of the Rieber gravestone with Mayor Bamberger with permission of both the mayor and the photographer, Inge Hermann. Special thanks go to Inge Hermann for her assistance in formatting the images. To the city of Schwaigern, for permission to quote from its book, *Schwaigern, Heimatbuch der Stadt Schwaigern*, I express my thanks as well.

Learning to read the old German handwriting was critical to this research, and I thank Dr. Hermann Stierle, Helga Engster-Möck, Elisabeth Biechl, Hans-Peter Rosenberger, and Dr. Jürgen Ackermann for their assistance in teaching me and deciphering difficult portions of German archival texts.

Because it wasn't convenient to fly to the United States every time I had a research question, I had the assistance of several researchers at various institutions. Special thanks to Gail McCormick, Dorothy Clark, Michael Blaakman, James M. Beidler, and Ralph Elder. Lee Shepherd (Virginia Historical Society), Randy Hackenburg, Glenn F. Williams, Donald A. Clark, Wallace L. McKeehan, and Andrew Hazekamp also fielded occasional questions. During my research trips to the United States, David Baugh (Philadelphia Archives), Chrissy Bellizzi and Bettina Hess (Horner Library of the German Society of Pennsylvania), and the staff of the Historical Society of Pennsylvania and Huntington Library graciously offered their help.

Textual material from Robert E. Lee correspondence is reprinted with the permission of the Virginia Historical Society, the quote from Douglas Southall Freeman's *R. E. Lee* with the gracious permission of Simon & Schuster, and the quote from Michael Korda's *Clouds of Glory* with the gracious permission of HarperCollins. The University of North Carolina permitted me to quote from the diary of Daniel Harvey Hill. The image of the Robert E. Lee letter is reproduced with the permission of the Virginia Historical Society, the map of Veracruz with the permission of the University of Texas at Arlington, and the image of Frederick Rupp's grave with the permission of Michael McCormick.

Carolyn Walker and Jill Swenson offered editorial advice on my work in progress. Brian Neugebauer, Angela Buckley, and James Rada offered feedback as beta readers.

My gratitude also goes to Malte Mory, my French horn teacher, who first suggested my research project would make a good book. Sometimes musicians have a good eye for literature as well.

Dieter, Alexander, and Dennis, thank you so much for your patience during this project.

CHAPTER ONE

A Nameless Hero

Robert E. Lee crouched by the cannon, concentrating on his targets, but his thoughts drifted to a wounded soldier behind him. The man's pain must have been excruciating.

It was Lee's first battle, and although he attended to his duties, he couldn't ignore the suffering around him. Here, at the Siege of Veracruz in the Mexican-American War, Lee collected his first experiences with military casualties. The strategy he'd forged with Gen. Winfield Scott now translated into smoke, blood, and crunching bone.

At an onshore naval battery in the dunes west of town, Lee directed the fire. He selected the targets on the city walls and fortresses, and the sailors fired. General Scott's goal was to break down those defenses.

Veracruz lobbed shells back into Lee's battery. The Americans ducked behind the embrasure for protection, but sometimes the shells struck the sailors' heads with an awful thud and decapitated them. It was a sound no West Point textbook ever described.

The man Lee was thinking about now lay in a trench behind the battery, covered with some brush as protection from the tropical sun. An incoming cannonball had shattered one of his legs, and while he was lying in the sand, another ball flew in and struck the same leg, fracturing it yet again.[1]

The double wound must have tortured him, especially when cannon fire shook the ground. But the man was stuck there for the time being; he couldn't be carried to the hospital. The officers had ordered that no one leave the battery, not even to fetch fresh water. Mexican fire made it too dangerous.

Hot, thirsty, and in agony, the man never complained.

Later, when enemy fire lulled, the officers deemed it safe to transport him to the hospital. That was the irony of the thing—it happened just when they all thought the soldier would be safe. Men were lifting him out of the trench onto a litter when a Mexican bomb struck him in the chest and exploded, dashing flesh and bone to smithereens. It killed the man instantly.[2]

To what extent did Robert E. Lee need to process his first experiences of battle? Did the images of Veracruz, and that death in the trench, still haunt him during the Civil War? Or did Lee find inspiration in the man's silent suffering? Two weeks later, he tried to work through his feelings in a letter to his oldest son, Custis:

> There was one poor fellow that behaved nobly. His thigh was broke by a cannon ball & he was laid in a trench at the rear of the battery for security, the balls & shells were flying so thick that he could not be borne away. A bush was stuck over him to keep the sun out of his eyes & all that we could give him was occasionally a cup of bad warm water. The men at the guns were hot & thirsty & drank up the water as fast as it could be brought. It was at some distance & the balls swept over the field & at such a furious rate that the officers would not let the men go for water except when they could not do without it. There the poor fellow lay till evening; when they got a litter & was bearing him off, when a shell fell & burst & a fragment killed him. He laid the whole day with the balls & bombs flying over him without uttering a complaint. His sufferings must have been very great, for the battery kept up a constant & brisk firing & the concussion from the 32 [pounders] & Paixhan guns shook the whole ground & must have pained him terribly. I doubt whether all Mexico is worth to us the life of that man.[3]

The last sentence contains surprising words for a man who later became an American military legend, one of the foremost generals in world history. Was he having trouble dealing with the horror of bloodshed? Or do his words reflect a mature effort to harmonize a single man's plight, and his feelings about it, with the harsh necessity of sending men to their deaths?

When the Virginia Historical Society acquired the letter in 1981, it inherited a national mystery. Who was that man worth all of Mexico? How could Lee balance the highest military goal of the United States against the fate of one soldier and find it lacking? While working through the emotional repercussions of his first battle, did he briefly flirt with pacifism? Or was Lee holding up the unnamed hero as a model of courage for his son? That one soldier has been an enigma ever since the letter became public.

Lee never named the man. He may have not even known his name.

We can't ascertain what was in Lee's mind, but we can at least crack the riddle of the soldier's identity. The trail leads us back to Europe and to one of its most unusual cold cases—an assassination that went unsolved for decades.

This is the story Lee never knew. It probably would have shocked him.

Part One

Murder in the Kingdom of Württemberg: 1835-36

CHAPTER TWO

Crime Scene Bönnigheim, 1835

When Mayor Johann Heinrich Rieber left the Waldhorn Inn in Bönnigheim on October 21, 1835, he didn't notice a man cradling a rifle and stalking him in the shadows. If he had, he might have had one last chance to save his life.

But the mayor was probably too distracted by his own grief to pay attention to his surroundings. He had spent the afternoon at the funeral of the town butcher, and that was a poignant reminder of his own loss. The funeral of his best friend—a school chum and local politician who had helped him promote a new school—had been held exactly one year prior. Ever since his friend's sudden death in October 1834, Bönnigheim's pastor had observed a change in the mayor—a new contemplative despondency. Rieber grieved at the butcher's funeral today and the pastor noticed it. He later described Rieber's mood as "especially solemn."[1]

Bönnigheim, a small town nestled among the vineyards of the Kingdom of Württemberg in what is now southwest Germany, survived primarily from wine production and the hospitality industry, profiting from the busy trade route that cut right through the city. It had elected Rieber mayor in 1823 when he was only twenty-nine years old. Initially touched by the town's expression of trust, Rieber soon found his youth and inexperience a liability; townsfolk felt freer to insult and threaten a young mayor than an older, more experienced official. Roving bands of boisterous youth created several crises in his early administration, disturbing the peace at night and even interrupting church services. Rieber responded by stepping up enforcement and penalties. Gaining the town's respect dominated his attention at the beginning of his life term, but now, at the age of forty-one, he had largely won that battle. A proactive approach to the youth by establishing the new boys' school and promoting education had become his new priorities; he even invested 900 *Gulden*—half the value of his own apartment—of his own money in the school.[2]

By the evening of October 21, 1835, the unmarried and childless mayor felt so exhausted he fell asleep during his dinner. The Waldhorn, or "Hunting Horn," was run by his older half-brother Karl Friedrich and his wife Rike ("REEKeh," short for Friederike). Rike served him in a side room. Germans in the nineteenth century ate warm suppers, like the *Spätzle* dumplings with lentils and sausage so typical for the region. At this time of the year, people also enjoyed drinking fizzing and lightly fermented new wine from the winepresses. Rike said Mayor Rieber had arrived between 7:00 and 7:30 P.M. He sat alone, ate some supper, and drank only half his pint of wine. He told her he was tired and then dozed for more than an hour in his armchair. Several townspeople—a shoemaker, a lathe worker, and two foresters—arrived and dined in the Waldhorn, but the mayor slept through their conversations. The other patrons left before Rieber did.[3]

Mayor Rieber had a stocky physique, an average height, and wore glasses. He was most certainly wearing the fashionable funeral attire of the day: black trousers, vest, and jacket, a broad black cravat at his throat, and a wide turnover collar.[4]

The two foresters in the Waldhorn, Ludwig Schwarzwälder and Eduard Vischer (pronounced "fisher"), enjoyed an evening to themselves. Their boss was out of town for the night. They had plenty to discuss. Hunting season had begun and the forestry department had recently started interviewing applicants for a position as a game warden. Around 9:30 P.M. the two foresters rose, pulled on their standard-issue dark green, black-collared forester coats over their yellow vests, and left.[5]

Ludwig and Eduard took the same route home that the mayor would take. Their destination was 140 yards away, where the end of the unpaved main street opened onto the Palace Square. A baroque palace, Bönnigheim's largest building, dominated the plaza. They not only worked in the palace, they also lived there. Once nobility—among them Germany's first best-selling novelist, Sophie von La Roche—had resided in the palace, but now it housed the regional forestry department administration and provided living quarters for some of its employees.[6]

Bönnigheim's palace with the St. George fountain in the foreground. Mayor Rieber walked past this fountain on the way home. (*Source:* Ann Marie Ackermann)

Neither man noticed anything unusual on the way home. Once in the palace, they climbed the stairs to their rooms and got ready for bed. Ludwig went over to Eduard's room to chat with him for a while.[7]

It was around 9:45 P.M. that the guileless mayor rose from his armchair, pulled on his heavy blue greatcoat, lit his lantern, and headed home. As soon as he stepped out the door onto the street, he would have smelled the heavy grape fragrance that always drifted through the streets and alleys, like mists of burgundy and the palest gold, whenever the winepresses operated. Bönnigheim had four presses within its city gates, and by late October 1835, they were all busy crushing the day's harvest of Silvaner, Elbling, and Trollinger. Wood creaked late into the night as men pushed the spindle handles of the massive beam presses, and the sticky, sweet nectar flowed into wooden collection buckets. It was a good year; the grape harvest in 1835 was larger than usual.[8]

From the Waldhorn, next to the town hall, Mayor Rieber turned right onto the main street. The mayor lived next to the palace in the Kavaliersbau (cavalier building), which he shared with the town physician, Dr. Nellmann, who lived and practiced above Rieber's apartment, and a forest ranger named Ernst Philipp Foettinger, who lived in a rear wing.[9]

It was dark and quiet outside on Bönnigheim's main thoroughfare. The soft, damp earth of the unpaved street muted the footfall of any other person. Rieber's lantern provided his main source of light. Bönnigheim did not yet have gas-lit streetlamps and the moon was new that night. The only artificial illumination came from the scattered, muted light of indoor oil lamps filtering through curtains. A few narrow alleys on either side of the street yawned like cavernous throats. But they appeared empty.

Mayor Rieber saw no one on the way.

About halfway home, he heard something. The report of two shots split the night. They sounded like they came from the churchyard and lower gate to his left. Rieber later told an investigator it bothered him that someone was shooting in town. But he didn't feel threatened and continued walking.[10]

In actuality, Rieber had been in danger ever since he left the Waldhorn, but unsuspecting, he forged ahead. As he passed the St. George fountain and reached the Palace Square, the night sky opened above him. If there was anything that distracted the mayor on the way home, it was the heavens above him. Halley's Comet had recently reached its nearest point to earth for this return, and not since 1378 had it sailed such a close course for observers in the Northern Hemisphere. The comet's tail cast a length twelve times the diameter of the moon. Here in southern Germany, rain and fog had veiled Halley since the beginning of September. One newspaper bemoaned the comet's modesty and its refusal to "flaunt its charms and instead [keep] them veiled in fog."[11] But today the weather had cleared, offering the first good chance in weeks to see anything, and the moon was new. If the mayor peered in any direction on his short walk home, it was likely up, not around.[12]

A high iron fence separated the public Palace Square from the palace's inner, private courtyard. To reach his home, Rieber had to pass through a fourteen-foot-wide, solid wooden gate between that fence and the "washhouse," where a forester named Stölzle lived. This gate led to the courtyard of Rieber's home. It was locked, but it had a small door, just large enough for a person to pass through, and that was usually kept open. The mayor passed through the door, turned right, and cut a diagonal path across the courtyard to his home. He was now only a few steps away from his front door in the Kavaliersbau.[13]

Wooden gates with doors are common architectural features in Germany. (*Source:* Ann Marie Ackermann)

At that moment, a man with a rifle slipped out of the shadows. He took a position near the corner of the washhouse, eased up his barrel, and took aim across the courtyard. If Mayor Rieber had looked back at that moment, the muzzle might have been the only thing visible in the darkness on the other side of the courtyard.

The man pulled the trigger.

This time, the crack of the rifle was much louder. Mayor Rieber whipped around to apprehend the shooter. But he couldn't see anyone.

The mayor didn't realize at first that he'd been shot. After a few steps, he was seized with pain, and only then did he realize he'd been the target. Someone had sprayed him in the back with shot pellets.

Rapidly losing strength from the loss of blood, the mayor first cried out for help. Dr. Nellmann, the town physician, lived above Rieber's apartment, and there was a chance he was there and could hear him. Rieber hollered "Doctor, doctor!" and careened into the Kavaliersbau. He staggered up one flight of stairs before he collapsed on the landing.[14]

As the echo of his shot resounded from the palace and Kavaliersbau, the man with the rifle darted around the washhouse into one of the dark alleys Mayor Rieber had passed on the way home. Then, heading north, he disappeared into a narrow passage between two houses. With those steps, the clock started ticking on nineteenth-century Württemberg's coldest case ever solved, and its only murder case ever solved in the United States by a third person.

CHAPTER THREE

Portents of Rebellion

Virginia and Texas, 1835–36

Within hours of the Rieber shooting in Bönnigheim, Robert E. Lee picked up a quill to scratch out a letter of woe to his friend and former supervisor, Andrew Talcott. Lee was coping with unexpected domestic duties and was aghast at the state of his wife's health. Mary Custis Lee had developed a postpartum infection and was bedridden. She couldn't care for their children, an infant girl and three-year-old boy who had come down with whooping cough. On October 21, 1835, the day Mayor Rieber was shot, Lee described Mary's condition: "She is still as weak & helpless as ever & confined to her bed."[1]

Mary's illness marked the beginning of an identity crisis for Lee, a crisis that caused him to question his career choice.

At the age of twenty-eight, Robert E. Lee enjoyed a coveted position as an army engineer. His path to the Army Corps of Engineers had been a tough, uphill battle against obstacles he had inherited at birth. Lee's father, the Revolutionary War hero Henry "Light-Horse Harry" Lee III, had excelled in the military during the Revolutionary War, served in the U.S. Congress and as governor of Virginia, and wrote George Washington's eulogy, penning the memorable words "first in war, first in peace, and first in the hearts of his countrymen."

But Light-Horse Harry had never been able to transfer any of those skills to the provision of his family. He mismanaged money, and when Robert was two, his father spent nearly a year in debtors' prison. Three years later, Henry Lee tried to defend a friend's newspaper press from a rioting mob. He was beaten senseless and then mutilated. Fiends stuck penknives into his flesh, poured hot candle wax into his eyes to see if he was still alive, and tried to cut off his nose. Henry Lee survived but was left crippled and an invalid. He sailed to Barbados the following year, hoping to improve his health in a different climate, but he never returned home to Virginia. He died on the return trip. Henry Lee's death left poverty and shame in its wake.[2]

Robert's mother, Ann Carter Lee, struggled to support her family and give her children an education. Self-denying and frugal, she taught Robert at home and sent him to a family-run grammar school. At a private secondary school in Alexandria, he learned Latin and Greek and excelled in mathematics. The lack of money to pay for college influenced the family's decision to send him to West Point, where he could obtain a free education. Stiff competition for admission never deterred Robert. With his family's help, he collected letters of recommendation from both congressmen and the secretary of war, John C. Calhoun, and eventually won his admission. When Robert graduated from West Point in 1829, he was second in his class and had received no demerits. His record opened the door to the Corps of Engineers.

Lee aimed just as high in marriage as he did in his career choice. Mary Custis, the belle of Arlington and granddaughter of George Washington by adoption, caught his eye, and he spent the summer of 1830, on leave from his first post in Georgia, wooing her. They married in 1831. She gave birth to their first son, George Washington Custis Lee, in 1832, and by late 1834, she was pregnant again.[3]

While the pregnant Mary suffered through the heat of the 1835 Virginia summer, Robert could escape to the cool breezes of Lake Erie and the northwestern wilderness between Michigan and Ohio. The Army Corps of Engineers sent him there to survey the disputed state boundary before the conflict developed into an armed clash between the two states. Lee traveled to Turtle Island, bisected by the state boundary, and Pelee Island on the Canadian side, where he used a lighthouse as a survey point.[4]

Mary gave birth to their daughter Mary in July, while he was away, and wrote to him, complaining of her health and imploring him to return home. He received her letter in Detroit. But her request exasperated him. He admonished Mary in a letter he sent home in August:

> But why do you urge my *immediate* return, & tempt one in the strongest possible manner, to endeavour to get excused from the performance of a

duty, imposed on me by my Profession for the pure gratification of my private feelings? Do you not think that those feelings are enough of themselves to contend with, without other aggravations; and that I rather require to be strengthened & encouraged to the *full* performance of what I am called on to execute, rather than excited to a dereliction, which even our affection could not palliate, or our judgement excuse?[5]

Lee remained at his job. But his homecoming in October wasn't what he expected. He realized immediately he had underestimated the severity of Mary's illness. Her pain was so severe she couldn't walk. Bedridden, she had shorn off her hair because she couldn't care for it. She wouldn't be able to get out of bed and walk again until the beginning of 1836. Mary Custis Lee remained sickly for the rest of her life.[6]

Whispers of guilt floated up through Lee's correspondence over the following months and years. He wrote of his wife's pain, her slow improvement, and of taking her to Virginia's spas over the summer to facilitate her healing. Robert and Mary reached a private truce. She would never again publically complain to him of her sufferings. But he would continue to nurse her for the rest of her life.

"I have never seen a man so changed and saddened," a relative commented.[7]

Lee's depression spiraled out into his career choice. He spent 1836 commuting to work in Washington, D.C., from his home at the Arlington House in Virginia. Lee would have enjoyed a post elsewhere, but he couldn't leave Mary. Now he despaired over a job whose prospects for promotion involved posts away from home. By February 1837, Lee toyed with the idea of resigning from the army and becoming a civil engineer.[8] He wrote to his friend Andrew Talcott again: "You ask what are my prospects in the Corps? Bad enough. . . . As to what I intend doing, it is rather hard to answer. There is one thing certain. I must get away from here. . . . I should have made a desperate effort, last spring, but Mary's health was so bad, I could not have left her & she could not have gone with me. I am waiting, looking and hoping for some good opportunity to bid an affectionate farewell to my dear Uncle Sam."[9]

But there was one event that buoyed Lee's spirits—the Texas Revolution in 1836. In another letter to Talcott, Lee called the reports of the revolution "great news" and "marvelous."

Emigrants from the United States had started it in October 1835, the same month as the Rieber shooting in Bönnigheim, but its origins had been long festering in Mexican and Indian history. When Mexico won independence from Spain in 1821, there was the problem of what to do with Texas, the vast, northern Mexican territory that lay west of the United States. To populate Texas and buffer itself from the Indian raids, Mexico set out the welcome mat for settlers from the United States, offering land grants. But it underestimated its newcomers. Mexico's settlement policy eventually backfired in a way that would change the lives of both Lee and the assassin from Bönnigheim.[10]

By 1835, the population of Texas was overwhelmingly "Texian," as the immigrants from the United States called themselves. When differences with Mexico developed over politics and a new Mexican constitution, Texians started a movement for separate statehood. Texian skirmishes with the Mexican military began the same month as the Rieber shooting and were largely successful. By November, Texians had driven out Mexican forces from everywhere but San Antonio.

Texian leaders organized a "Consultation," or convention, in early November. They approved a resolution calling for the reenactment of the old Mexican constitution. It wasn't exactly a Texian Declaration of Independence. That would come later, in March 1836. But it came close. Mexican President Antonio López de Santa Anna viewed it as an act of treason.[11]

Branch T. Archer, chairman of the Consultation, was fully cognizant of the role that the Texians were playing in history. He borrowed the rhetorical thunder of the Bible in his opening address: "[T]he destinies of Texas are placed in your hands. . . . In the words of the Hebrew prophet, I would say, 'Put off your shoes, for the ground upon which you stand is holy.' The rights and liberties of thousands of freemen are in your hands, and millions yet unborn may be affected by your decisions."[12]

Archer was certainly not thinking of Virginia or Germany when he drew a circle around the thousands and millions of lives he envisioned as affected by the Consultation. He could not have known that the events in Texas pivoted the rudder and reset the sails on a political frigate that would one day overtake both Robert E. Lee and the assassin of Bönnigheim. Their courses would converge in Mexico.

CHAPTER FOUR

A Town Reacts

When the gunshot in Rieber's courtyard pierced the stillness of the night, Bönnigheim's residents rose from their beds, peered through windows, and strained their ears. Mayor Rieber's closest neighbors were not only the first responders. During a time when the regional detective lived more than an hour away, and before the emergence of a modern local police force, citizens sometimes took the first steps in collecting evidence and noting the details of the case, and the investigating magistrate welcomed their efforts.

The night watchman was making his rounds when he heard the shot in Rieber's courtyard. But he wasn't near it and didn't respond. Bönnigheim residents had a tradition of shooting in the autumn; gunshots, even within the city limits, were nothing unusual.[1]

Louise Hepperle, the cooper's daughter, lived on the churchyard. She had just put out her light and was ready to go to bed when a strange rattling noise outside her father's house drew her to the window. Louise immediately thought of two young men. One of them fancied Catherine, the girl next door, and they were probably up to something. Then two gunshots, very close and in quick succession, sounded from the corner of the churchyard.

Louise yanked open her bedroom window and found Catherine staring out of hers.

"Catherine, that was meant for you," Louise said.

Catherine laughed and said she didn't think so.

"Oh, God!" a male voice in the churchyard moaned.

At that moment, the twenty-four-year-old Louise realized something serious had happened. She couldn't see the man in the courtyard and still suspected he was Catherine's admirer. But whoever it was, he left the churchyard.

The clock struck ten not long afterwards, so Louise could at least place the shots before 10:00 P.M.[2]

The crack of a gunshot roused Philipp Foettinger, the forest ranger who lived in the rear wing of Mayor Rieber's house. He and his wife had already retired for the night. The Foettingers heard three shots, two in close succession, followed by a third single shot several minutes later. They estimated the time of the shots as sometime after 9:00–9:15 P.M.[3]

Juliane Stölzle lived in the "washhouse," a smaller building kitty-corner to the mayor's home and only a few yards from his front door. She was home alone with her maid, washing dishes in the kitchen, when she heard the report of a rifle. Her husband was out late working in the winepress, and Julianne had served him and a group of grape harvesters a quick supper before they returned to the press around 9:00 P.M. Then she went to her brother-in-law's home to pick up some milk. When she came back with her milk pail through the back door, everything was still. She noticed nothing unusual.

Frau Stölzle guessed she heard the shot between 9:30 and 9:45 P.M. Her kitchen was on the other side of the house from Rieber's courtyard, and when she heard the report, she left her light on in the kitchen, crept out into the dark alley behind her house, and sneaked around the corner to the walkway leading to Rieber's courtyard. She must have missed encountering the fleeing criminal by mere seconds because his escape route led behind her house. Now, in the walkway, Frau Stölzle stood by the gate, close to the place the rifle had been fired just a couple of minutes before.

"I saw a man in the courtyard," she later told the investigator, "who said several times 'Oh God, oh God' and then cried out 'Doctor, come! Doctor, come!' . . . I thought it must be someone who had injured himself shooting."[4]

But Frau Stölzle didn't recognize Mayor Rieber in the darkness. She watched the man stagger to the Kavaliersbau door and wrest it open, and then heard his heavy footsteps on the staircase. It sounded to her like he was taking two to three steps at a time. She assumed he was going to Dr.

Scene of the crime, taken from the palace. Mayor Rieber was a few steps in front of the door to the building on the left. The murderer stood by the corner of the washhouse to the right. The gate no longer exists. (*Source:* Ann Marie Ackermann)

Nellmann, on the upper story, to seek medical attention, so she returned to her home and went back inside.[5]

A butcher and his wife, whose house faced the Palace Square just two blocks north of the mayor, were also in bed when they heard a single shot, followed by the sound of someone whimpering. It sounded like it came from the direction of the palace. The butcher could at least provide a more accurate estimate of the time than either Louise or Frau Stölzle. He said the shot occurred at around 9:45 P.M. He thought it was a drunk shooting a weapon. The couple stayed in bed.[6]

Christof Wenz, a twenty-six-year-old vintner and cavalryman on leave from his regiment, had worked late with the grape harvest. He deposited his wooden harvest tubs at a pub on the Palace Square around 9:00 P.M. and then went inside for forty-five minutes to relax. When he left, he heard shots from the churchyard. He walked over to his house, just two houses away, and entered his barn. He was preparing the feed for his livestock, not three minutes after he heard the gunfire from the churchyard, when he heard another shot from the other direction. It sounded like it came from the St. George fountain just north of the palace. But what disturbed Christof was the sound that followed the report.

It sounded like someone was crying, "Oh, Jesus! Oh, Jesus!"

Christof walked out to the street in front of his house, where he had a clear view of the palace courtyard, and beyond it, Mayor Rieber's house, but he didn't see anything. His next-door neighbors were looking out their window and they had a brief conversation with Christof about the shot. The neighbors convinced him it was nothing and he should go to bed.

Christof retired at 10:00 P.M. But his night was far from over. An hour later, he would be routed out of bed.[7]

The two young foresters who had dined in the Waldhorn, Ludwig Schwarzwälder and Eduard Vischer, had returned to their apartment in the palace. Nothing unusual caught their attention on the way home. In fact, Ludwig didn't remember having seen anyone. They had been carrying a lantern, he later admitted to the investigator, implying the obvious. It was hard to discern details beyond the halo of lantern light.

Only ten minutes had passed since they had left the Waldhorn. Both had gotten undressed. Eduard was already in bed and Ludwig was in his room talking to him when they heard a shot close to the palace.

"Now rascals are shooting in town!" Eduard remembered his colleague saying.

Ludwig dashed down two flights of stairs and flung open the palace door. Standing there in his nightshirt, he heard "lamentable screaming" in Mayor Rieber's courtyard.

"What's going on out there?" he called out.

No one answered.

The spinster Cotta, who lived in the palace on the floor below him, appeared and told him the mayor had been shot.

Ludwig dashed back up the stairs to tell Eduard. Both foresters threw on their clothes and ran over to the mayor's home. When the two foresters climbed the steps in the Kavalierbau and entered Mayor Rieber's apartment, they found Dr. Nellmann already attending him. Ludwig stayed to assist the doctor, but Eduard left to do a little investigating on his own.[8]

In the apartment above the mayor's, the blast and sound of someone screaming had roused Dr. Nellmann from his bed and brought him to his window. The sight of a man with a lantern in the courtyard galvanized the physician. He scrambled into his clothes and ran down the stairs, only to find Mayor Rieber collapsed on the landing. Nellmann and his wife carried the mayor into his apartment and onto his bed. Blood was already saturating his shirt.

Now the doctor's real work began. To perform a physical examination, he would first have to remove Mayor Rieber's clothing. According to a nineteenth-century German medical treatise on treating gunshot wounds, this was best done with scissors. The physician was to open the clothing along the seams, pull off the pieces of cloth first from the healthy limbs, then the injured ones, taking care to move the patient as little as possible. The extent to which blood had already saturated each piece of clothing constituted the first important finding. That would tell the doctor where the hemorrhaging was most severe.

Only then should the physician examine the wounds themselves. Which were still bleeding? Were the wounds secreting other fluids? How many entry and exit wounds were present? The physician needed to check for deformities and dislocations, and then palpate the immediate vicinity of the wounds for possible subcutaneous emphysema (trapped air under the skin), air escaping from the wound track, or crackling noises from shattered bone.[9]

What Dr. Nellmann found caused him to classify his patient's condition as dangerous. Several gunshot wounds perforated Mayor Rieber's upper and lower back. One went all the way through, exiting from the mayor's chest. And at least one bone was fractured. In Rieber's clothing, Nellmann found more than just blood. A piece of lead dropped out of the mayor's vest. The physician set it aside as potential evidence to turn over later to the investigator. He then needed to clean and dress the wounds.[10]

Dr. Nellmann turned briefly from his patient to bark some orders. He sent his maid over to the Waldhorn inn to notify the mayor's relatives. Then he sent her over to Christof Wenz's house with a message the young cavalryman should deliver to the nearby town of Besigheim. To start an official criminal investigation, he needed to apprise the Royal District Authority of the shooting. The Royal District Authority in Besigheim,[11] a regional department under the king's authority, administered several cities, including Bönnigheim. It had the closest investigating magistrate who worked as a detective.[12]

Karl Friedrich, the mayor's brother, was in the Waldhorn wine cellar, examining barrels with his cooper, when Dr. Nellmann's maid arrived. Someone called down the stairs to tell him his brother had just been shot. He sent his wife Rike and one of her maids to his brother's until he was free. His family nursed Mayor Rieber throughout the night.[13]

It was 11:00 P.M. by the time Dr. Nellmann's maid banged on Christof Wenz's door, handing him the doctor's message—a report to the District Authority:

> October 21, 1835
>
> The undersigned hereby makes the following hasty report that Mayor Rieber was wounded this evening while he was walking home, by someone whose identity is yet unknown, who fired at him with buckshot. Because the wounds appear to be dangerous, the presence of the District Authority physician would be highly necessary.
>
> [Illegible],
> Nellmann
> City Physician[14]

Although the storks that roosted on Bönnigheim's palace needed to fly only three-and-a-half miles to reach Besigheim, where the District Authority physician lived and worked, the closest route for a horse was nearly five miles long. It took Christof over the fields to the south, then downhill and eastward through orchards and vineyards. The path led to the Enz River and across a bridge. Besigheim, a walled city atop a steep hill, lay on the peninsula formed by the confluence of the Enz and Neckar Rivers. Christof's destination, the District Authority building, sat perched high above the Neckar along the town wall. In the daytime, it was a one-and-a-half hour trip by horse and carriage. Now the cavalryman had to maneuver his horse through the mud left by the recent rains, and in the darkness of a new moon with only a comet for lighting. Christof Wenz arrived in Besigheim at 12:45 A.M.

The Royal District Authority's chief administrator read the note and dispatched Christof to the one person within its administration who was in charge of investigating serious crimes: the investigating magistrate. He lived several streets away in the District Authority courthouse, just across town on the Enz side. Dr. Nellmann's message was enough to galvanize the magistrate into action. He ordered the District Authority physician to Bönnigheim, asking him to leave immediately, and made plans to travel himself to Bönnigheim the first thing in the morning.[15]

In the meantime, the people in the mayor's apartment didn't want to wait for the District Authority physician to arrive from Besigheim. Ludwig Schwarzwälder, the forester, and a city councilman left Mayor Rieber's apartment to fetch Bönnigheim's surgeon, Heinrich Böhringer. They entered his living room to find the surgeon treating a young man named Christian Wachter. He had just lost his left thumb to a firearm accident in the churchyard. His pistol, probably loaded with too much powder, had exploded.

"Who would have thought," Christian whined, "that this was waiting for me today?"

Ludwig realized the obvious. Anyone known to have been shooting a firearm in town the same night the mayor was shot would have to face the investigating magistrate later. "There will be even more waiting for you," the forester said.

"Certainly not!" said Christian.

Ludwig didn't probe him any further. He and the councilman asked the surgeon to report to Dr. Nellmann.[16]

Herr Böhringer would have gone there anyway. Christian's wound was dangerous. He didn't have the medical training that Dr. Nellmann did— he wasn't even a doctor—and didn't feel comfortable treating the wound himself. He brought Christian home and went to Dr. Nellmann's apartment, intending to ask Dr. Nellmann to make a house call on Christian. But on the way up the stairs to the doctor's apartment, the surgeon found Dr. Nellmann in Mayor Rieber's apartment instead. Dr. Nellmann told the surgeon the mayor had been shot.

"Just bandage up your patient the best you can," the doctor said. "I can't leave!"

Heinrich Böhringer returned to Christian's home. Documents don't record him treating the mayor himself, perhaps because the District Authority physician arrived at Mayor Rieber's house during the night.[17]

The citizens of Bönnigheim didn't wait for the investigating magistrate from Besigheim to arrive. They called an emergency meeting at the city hall in the middle of the night. Their discussions weren't recorded, but the meeting apparently had to do with more than just organizing the city administration during the mayor's absence because by daybreak, citizens had fanned across the town to look for evidence of the shooting of their beloved mayor. They took the first steps of the investigation into their own hands.[18]

The city scribe hauled the friend of the young man who injured his thumb to the city hall and interrogated him. The man denied having anything to do with shooting Rieber. The scribe had a messenger forward a transcription of the questions and answers to the investigating magistrate in Besigheim even before the sun rose.[19]

Both the forester, Eduard Vischer, and the night watchman searched Mayor Rieber's courtyard. The forester looked for the wadding used to load the period front-loading rifles. Because a rifle ejects the wadding along with the bullet or shot pellets, and because the wadding doesn't fly as far as the projectile, its landing place offers a proximate indication of where the shooter stood. But in the darkness neither man found anything.[20]

A local policeman started questioning Bönnigheim residents and located Louise Hepperle, the cooper's daughter who lived next to the churchyard, as a potential witness.[21]

A city councilman searched the churchyard and found eight pieces of a pistol, bloody and strewn over the distance of thirty paces. He collected them and brought them to the city hall. The scribe wrote another note to the investigating magistrate at 4:00 A.M., informing him of the find.[22]

He also found several pieces of a finger, including a fingertip and fingernail, and collected them as well.[23]

One block north of Mayor Rieber's house, one young man sleeping through the night would turn out to be the best witness of them all. Walking home from the same pub the cavalryman Christof Wenz had visited, he saw a man fleeing from the scene just seconds after hearing the shot. But he didn't associate the gunshot with a crime; random shots were common during the hunting season. Several days would pass before he realized the significance of his observation.

CHAPTER FIVE

The Detective's Hourglass

The assault on Mayor Rieber turned the investigative hourglass. For Eduard Hammer, the sand began flowing at 2:00 A.M. That's when the Bönnigheim cavalryman, Christof Wenz, pounded on his door to deliver Dr. Nellmann's report. As the district investigating magistrate, Hammer knew that every minute counted; statistically, he could expect to solve a case within a few weeks or see it go cold. The first hours, like the switches on a railroad track, could affect the outcome of his investigation. Hammer couldn't have known it at the time, but the case he was about to start probing would become nineteenth-century Germany's record-breaking cold case—its longest-running nineteenth-century cold case ever solved.

Magistrate Hammer went to work.

His most pressing task was to obtain and preserve medical evidence. He dispatched the messenger to the District Authority physician, Dr. Hauff, with a note directing the doctor to travel to Bönnigheim at once and examine Mayor Rieber. Dr. Hauff was like an early modern medical examiner. He provided reports on the state of a victim's injuries—critical medical evidence for the court. And in murder cases, he performed the autopsy and provided an expert opinion on the cause of death.[1]

Magistrate Hammer needed to investigate the crime scene and interrogate witnesses as soon as the day broke. In preparation, he opened a file and packed all the material he needed for an attempted murder investigation. Paper, quills and pencils, ink, a pedometer, and measuring tape are just a few of the things that the leading forensic handbook in the German language of the nineteenth century recommended an investigating magistrate bring for his fieldwork. Hammer also organized a scribe to record the questions and answers during the interrogations.[2]

The forty-two-year-old investigator combined keen intelligence with compassion. Hammer could be severe in applying the law, but was able to respect the criminal as a person. After having completed a university education specifically aimed at training judges, Hammer had gathered administrative experience in several other cities before landing his first job as an investigating magistrate[3]—the title for a nineteenth-century German detective—at the age of twenty-eight. He then distinguished himself with an academic publication on judicial administration. In 1829, Hammer came to the District Authority of Besigheim as an official investigator. Later in life, Hammer was promoted to chief judicial counselor in Ulm, one of the largest cities in Württemberg, and elected to the state legislature. In 1841, King Wilhelm I of Württemberg knighted him, bestowing membership in the Order of the Württemberg Crown and a coveted name change to "von Hammer."[4]

Shortly before 7:00 A.M., a second messenger pounded on his door with the messages from the District Authority physician and Bönnigheim's city scribe. They provided critical information: The wounds were life-threatening; it was a serious crime. The messages also provided Hammer with his first lead in the case. Christian Wachter and Philipp Häberle were the names of the two men shooting a pistol in the churchyard. Bönnigheim's city council had sent along a transcript of its interrogation of Häberle.[5]

October 22, 1835, dawned clear. Magistrate Hammer harnessed his span of two horses to his carriage and made the uphill journey to Bönnigheim. When he arrived in Bönnigheim at 8:30 A.M., Mayor Rieber was doing better, but Dr. Hauff felt his condition was critical enough to postpone any interrogation of his patient. Hammer swore in two city council members to assist him in the investigation and witness the interrogations. He then turned to his first witness, Dr. Nellmann.[6]

The magistrate's scribe recorded the questions and answers in a brown, leather-bound protocol book and numbered each question. He prefaced the transcript with particulars about the witness: *Johann Andreas Nellmann, practicing physician, domiciled in Bönnigheim, married, forty-three years old.*

"What can you state about the occurrence in which Mayor Rieber was injured?" Magistrate Hammer asked.

"Last night, I was already home and in bed when I suddenly heard a loud shot near my house around 9:45. Then I heard a person crying out— he used the words 'Oh, Jesus, oh, Jesus, come help me, I've been shot.' I got up, looked out the window and saw a man with a lantern close to the house, not even five paces distant, and thought, 'Somebody has injured himself while shooting.'"

Dr. Nellmann explained that he got dressed and ran downstairs.

"On the lower story, where Mayor Rieber lives, I found a man lying on his back who could hardly speak and whom I recognized, only when I approached him, as Mayor Rieber." The doctor and his wife found the key to Rieber's apartment in his coat pocket and carried him to his bed.

"Rieber was very weak and bleeding severely; the blood ran out of his breeches, and as we undressed him, his entire shirt was soaked in blood." The doctor told how he sent his maid to notify the mayor's relatives, dressed the mayor's wounds, and notified the police.

"Besides the wounded man whom you saw through your window, did you see no one?" Magistrate Hammer asked.

"No, nobody."

"How far from your home was the shot fired?"

"It must have been ten to twelve paces from the house, it wasn't any further; it was a frightful blast."[7]

As Dr. Nellmann signed his statement, the city scribe interrupted to say that the mayor felt weak and requested more time before being questioned. The magistrate and his assistants now moved over to the churchyard, where the councilman had found the pistol pieces. Both city council members knew the two young men in the churchyard shooting, and neither thought either of the men would go so far as to shoot the mayor. But they did confirm that Philipp Häberle owned a pistol.

Obviously, if the young men had shot the mayor, they would have had to have used a second weapon. The explosion had destroyed one pistol even before Mayor Rieber was shot. Did the two men shoot another pistol first and then use Häberle's pistol to shoot the mayor? Hammer arrested Häberle and held him over in the town jail for questioning. He then searched Häberle's house. The magistrate specifically looked for objects with bloodstains, guns, and firearm accoutrements. Hammer seized the pistol, but couldn't find anything else suspicious.[8]

The party then moved to Louise Hepperle's house, where Hammer questioned her. She confirmed that Christian Wachter fancied her neighbor Catherine Maier. Louise was sure both Christian and his friend Philipp Häberle had been in the churchyard. They had probably been firing the pistol to get Catherine's attention.

"Why did you think of Häberle when Wachter is the one who fancies the Maier girl?" Hammer asked.

She laughed. "Because they have always been friends and do everything together."

The magistrate believed her and made a note in his protocol. *The girl expresses herself without inhibition and appears completely unsuspicious.*[9]

The rising sun offered the first good opportunity to search Mayor Rieber's courtyard. It would have been hands-and-knees work. Now, with better light, the magistrate had more luck than the forester who had searched during the night. Near the gate leading to Rieber's courtyard, Hammer found wadding, the padding used between the gunpowder and shot pellets. It appeared to be made of deer fur.

A closer inspection of Rieber's gate revealed two fresh, splintered impressions in the wood that did not go all the way through the door. Hammer measured them. The first one looked like it came from so-called *Rehposten*, or buckshot, the second from large pellets sized 0 or 1, used for hunting foxes and badgers.[10] On the door in the gate, he found a similar mark; it looked like one pellet had grazed the open door before it embedded itself in the gate. Hammer couldn't find any lead in the wood, but he measured the impressions.[11]

The assassin's footprints in the rain-soaked earth might have still been visible at 9:45 P.M., but everyone who came to the mayor's assistance during the night—the foresters, the maids, the District Authority physician, and the mayor's relatives—entered through the same door in the gate the assassin had used—and trampled over them.

Now the detective went inside to interview Mayor Rieber. He first examined the mayor's clothing. Rieber's shirt, especially on the right side, was completely blood-soaked. Hammer counted and measured twenty-eight holes in the shirt alone. The largest was 0.7 by 0.3 inches, indicating buckshot, and the smallest one 0.1 inches in diameter, indicating birdshot. On the right side of the waistband and seat of Rieber's pants, he found five additional openings, both large and small. Hammer dictated his impression to his clerk that buckshot caused one big one and birdshot the four smaller ones.[12]

Rieber's greatcoat was made of thick blue material and was well padded. Hammer located twenty round holes. Two, Hammer wrote, "were clearly made by lead [pellets] larger than birdshot, by buckshot." Birdshot had also bored one opening through the mayor's suspenders. The mayor's vest, which Magistrate Hammer examined a day later, contained eleven holes of varying sizes.

Magistrate Hammer then made a cursory examination of Rieber's injuries, dictating his findings to his scribe. To avoid having to move the victim, he refrained from examining all the wounds. Hammer dictated a description of one exit wound in the chest below the right nipple; a second wound under the nipple, caused by a penetrating pellet that did not exit the skin but left visible injury underneath; and entry wounds in the lower back and right upper arm.[13]

It was only then that the magistrate attempted to question the mayor. Rieber had trouble breathing and delivered his answers in brief "paragraphs," punctuated by pauses. But he started talking before Hammer even posed a question, so Hammer's scribe, poised with his quill and protocol book, recorded the statement right away.[14]

"Around 10:00 I quit the Waldhorn after dining, and went home with my lantern, came to the gate that leads into the courtyard, and when I was only 3–4 paces from my residence, a shot was abruptly fired.

"I didn't realize immediately the shot was intended for me and reckoned it was a shot like those that occur in autumn; I leaped 3–4 paces back to apprehend the shooter, and then I noticed I had been shot.

"I cried out: 'Oh, Jesus, I've been shot! Help me, doctor, doctor!'

"I made my way up my staircase, almost to my apartment, but then I couldn't stand any longer and collapsed. In the meantime, the doctor and his wife came. They first wanted to bring me into their apartment, but according to my wishes they brought me into my room and to my bed."

"How far away from you might the gunman have stood as he fired?" Magistrate Hammer asked.

"He must have been standing near Stölzle's washhouse."

"Did you see anybody before or after the shot?"

"No, nobody at all, I didn't even hear anyone run away after the shot."

The magistrate dictated an explanatory note to the file: *From the corner of the washhouse of the forestry worker Stölzle, the path leads diagonally to the door of Rieber's house and it is 26 paces from this corner to the door.*

Magistrate Hammer continued: "Are you not able to ascertain the precise time at which you were fired upon?"

"It was past 10:00, but not yet 10:15," said Mayor Rieber.

"Do you suspect anyone of causing you your injuries?"

"Indeed, I cannot say; I was, of course, a major informer against a very bad character here, Carl Gartmann, who has already stolen a plentitude—twice—and I rejected him not long ago as a contract employee when he applied for the position. It could have been him, but I have no further suspicions."

That was another lead.

Mayor Rieber continued: "But I did notice, as I went home, two shots from the side, one to my left and the other by the Lower Gate [the southern gate in the city wall], and I thought, 'Now the scoundrels are shooting at night at 10:00.'"

At this point, Hammer dictated a note to his scribe: *In answer to a comment by one of the persons present that the gentlemen of the forestry department, who left the Waldhorn shortly before Rieber did, stated that the clock struck 10 after Rieber arrived home, Mayor Rieber replied: "I cannot say precisely."*

"Was the shot loud?" asked Magistrate Hammer.

"Yes."

"Did you see the fire of the discharging rifle?"

"Absolutely nothing. It happened to my back, so I couldn't notice anything."

"Do you now have anything else to state?"

"No."

But then Mayor Rieber went on: "Perhaps it was unwed youth, especially soldiers on leave; we recently decided in the city council, because windows were broken at night, that no such youth should be permitted to be out on the streets after 10:00 P.M. and violations should be punished with the jailhouse. We also informed the townsfolk about several soldiers involved in a beating in [the neighboring town of] Lauffen. It could have been one of them, but I really can't say."[15]

Rieber was too weak to raise his arm to sign his statement. The magistrate noted that and terminated the interview.[16]

In the afternoon, Magistrate Hammer questioned more witnesses. The foresters, the schoolmaster, and Catherine Maier, in whose honor the youth had fired their pistols, corroborated Luise's testimony about the timing of the two shots in the courtyard. He talked to the mayor's brother at the Waldhorn inn, but he had no idea who shot his brother or why.[17]

Hammer asked one of the councilmen to rake the mayor's courtyard and sift the dirt through a sieve. This process revealed one overlooked piece of lead. It was deformed—common for shot that has been fired, but it was definitely buckshot. More importantly, the piece weighed 3.65 grams[18]—more than it should have for its size. That meant it contained more lead than usual. Did the assassin make his own ammunition? Hammer noted the fact because possession of tools like casting ladles and shot molds might prove valuable as evidence.[19]

Although his wounds had mostly stopped bleeding, Rieber's condition worsened. By all appearances, at least one wound track perforated the entire thickness of his right lung. And based on the position of the other back wounds, the physician probably couldn't rule out further penetration of the lungs.[20]

Even in the nineteenth century, physicians knew to expect a condition called "pneumothorax," or a collapsed lung. They knew once a bullet or shot pellet had pierced lung tissue, air escaped from the lungs. Only rarely did that air seep through the wound track and out the skin with a telltale hissing noise. More often, the air from the lungs or from the outside, coming through the wound track, got trapped between the outer pleural linings of the lung and could, with increasing pressure, cause the lungs to collapse and suffocate the patient.[21]

Today pneumothorax can be readily diagnosed and treated. But in 1835, without diagnostic instruments such as X-rays or computer tomography, physicians could make only a probable diagnosis of lung perforation, adjusting their diagnosis over time based on their patient's course.[22] Difficulty breathing was the main symptom, and Mayor Rieber was already experiencing that.[23]

There weren't many treatment options available in a German country doctor's early nineteenth-century medical toolbox. Insertion of a chest tube or reopening the wound to drain off the excess air was one possible approach.[24] But if too many wounds perforated the lungs, it complicated the picture. If the shot pellets had left an opening between the lungs and pleural space, then extracting air from the pleural space would just draw more air from the lungs and defeat the purpose.

Doctors Hauff and Nellmann adopted a wait-and-see approach and discouraged visitors. Only a few guests are documented. One was the young assistant pastor, Dr. Christoph Ulrich Hahn. The conversation between the mayor and pastor would become topics of Hahn's eulogy in two days' time. Rieber confided to Hahn a premonition that his wounds would prove fatal. Hahn had the impression that the death of the mayor's friend a year before had somehow prepared the forty-one-year-old Rieber for his own. Rieber also spoke words of forgiveness for the unknown assassin and found comfort by wheezing the refrain of a then-popular German funeral hymn:

> Jesus, fountain of my sole relief
> Upon my Savior, I depart in peace.[25]

Mayor Rieber's one full sibling, his younger brother Louis, was the last visitor. Louis, a pastor from a neighboring town, had been gone the entire day at his brother-in-law's funeral, and when word reached him about the shooting, he was barely able to make it to Bönnigheim in time to bid his brother a final farewell.[26]

In the early hours of predawn on October 23, around the time Bönnigheim's clocks chimed the quarter hour of 4:15 A.M. in muted tones, the crime Magistrate Hammer was investigating quietly passed from attempted murder to murder. The next day would bring an autopsy and new physical evidence.[27]

CHAPTER SIX

Queen of the Carolina

From a detective's standpoint, there wasn't a worst time to investigate a murder. Württemberg's criminal law and procedure were in transition, and that transition bound investigators with such a short tether that their success rates plummeted.

Württemberg still clung to a three-hundred-year-old criminal code, the *Constitutio Criminalis Carolina*. When the Holy Roman Emperor, Charles V, enacted it in 1532, it was hailed as a milestone in European criminal law. "The Carolina," as it was dubbed, unified criminal law in German-speaking countries. By restricting the court's discretion in collecting and assessing evidence, it gave birth to German criminal procedure. It also contained some seemingly modern insights, such as a distinction between murder and manslaughter. And by requiring inspection of the body in cases of murder and expert medical testimony for crimes involving death or injury, it gave birth to forensic medicine.[1]

But under the Carolina's surface swirled disturbing undercurrents. It recognized witchcraft as a capital crime and in doing so, contributed to the wave of witch trials that swept over Europe.

It also borrowed its rules of evidence from Roman canon law, under whose law of proof witness testimony, and the confession, in particular, reigned supreme. Circumstantial evidence—a bloody handprint on the wall, stolen loot in the suspect's closet, mud on his shoes, and the like— was considered so unreliable the law throttled it and stuffed it into a cramped cage. It could be introduced to corroborate testimony. But under the Carolina, a judge could never convict based on circumstantial evidence alone. A murder conviction had to rest upon one of two types of proof: *two* eyewitnesses or a confession. Two eyewitnesses to a stealthily planned murder might come along once in a detective's career. For all practical purposes, confession was the chief aim of an investigation. *Confessio est regina probationum*, lawyers said. Confession is the queen of proof.[2]

To induce confessions, the Carolina permitted torture. The procedure first called for the *territio*, or a verbal threat of torture, sometimes combined with a tour of the torture chamber and its instruments. Often that sufficed to scare a suspect into confessing. But if *territio* didn't work, the investigator moved on to *tortura*, the application of the instruments, in five increasing degrees. Methods included thumbscrews (vices to crush thumbs), Spanish boots (vices for the feet, often spiked on the inside), the rack (a frame with rollers to which the suspect was bound and stretched), spiked chairs, and the *strappado* (hanging the suspect by the arms behind the back).[3]

By 1835, the year Mayor Rieber was murdered, a wave of statutory reforms inspired by the Enlightenment was sweeping through European criminal law. Torture was one of the first things to go. Württemberg abolished it in 1809.[4] At the same time, German-speaking countries recognized the need for a new criminal code, one that allowed an investigator to build a case based on circumstantial evidence.[5] But Württemberg's new code for criminal procedure got hung up in legislative deliberations and never got enacted until 1843, eight years after the Rieber assassination.[6]

Between the prohibition of torture in 1809 and the recognition of circumstantial evidence in 1843, the odd marriage between the Roman-canon rules of evidence and abolition of torture effectively slammed several doors in Eduard Hammer's face. In the neighboring state of Baden, where similar legislative reforms took place, statistics collected by the high court during the Vormärz period (1830–48) painted a picture of criminals slipping through the investigators' fingers. When Baden abolished torture, the acquittal rate soared to a dizzying 43 percent. It sank to under 10 percent only after Baden instituted legislative reforms permitting convictions based on circumstantial evidence.[7]

The hurdles were high. To obtain a conviction, Eduard Hammer would have to find two witnesses to identify a suspect, or find a suspect who confessed. And even if he found a suspect, the magistrate's chances of obtaining a voluntary confession without torture were slim. The Carolina punished murder with the death penalty. Why would anyone voluntarily confess? But Magistrate Hammer would have to try anyway.

Circumstantial evidence did play one important role, at least in the investigation. Even though he couldn't base his case on it, Hammer could still use it as a lead. A good piece of circumstantial evidence might lead him to a suspect or force a witness to talk.

Hammer's first lead was unusual because *two* men had fired shots in the churchyard right before the mayor's assassination. Were they guilty? Could he get both to confess?

On the morning of October 23, Hammer did three things. He first searched the homes of all the possible suspects Mayor Rieber had mentioned to look for firearms and accoutrements. Who had buckshot and birdshot? Who made their own ammunition? He found several items, but on further questioning, only one provided a good lead.[8]

Friedrich Bleil, a young man who'd often gotten into arguments with Mayor Rieber, had obtained a passport just a few days prior. He had traveled to Heilbronn, a port city on the Neckar, the day before the murder. The city messenger told Hammer that Friedrich had given him his suitcase early in the morning on the day before the murder and paid him to deliver it to Heilbronn. His intentions were to travel from Heilbronn to Mannheim, but he had to go to Besigheim first. Apparently, he had found work in Mannheim. Mannheim, the city in which the Neckar flows into the Rhine, was then in the Grand Duchy of Baden, a separate country. Might the young man have slipped back to Bönnigheim to commit a murder before escaping down the Neckar to another country?[9]

Friedrich had been living at home with his father, an aging vintner. When Hammer searched the father's home, he found several pieces of lead and a ladle. That raised further questions. Did Friedrich make his own ammunition?

Answering those questions was Hammer's second task of the day. He interrogated several witnesses. First he hauled Friedrich's eighteen-year-old sister Juliane over to the city hall for questioning.

"In your father's house, various pieces of lead were found. Where did they come from?" Hammer asked.

"I don't know."

The scribe made a note to the file that the witness thought about it for awhile, and then changed her mind. What she said pointed to a childhood pastime, not a crime.

"Those little pieces of lead I got a long time ago, several years ago, from the vintner Siegel's daughter. She cast little rings—earrings—and I asked if she could give me a few pieces."

"At Bleil's house, there was also a ladle and a lead ball. Where did those objects come from?" Hammer asked.

"Old ladles like that we probably just had lying around. I don't know anything about a lead ball," said Juliane.[10]

Hammer didn't press it. But was she telling the truth?

Hammer now had Juliane's sixty-two-year-old father brought to the city hall to see what he had to say.

"When did your son Friedrich leave here?" asked Hammer.

Caspar Bleil said his son had left early Tuesday morning—the day before the murder—to go to Besigheim, where he picked up his passport. Then he traveled to Heilbronn, and from there, down the Neckar to Mannheim, where he had a job. The father hadn't seen the son since then; Friedrich hadn't returned to Bönnigheim.

The father's testimony corroborated the city messenger's statement.

"Where did the lead that was found in your house come from?" Hammer asked.

"A long time ago, they wanted to cast earrings. The neighbor's children and mine."

"Isn't there a lead ball, too?"

"Yes, I have several of them at home. I found them once in the ground. They've been lying around the house for a long time."[11]

The testimony about the earrings, at least, corroborated Juliane's testimony. The lead pieces might have been nothing more than part of a childhood attempt at making jewelry. But to be certain, he interrogated the Bleils' neighbors, the Siegels. Frau Siegel confirmed that her daughter Martha used to make earrings from lead.[12]

To rule out that Friedrich might have used the lead balls as ammunition against Mayor Rieber, Hammer commissioned the local commandant of the gendarmes to travel to Baden with one of Bönnigheim's councilmen and interrogate Friedrich.[13]

Then Hammer turned to his primary task for the morning: to clarify the churchyard shooting. He went to Christian Wachter's house and grilled him. Christian was bedridden after his thumb injury, but was at least able to talk.

The pistol that exploded belonged to him, Christian explained. They had each had their own pistols that night.

Hammer homed in on their motive for firing their pistols. Shooting within the town limits was illegal, so why had they done it?

"My friend said we should shoot there," Christian explained. Philipp Häberle's sister had told him that Catherine Maier, who usually worked in Stuttgart, was back in Bönnigheim that night, Christian explained.

The route that the two men took to the surgeon's house after the accident bothered Hammer. Instead of taking a direct route down the street to the west, they had taken a detour around the block, heading south, then west and finally north on the main street. The route brought them past the St. George fountain and close to Mayor Rieber's house at the exact time he was shot.

Why the detour?

"We didn't know where we were running," Wachter said. "I was in shock and neither of us knew what we were doing."

The crime scene sketch suggests another reason. The most direct route from the churchyard to the surgeon's house led right past Catherine's house. Perhaps Christian didn't want to parade his humiliation under her bedroom window.

But Christian had observed one thing unusual on his circuitous route to the surgeon. He heard a shot as he and his friend were running down the fire wagon alley toward the palace. Then, as they turned north onto the main street, there was a man standing at the St. George fountain—just standing, not doing anything else. Christian didn't know who it was.

"Where did the shot come from?" asked Hammer.

"I don't know. I was in pain. I can't say where the shot came from. I ran down there as soon as I fired my shot. I didn't know where to and just ran into the alley and then ran to Böhringer [the surgeon]."

"Describe the person you saw."

"It was a man, but what he was wearing, I don't know; because of my hand, I didn't really see anything. I think he had on a jerkin; I didn't see how heavy or thin or how tall he was."

Could this have been the assassin? If so, he might have been carrying a weapon.

"Did you see this person holding or carrying anything?" Hammer asked.

"I didn't see his hands, but he didn't have anything on his shoulders or head, but at the moment, I was running because of my hand."

The man was just quietly standing in the middle of the street when they ran by, Christian explained. He didn't say anything as they passed him. Christian couldn't remember in which direction the man was looking.[14]

Christian Wachter's explanations made sense and, for the most part, they corroborated Philipp Häberle's statement, even though the two had been interviewed separately. So far, this lead wasn't panning out.

Hammer needed a new lead, even if it were only circumstantial evidence.

The doctors who performed Mayor Rieber's autopsy the following day found just that.

CHAPTER SEVEN

Buckshot in the Scales of Justice

At 8:00 A.M. the next morning, Dr. Jung, the District Authority surgeon, picked up his scalpel to start the autopsy. The day before, Magistrate Hammer had locked Mayor Rieber's body in his apartment and placed the body under watch, as required by law, to make sure the mayor was really dead. Only after a day had passed without the body waking from the dead could they start the autopsy.[1]

The Carolina required autopsies in cases of unnatural deaths. Although the statute provided that qualified persons, such as surgeons, conduct the autopsy if they were available, it regulated only external examination of the body. By 1835, medicine had advanced and District Authority physicians also performed internal examinations to clarify the cause of death in criminal cases, although the law didn't standardize any of the procedures.[2]

The investigative team gathered on Saturday morning in Mayor Rieber's apartment, one day after his death. Dr. Hauff, the District Authority physician, assisted Dr. Jung with the autopsy. Hammer witnessed the procedure while Hammer's scribe transcribed the magistrate's dictation of the findings.

The autopsy began with an external examination of the corpse. It revealed a man of stocky physique and average height. The body was well formed and well nourished and had no abnormalities or fractures except for several wounds the physicians described.

The doctors found ten entrance wounds. Nine were in Rieber's upper back, all within the radius of a "dessert plate," and spread equally between the left and right side of the spine. Most of the wounds were small, but one was as large as 0.7 inches in diameter, about the size of an American dime. The tenth entrance wound was in the right arm. The doctors also found an exit wound below the right nipple.

Internal examination revealed extensive damage. After the physicians opened the mayor's chest cavity, they found three rib fractures. One rib had embedded itself in the spinal canal. Dr. Jung removed two buckshot pellets, one impacted in a rib and another in the sternum. They had penetrated inwards from the back.

The heart itself was uninjured, but the cardiac sac sported one hole the size of a large pea and several smaller ones the size of large mustard seeds. Two wound tracks penetrated the entire depth of the lungs from back to front. The lungs appeared collapsed, suggesting pneumothorax.

On opening the abdominal cavity, the physicians found two more wound tracks. One, with a diameter about the size of a dime, had bored through a lower lobe of Mayor Rieber's diaphragm. A second track, with a diameter about the size of a quill, had penetrated the liver and torn tissue along its entire length. Dr. Jung dissected the liver but couldn't find the projectile.

The surgeon incised the wound track in Rieber's right upper arm. There he located two more pieces of lead embedded in the bone tissue and removed them.

In his autopsy report, Dr. Jung concluded that the injuries to the lungs, cardiac sac, diaphragm, and liver were the cause of death; they had contributed to paralysis of both the lungs and heart.[3]

Eduard Hammer knew instinctively the shot pellets in Rieber's body were a significant lead. It was now time to examine them.

He now had several pellets recovered from the autopsy. He also had collected the pellet Dr. Nellmann had found while undressing Rieber and the pellets the councilman found in the dirt sifted from the ground in front of the mayor's door. Hammer found yet another lead pellet, embedded in the frame of the gate to Rieber's courtyard, that had flown astray during the shot. It was embedded forty-one inches above the ground. He searched the ground for a cartridge but didn't find any. Even where he couldn't find the ammunition, Hammer estimated the pellets' sizes based on the holes they left in the gate and in the mayor's organs.[4]

All of those findings pointed to one thing: The killer had used a variety of shot sizes, a mixture of buckshot and birdshot. But buckshot comes in various sizes, and establishing the exact size could help pinpoint the ammunition's origin. If the murderer had purchased the buckshot in Bönnigheim, it could make a good lead. Because the pellet the councilman found in front of Mayor Rieber's door weighed more than it should have, it might have pointed to irregular or homemade shot.

Hammer asked one of the councilmen to do some important ballistics legwork. He should visit all the stores in Bönnigheim. Hammer needed to know what size buckshot they had in stock and if any had sold shot recently to someone who wasn't a hunter. If they had, Hammer wanted the buyers' descriptions.[5]

In the meantime, the magistrate released Philipp Häberle from jail. He didn't consider either of the two young men in the churchyard guilty and listed a number of reasons why. Although firing weapons in town was illegal, it appeared to be a custom in Bönnigheim. Philipp and Christian had fired their weapons to salute a young woman, not to hurt anyone. Christian had been understandably in pain after losing a thumb and it was unlikely anyone would think to commit a murder having just lost an appendage that's necessary to hold and aim a weapon. And certainly, both men must have realized they would have fallen under suspicion because they had shown up at the surgeon's house with a pistol injury only minutes after the mayor had been shot. No one could be that dumb.

Hammer's decision was correct. It would take another thirty-seven years to prove it, but neither Philipp nor Christian shot the mayor.[6]

The councilman came back from his assignment. He had located three stores with buckshot in stock, but they hadn't sold any recently to anyone except to local hunters. A fourth store had recently sold shot, but it stocked only birdshot.

Now the presence of buckshot in Rieber's body and gate narrowed the field even further. The merchants stocked less buckshot than birdshot and might remember to whom they had sold buckshot. Hammer sent both councilmen back to question the store owners more thoroughly about sales of both buckshot and birdshot. He also asked them to bring back samples of buckshot from each store.[7]

The store samples were a major lead. Hammer weighed them, and none of them matched the weight and size of the buckshot found in Rieber's body. The buckshot from Rieber's body weighed 3.721 grams. The shot from the stores was larger and heavier. It weighed between 5.606 and 5.728 grams. Neither the pellets found in the courtyard nor those from the mayor's body corresponded to standard weights and sizes.[8]

That meant one of two things. Either the assassin had purchased his buckshot outside of Bönnigheim, or he made his shot himself. Hunters often saved money by making their own shot, either by dropping hot lead into cold water—the process forms round balls—or by pouring lead into a mold.

Wadding was usually made from felt or cloth. Might the buckshot, coupled with the deer hair wadding found by the corner of the washhouse, point to a deer hunter?[9]

It was a good lead. Combined with what happened next, it had the potential to break the case. Magistrate Hammer received a tip that someone had actually seen the assassin fleeing the scene of the crime.

CHAPTER EIGHT

Like Cain Will You Wander

Anyone can trim a quill to a sharp point and dip it into an inkwell. It is what happens afterwards that separates the poet from the scribe, the composer from the minstrel, and the preacher from his flock.

The task of holding the funeral service for Mayor Rieber on Sunday fell to the assistant pastor of Bönnigheim's sole Protestant church. Christoph Ulrich Hahn was the same pastor who had visited the mayor on his deathbed.

For any pastor, this service would be extraordinary. The death of a mayor alone would suffice to make a funeral different: A clergyman could expect to hold a mayoral funeral perhaps once or twice in his career. There was also the fact of the murder, a heinous crime. The congregation would probably be more agitated than usual. What perhaps bothered the pastor most was his suspicion that the assassin lived in Bönnigheim. If he did, the chances were good that he was a member of Hahn's church. Of Bönnigheim's 2,244 souls, all but six were Protestants.[1] The wording of Hahn's eulogy indicates the pastor had considered the possibility the assassin would attend the service and hear his eulogy.

So how should a pastor deal with a wolf in his flock?

That question made this funeral unique.

The pulpit might offer Hahn's only chance to speak to the assassin. His eulogy, then, would have two target audiences: the mourners and the murderer. And once he dipped his quill into the ink, the curate would have to forge the right words for both.

Hahn was quite well trained for this kind of task. He descended from a long clerical line that enjoyed some degree of fame. One of his uncles was a regional cofounder of a Lutheran reform movement called Pietism; another was a professor of theology at the University of Heidelberg. Pastor Hahn had an academic bent; he had earned a doctorate and enjoyed researching and publishing. Later in life, the kings of Prussia and Württemberg awarded him gold medals for his contributions to the arts and sciences. Hahn went on to found the German Red Cross and sign the First Geneva Convention as the representative for Württemberg.[2]

At the time of Mayor Rieber's funeral, Pastor Hahn was not quite thirty years old. He had already been in Bönnigheim for two years, and in that time founded the boys' school there with Mayor Rieber.[3] Photographs of Hahn during his later years depict a heavy-lidded, thin-lipped man with round, wire-framed glasses. He had dark eyebrows and a full head of hair he combed back. At the funeral, Pastor Hahn would have worn a black robe and the customary two white Geneva bands, rectangular strips of cloth about eight inches long that hung from his throat in an upside-down V.[4]

Pastor Christoph Ulrich Hahn, founding father of the German Red Cross and signatory to the first Geneva Convention. Photographed by F. Brandseph ca. 1870. (*Source:* Courtesy of the Württembergische Landesbibliothek, Graphische Sammlungen.)

Mayor Rieber's burial took place before the church service. The afternoon of Sunday, October 25, 1835, was sunny with a high around 48°F,[5] but the ground was probably still soggy from the previous three weeks of rain. A choir sang at the cemetery.

Afterwards, the congregation walked back through the city gates and gathered again in the church, where the mourners first sang the hymn Hahn selected—the same hymn Mayor Rieber had recited on his deathbed.[6]

From the pulpit, Dr. Hahn addressed his first target audience, the mourners:

> It is a highly painful, a very sad occurrence, my dearest and venerated bereaved, that brings us here together.
>
> A boldfaced murderer has suddenly torn our beloved friend from us in the midst of his labors, in the best years of his life, in the full vigor of his health, and has delivered us a wound that will not heal so quickly.
>
> Human solace cannot still our pain; we must tarry to that fountain of all solace and all tranquillity that springs forth to meet us so clearly in God's Word. . . . He has already prepared the balsam to heal the wounds.[7]

Following his scripture commentary, but before turning to the murderer, Hahn addressed the deceased, slipping into the *du* form, the intimate form of the German word for "you": "Thank you for all the love and friendship that you have so gladly shown us, even with sacrifice; thank you for all your toil and labor for the good of this city, from which you never shied away; thank you for the joy that we so often experienced in your presence."[8]

Now Hahn needed to steer a course between churning whirlpools. His aim was to save a soul. Presumably, he wanted to reach the murderer and persuade him to take advantage of pastoral confidentiality, to confess and receive counsel. Frightful rhetoric about the state of the murderer's soul might vent some of the congregation's anger and spur the sinner to reexamine his spiritual state, but if the pastor wanted the sinner to seek atonement in his office, he would also have to paint a picture of that open door.

In the end, Hahn chose the following words:

> But that which is solace to us, in the difficult trial to which the Lord has subjected us, must be dreadful to him through which this black deed was

perpetrated. The Lord knows everything; behold, He even knows what you have done in the dark night. He knows everyone; behold, He even knows you. And whether you hide in the darkness of the night; before Him the night is day, and darkness the light; and whether you flee to the east or to the west, to midnight or midday; He knows how to find you; and even if you have committed your deed so cleverly, He can turn your godless cunning to shame. Peace will never abide in you as long as you carry your deed with you; your own conscience will indict you and leave you no rest; the bloody figure of the victim will pursue you day and night, everywhere you go. The deep, heart-rending sighs the victim of your revenge exhaled, his tears, yes! and even his words of forgiveness he spoke for you more than once on his deathbed—they will lie on your heart like a hundredweight: your own unease will betray you and bear witness against you. Vagabond and transient, like Cain, will you wander. . . . But if your deed should remain undiscovered, how much more woe to you when the last hour strikes for you and you, with your unatoned sin, tread unreconciled before the throne of the Judge who has eyes like tongues of fire and before whom human reckoning is naught. Yes, Lord, don't count this sin against him until that day of the Last Judgment; lead him to the recognition of his misconduct while he still is on this earth, while it is still day, and before the nighttime comes when no man can work.[9]

In the days and months that followed, if Christoph Ulrich Hahn ever waited for someone to knock on his door and bare his soul, he probably waited in vain. He erred in his presumption. The assassin didn't live in Bönnigheim. His home was three hours away by horse and carriage.[10] In all likelihood, he never returned to Bönnigheim to hear the eulogy.

Pastor Hahn's eulogy was prophetic in one respect. The assassin would wander, farther than most known murderers of the nineteenth century. And that man would have been pleased to hear of a new suspicion growing in the hearts of Hahn's congregation, one directed away from him. Perhaps it was Hahn's words, "your own unease will betray you and bear witness against you," that caused the people of Bönnigheim to cast their eyes about. And their eyes settled on one young man. A twenty-five-year-old comb maker, Frederick Rupp, became the suspect of Bönnigheim's rumor mill. A forester's diary chronicles the gossip, but its author doesn't give the reasons for it.[11] The city couldn't know it yet, but its rumor mill was a paradox. The townsfolk were wrong, but without their false accusations against the comb maker Rupp, the case would never have been solved.

Mayor Rieber's grave, ca. 1970. (*Source:* Courtesy of Jochen Richer, Bönnigheim.)

CHAPTER NINE

Witness!

It was time for a shift in strategy.

Hammer's first leads about the youth shooting in the courtyard had gotten stuck like a wagon wheel in the mud. He spent the Tuesday following Mayor Rieber's funeral focusing on new witnesses and the murder weapon.

Christian Wachter had seen a man near the St. George fountain directly after Mayor Rieber was shot. But he hadn't seen the man carrying anything. Despite his searches of various suspects' homes, the magistrate hadn't yet found a murder weapon. Now he drained the St. George fountain, just north of the palace, to see if the murderer had dumped anything in it. He found nothing.[1]

Mayor Rieber had mentioned a thief and several soldiers who had gotten embroiled in a fistfight in a neighboring town. Hammer then grilled them, but couldn't place any of them at the crime scene. The thief had been at home with his family at the time of the shot, and his family corroborated it. The soldiers had alibis. One of them had visited his girlfriend near the upper city gate. He had been helping her family with chores when they heard the shots.[2]

But another soldier, Jakob Hofmann, had something interesting to say. He hadn't been at Rieber's courtyard that night; his commander had given him a mission, and then he went to bed. A few days later, while they were working the winepress together, another soldier told him an interesting story. He claimed to have seen the assassin fleeing the scene. The soldier's name was Jacob Wiedmann, and he lived a block north of the mayor's house.[3]

Hammer summoned Jacob Wiedmann to the city hall for an interrogation. The scribe transcribed each question and answer into the protocol, dipping his quill and scratching out the words in the old German, Gothic handwriting: "*27 October 1835. . . . Jacob Wiedmann, son of the lathe worker Philipp Jacob Wiedmann, resident. Soldier in the 6th Infantry Regiment, single, 26 years old.*"

Magistrate Hammer coupled his first question with a stern warning: "What can you say about the circumstances in which Mayor Rieber was wounded? In this important matter, every subject has the duty to testify and you are required to state the truth all the more, just as if you [were swearing on the Bible.]"

"I went home from Carl Friz's house at 9:45 P.M.," Jacob said, "and I passed the [St. George] fountain as I entered my alley. As I was walking past my garden, there was a shot, and I think there were two other shots back by the [St. George] fountain. And when I reached my stairs, a man wearing a brimmed cap slipped out of the corridor between my father's house and Christian Altmann's."

Hammer made a note to the file that the corridor was so narrow a heavy person would have to turn sideways to get through.

Narrow corridors between houses are common in the historic district of any German town. (*Source:* Ann Marie Ackermann)

"How long after the shot was that?" Hammer asked.

"Right after the shot, suddenly. I had hardly arrived at my stairs; I walked about fifty paces between the shot and when the man came out."

Fifty paces didn't quite make sense. The Wiedmanns' garden was next to their home; the distance would have been twenty paces at most. Fifty paces corresponded to the distance from the fountain to the house, not from the garden to the stairs. But as the investigator discovered, the residents of Bönnigheim had a tradition of shooting firearms in town during autumn. If hearing a shot wasn't an unusual event, maybe the witness didn't take note of where he was when he heard it. It was only later that Jacob Wiedmann learned the significance of his observations. Was he having trouble remembering precisely where he was?

"Describe the man you saw more precisely," Hammer probed.

"I didn't see his face. I only saw that he was wearing a greatcoat and a brimmed hat."

"Where did the man go once he left the corridor?"

"He crossed over [the alley] to the Müllers' house. I saw him go further—there's an alley that leads on from there."

"Did you see whether the man was carrying anything?"

"No. I didn't see anything," Jacob said.

"Did you see a rifle on him?"

"No, I didn't."

"How was the man walking?"

"Really fast. He wasn't running, but walking as fast as possible."

"How tall did the man appear?"

"Half a head taller than I am."

Jacob was five feet four inches tall. That would have put the man's height at about five feet eight inches.[4]

The man's location and behavior were suspicious, and Hammer was trying to home in on the presence of a weapon: "What was the man doing with his arms and hands?"

"He was walking really fast and his hands were swinging."

"Was the man fat or thin?"

"He was medium."

It's not difficult to read the magistrate's thoughts in his line of questioning. *Might it be that the witness just didn't see the weapon?*

"Was it dark when you saw this person?" Hammer asked.

"Yes, really dark," Jacob said.

"How far away from you was he when he walked by?"

"About six paces."

"How long did you watch him walking?"

"Just across the alley, about twenty paces."

"What color did the greatcoat and cap appear?" Hammer asked.

"I can't really say."

"To whom did you first report your observation?"

Jacob had told his father and one other person the day following the shooting.

Hammer was frustrated. This was a good lead, but it was coming in five days too late. Nearly two centuries later, his next question rises from the yellowing, archived pages of the protocol book with a sting, like salt and vinegar: "Why did you neglect to report this immediately?"

"I didn't know what it was; lots of shots like that one get fired and a lot happens in the alley at night," Jacob said.

"Where does the route lead that the man you saw that night took?"

"You come to an open place and that connects to a street."

"Do you know if anyone besides you saw the man?" Hammer asked.

"That I can't say."

"Who do you think the man might be based on his appearance, his gait, and his clothing?"

"I have no idea. I can only say I didn't see his face, and he was walking fast and loudly."

Magistrate Hammer asked Jacob if he would be willing to swear under oath. Jacob gave his consent. Then the investigator changed tactics. He began to home in on the timing between the shot and the man's emergence from the corridor.

"How long was it between the last shot and the two shots you already mentioned?" Hammer asked.

"When I left the Friz house, the two shots were fired, not even a quarter hour before the last shot."

It shouldn't have taken anything close to a quarter hour to get home. The Friz house was only about a hundred paces from the Wiedmanns' home. Jacob must have been ambling on his way home. More likely, he had paused to take in Halley's Comet. The timing suggests he was the man Christian Wachter saw, just standing in the middle of the street by the

St. George fountain. Hammer didn't ask him about Halley's Comet, but the street there opens to the north and was the only place on Jacob's walk home that would have offered a view of the northern sky and the comet. Anybody might have paused there to take in the sight.

"From what direction did the two shots come?"

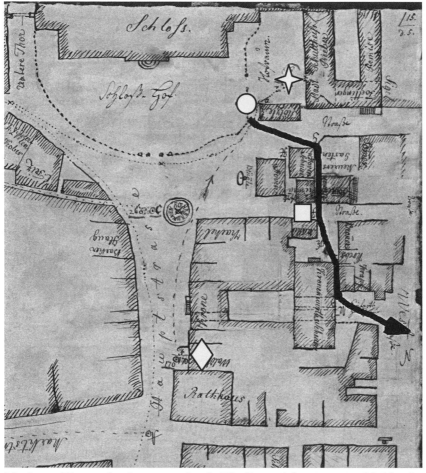

Magistrate Hammer's crime scene sketch. The line and figures were added by the author to make Hammer's marks more legible. The line indicates the direction Hammer noted for the murderer's flight. The diamond shows where Mayor Rieber had been dining, the star Rieber's location when he was shot, the circle the approximate location of the murderer when he fired, and the square Jacob Wiedmann's approximate location when he saw the man. (*Source:* Investigative file; courtesy of the Landesarchiv Baden-Württemberg, Staatsarchiv Ludwigsburg.)

"They must have been back there in the churchyard," Jacob said.

"While going home, did you see or hear anything on the *Hauptstrasse* [main street]?

"No, nothing. It was completely still."[5]

Hammer terminated the interrogation and made a note that the alley into which the man disappeared led to the west side of the town. That was probably the escape route.

Magistrate Hammer now focused on finding more witnesses along that route. Over the next couple of days, he interviewed all of Jacob's neighbors. Several had heard the shot, but they'd been in bed. They hadn't noticed the fleeing man. Hammer also asked Bönnigheim's residents if they could identify the suspect based on his clothing, but Jacob's description wasn't precise enough. Many men wore greatcoats and brimmed hats. Still, Jacob Wiedmann was the best lead Magistrate Hammer had. It was so good, in fact, that Hammer summoned Jacob the following day, put him under oath, and asked him to swear to the veracity of his witness statement. It was a step Hammer hadn't taken for any other witnesses.[6]

That makes it all the more puzzling that Hammer didn't pursue the lead any further. Perhaps he assumed if Jacob saw no weapon, the man wasn't a good suspect. If so, he was making a huge mistake. Hanns Gross, the nineteenth-century Austrian professor and father of forensic science, pounded this point into his readers' minds in his groundbreaking textbook on criminal investigation. "Never," Gross wrote, "should [an investigator] get confused by the fact that several witnesses assert a suspect walking by 'most definitely had no rifle on him'. . . ." That was because the takedown rifle was a popular murder weapon in the nineteenth century.[7]

Takedown rifles could be quickly disassembled into pieces, sometimes within seconds. And because they were illegal, they were often hand-constructed. They were particularly popular with poachers. Gross explained in his textbook:

In light of the ingenious, compact constructions of these rifles, I can completely understand why one old hunter half-jokingly once said: "A clever poacher carries his rifle folded up in his vest pocket." [It is amazing] how quickly, reliably, and securely a completely usable rifle can be assembled from numerous pieces and disassembled again. These circumstances make it clear why such weapons remain "completely undiscoverable" in numerous

poaching and murder cases. . . . [If witnesses say they saw no weapon,] the
rifle might have been distributed among various pockets, if not in the vest
pocket, or hidden in the upper parts of the pants (on the thighs), without
having been noticeable from the outside.[8]

Criminals misused takedown rifles frequently enough that Württemberg outlawed them in 1821, fourteen years before the murder.[9] If Magistrate Hammer considered the possibility of the poacher's weapon of
choice, he didn't mention it in the file. But what better place was there to
break down a rifle and hide the pieces than a dark corridor between two
houses? What Hammer didn't know was that the murderer had a career
that would have acquainted him with this type of weapon.

Instead, the detective and city administration focused on another facet
of the investigation. Hammer had been piecing together a biography of
the murder victim, a critical strategy that often reveals the motive for the
crime. But looking for the motive in this victim's life story was like playing
a game of blindman's bluff. Because Johann Heinrich Rieber had never
been married and had no children, Hammer could rule out a family quar-
rel. Mayor Rieber's career had been unremarkable. At the age of fifteen,
after having become an orphan, he had apprenticed as a scribe with one of
Bönnigheim's city officials. That led to positions of increasing responsibility with other cities, and when Bönnigheim's top administrative position
became vacant, his friends had encouraged him to return to his home-
town to run for mayor. Finding no discernible motive in the mayor's background, Hammer turned to witnesses for more information.[10]

He interviewed Mayor Rieber's relatives and collected information
about citizens who'd been unhappy with the mayor's administration.
Rieber's relatives could recall no recent discord in his private life.[11]

Hammer remembered a Bönnigheim defendant from a year prior, the
butcher Ferdinand Krafft. He had been convicted of insulting Mayor
Rieber and was sentenced to thirty-three days of house arrest. The mayor
of the nearby town of Hofen said he'd heard a disturbing rumor about
Krafft. When Krafft had visited an inn in the neighboring town of Walheim, he had apparently threatened to shoot the mayor.[12]

But when Hammer interrogated the butcher, he had an airtight alibi.
At the very moment the shot was fired in the mayor's courtyard, Krafft
was sitting in Bönnigheim's biggest inn, on the main street, talking with a

tanner who wanted to buy animal hides from his butcher's shop. At 10:00 P.M., a man burst through the door of the inn and announced the mayor had been shot. A guest at the inn told Hammer he had been sitting at a table with Krafft that night, and between 9:30 and 10:00 P.M., Krafft had never left the table. The innkeeper and yet another guest confirmed it.[13]

Hammer tracked down the source of the rumor only to find it was false. The innkeeper in Walheim was willing to testify under oath that Krafft had occasionally visited his inn to sell meat but had never made a threat against Bönnigheim's mayor. The magistrate dropped the butcher from his suspect list.[14]

Like several badgers escaping from the myriad entrances of their labyrinth den, new rumors emerged as soon as Eduard Hammer finished hunting down the one about Krafft. The townsfolk now suspected the forest ranger, Ernst Philipp Foettinger, who lived in the wing behind the mayor's apartment. But, as Magistrate Hammer noted in his file, the rumor was groundless. Hammer had interrogated him. Foettinger had been at home at the time of the shooting and his family could corroborate that.[15]

Then a vintner named Gottfried Kölle got his fingers caught in the cogs of the rumor mill. One day, after drinking too much of the fruit of Bönnigheim's vines, he made a slurred announcement in a winehouse about having shot the mayor. One of the guests reported the comment to the city hall, which reported it to the investigating magistrate on October 28. Hammer promptly arrested the vintner and held him over in the town jail for questioning.[16]

When Hammer interrogated Kölle the next day, the prisoner said he had no memory of what he had said while under the influence, but he was sure of one thing. He had not shot the mayor. The whole town knew him and knew he would never do such a thing. In fact, at the moment Mayor Rieber had been shot, Kölle had been in bed. When Hammer questioned Kölle's wife, she confirmed that. He had gone to bed around 7 P.M. on October 21. She'd also heard the rumor about her husband making a drunken comment in a tavern, "but," she added, "no one in all of Bönnigheim believes my husband killed the mayor!"[17]

The two city council members assisting Eduard Hammer came to Kölle's defense: They said he had a good reputation; he just pulled jokes when he got drunk. They didn't believe he could have killed Mayor Rieber either. On October 31, Hammer interviewed the man who had reported the comment. He knew Kölle well and also didn't think he meant it when he said it. Other witnesses in the winehouse had heard the comment too but said Kölle hadn't been serious.[18]

Hammer observed Kölle's behavior carefully during his confinement but couldn't detect any signs of guilt. He released the vintner and summarized his findings in a memorandum to the criminal court, suggesting that if the court found it necessary, he would reopen his investigation into the vintner as a suspect. The court never requested that Hammer do that.[19]

While Hammer was finishing up his investigation of Gottfried Kölle, he switched to a proactive tactic. When the city of Bönnigheim decided to offer rewards for information leading to the identification of the murderer and for solid leads, Magistrate Hammer went to the press with a plea for help. On October 31, he published an announcement of the reward in the local newspaper.[20]

Besigheim. (Call for witnesses.) Mayor Rieber of Bönnigheim was severely wounded by a shot in the back with buckshot and birdshot as he was going home on Wednesday, October 21 of this year between 9:45 and 10:00 P.M., carrying a lantern, only 3–4 paces from the entrance to his home, and died of the results of the injury in the course of 30 hours.

The undersigned directs this request to agencies and private persons for their sincere cooperation in discovering the author of this crime, and the request is all the more urgent because according to the deed's outward appearances, it was committed with a rare degree of outrageousness, and to date, nothing can be found in either the private or public life of the deceased that even appears to serve as motive. For reporting such facts through which the criminal is discovered, a reward of 200 *Gulden* will be paid, and for reporting facts that sufficiently justify further investigation, a reward of up to 100 *Gulden*.

October 31, 1835; Court of the Royal District Authority
Hammer[21]

The 200 *Gulden* reward amounts to nearly U.S. $5,000 today. If Hammer hoped that amount would motivate someone to reveal a secret and break the case, he was disappointed. No useful leads came in from the public as a result of this plea.

In early November, the commandant of the gendarmes traveled to the

Grand Duchy of Baden and on November 8, interrogated Friedrich Bleil in Mannheim. But Bleil had an alibi. He had already arrived in Mannheim on October 21, the day Mayor Rieber was shot, and had been there that evening. Mannheim's city administration confirmed his presence in the city on that date. Hammer scratched him from the suspect list.[22]

In the end, Hammer made the right decisions about Bleil, Krafft, Foettinger, and Kölle. But it took another thirty-seven years to find out who the real suspect was—and confirm the innocence of the men on Hammer's suspect list.

In the first week of November, Magistrate Hammer tried one more tactic: he wrote to a neighboring District Authority court to ask for assistance in identifying stores that had recently sold buckshot or birdshot to Bönnigheim residents or to "suspicious persons." The court wrote back to say it had inquired and there had been no suspicious sales.[23]

But the court and shop owners in the other district had no information with which they could categorize a buyer as suspicious: Nowhere in his letter to the neighboring authority or in his call for witnesses did Hammer provide a description of the man Jacob had seen. He never tried to collect information about people who made their own ammunition or about all recent sales of buckshot or birdshot. He never made Jacob's description public.

That may have been the biggest error in his investigation.

Decades later, information from U.S. military records would corroborate Jacob's estimate of the man's height. In all likelihood, Jacob had seen the murderer. A more detailed inquiry might have helped because the murderer was indeed from the neighboring District Authority where Hammer had made his inquiry.

CHAPTER TEN

The Birth of Forensic Ballistics

Tiny scratches etched into the soft lead of the shot pellets. That's what Magistrate Hammer found when he took a closer look at two of the projectiles removed from Rieber's body. Pellets can flatten when they're shot, and it was on their flattened sides that he found them: "irregular striations . . . on both a buckshot and birdshot pellet," he noted to the file.[1]

It was a clue, and in Hammer's hands, it became a good clue.

Sometimes, in desperation, an investigator will invent a new technique. That's exactly what the investigating magistrate of the District Authority of Besigheim now did. The scratches on the pellets became the vehicle through which Eduard Hammer displayed his analytical brilliance. For a brief moment, his investigative genius shone like a supernova before the case went cold. If for no other reason, the murder of Johann Heinrich Rieber deserves a footnote in the annals of forensic science for what Hammer did next.

A modern forensics firearm examiner would try to use those striations to identify the individual weapon that shot the pellets. Even in 1835, every gunsmith knew what caused those scratches. Hammer recognized them too. Some firearms, like rifles, have spiral grooves on the surface of the bore, the inside of the barrel. This so-called "rifling" throws the bullet into a spin, imparting a more accurate flight path. But the grooves leave rifling marks on the projectiles, little striations like the ones Hammer had just discovered.

Not all firearms have rifling. Shotguns don't. Usually shotguns are used for shooting shot. Firing shot through a rifle could damage the rifling and ruin the rifle. But in a murder case, there is no telling what a suspect might have done. Any person angry enough to point a firearm at another person and pull the trigger might not care about damage to the weapon. In fact, using the wrong type of weapon could be a ploy to throw law enforcement off the trail.

Professor Hanns Gross, the Austrian father of forensic science, put it this way in his nineteenth-century handbook:

> No one wants to ruin a rifle barrel by using it to shoot shot pellets unless the act involves a special intent, in which case the person will hardly care about maintenance of the rifle barrel. . . . Anyone investigating gunshots cannot be careful enough in drawing conclusions about the suspect firearm, based on the projectiles found, and the converse. A premature assertion, "Here a shotgun was used because shot pellets were found," or "Here a rifle was used because a bullet was fired," can never be justified and can lead to serious mistakes.[2]

Hammer had no intention of making a mistake like that, but he first needed to rule out whether something other than the rifling in the murder weapon had scratched the pellets. It was Mayor Rieber's bones he was concerned about. So the magistrate's first step was to have the physician and surgeon who performed the autopsy examine the striations on the pellets. When both agreed the scratches were not caused by bone tissue, Hammer called in a gunsmith from a neighboring town as an expert witness. And the gunsmith's conclusions appeared to offer the lead Hammer needed to break the case.[3]

If a collision with bones didn't cause those scratches, the gunsmith explained, they had to have come from a rifle. He could think of no other explanation. And they didn't come from just any old rifle. The scratches originated from an unusual type of rifling. Period rifles usually had six to twelve grooves in their barrels, but some had up to 120 hairlike grooves, so-called "fine grooving." That type of rifling was rare, but it was precisely what had etched the striations in the pellets from Rieber's body.[4]

This was an excellent lead. Fine grooving narrowed down the field of possible murder weapons significantly, and with luck, breaking the case promised to become a simple matter of locating a rare fine-grooved rifle and its owner.

Hammer issued an order. All residents in Bönnigheim had to turn over

Fine-grooved versus conventional rifling. (*Source:* Courtesy of Volker Schäfer, Landeskriminalamt Baden-Württemberg.)

their long-barreled firearms to the city hall for inspection. Although the Kingdom of Württemberg did not then require licensing for weapon ownership, it had already restricted the average citizen's right to own a rifle. Secret ownership of a rifle was criminalized. Hunters or members of a shooting club could own rifles. But any citizen who didn't fall under a statutory exception had to take an oath that he didn't own a rifle. For that reason, Hammer could compile a list of known rifle owners in Bönnigheim and ask them to turn over their weapons.[5]

Hammer collected forty-eight firearms. The gunsmith then checked their bores. Any with smooth bores and normal rifling were eliminated. Only two appeared to have fine grooving. Both of them belonged to the same man, Ludwig Schwarzwälder, the forestry assistant who lived in the palace next door to Mayor Rieber and who had responded to the shooting. The fine-groove rifling in the bore of one of his rifles looked blunted by wear and appeared somewhat irregular. The gunsmith had to completely dismantle the other rifle to tell for sure, but what originally had appeared to be fine-groove rifling turned out to be just scratches caused by the rifle butt. The gunsmith could rule out that firearm as the murder weapon.[6]

To check if Ludwig's other rifle might have been the murder weapon, Hammer loaded it with buckshot and birdshot and test-fired into a 22.5-by-17-inch sack of sawdust. He retrieved the shot from the sack, and together with the gunsmith and two "knowledgeable" judicial officers, compared it to the pellets extracted from Rieber's body.[7]

Now the gunsmith could rule out the rifle. "One cannot conclude that the buckshot found in the body was fired from the test rifle. That is apparent from the buckshot fired today. The rifling in the rifle is not as sharp-edged as the distinct grooves on the buckshot from the body." Hammer and the two law enforcement officers agreed, based on their own comparisons. Ludwig's second rifle wasn't the murder weapon either.[8]

But it made sense. Ludwig had a pretty solid alibi: He had been talking to his colleague Eduard in Eduard's bedroom when both heard the shot. Magistrate Hammer had interviewed both men separately, and their stories were identical. After he examined the rifle, Hammer interrogated them one more time but only came to the same result. The forestry assistant Ludwig Schwarzwälder wasn't the murderer. Hammer summed up in a memorandum to the file: "As important as the results were, and as promising as [the technique] appeared, they didn't bring any success with the weapons collected in Bönnigheim."[9]

Today, Volker Schäfer, a firearms examiner with the state police (*Landeskriminalamt*) in Baden-Württemberg, calls Eduard Hammer's test-firing and comparisons "a very formidable investigative technique"[10] for its time. A brief stroll through the history of forensic ballistics explains why. Eduard Hammer stands out like a man half a century before his time.

Alexandre Lacassagne, a French pathology professor who founded his own school of criminology in Lyon, is considered the father of forensic ballistics, the fine art of identifying a firearm based on the striations on its projectiles. Lacassagne performed autopsies in two murder cases in February 1888 and removed bullets from both bodies. Like Hammer, Lacassagne noticed striations etched into the bullets. Like the German detective, the French pathologist called in a gunsmith for assistance in interpreting them. And like Hammer, Lacassagne test-fired suspect weapons and compared their projectiles with those from the victims' bodies. In both cases, the evidence pointed to revolvers recovered from the suspects. The bullets from one victim's body had seven striations. The suspect revolver had an unusual number of rifling grooves, namely seven. In the second case,

Lacassagne examined and measured the striations with a magnifying glass and recorded uneven surfaces scoured inside the striations. The pattern was the same on the test-fired bullet. In both cases, the suspects were convicted of murder. Lacassagne became the first person to identify a murder weapon based on the rifling marks on its projectiles.[11]

Realizing he had stumbled on to a new technique, the pathology professor and one of his students began testing various makes of French, American, and British revolvers by test-firing them and examining the striations they produced. They compiled a table of twenty-six revolvers with descriptions of their projectiles and published it, together with a discussion of both murder investigations, in the French journal *Archives de l'anthropologie criminelle* in 1889. That was the birth of what a later scientist dubbed "forensic ballistics."[12]

The literature prior to Lacassagne's publication contains several successful attempts to identify or eliminate a suspect weapon on the basis of projectiles removed from the victim's body, but none of them were based on striations. In 1794, a man was shot in the head by a burglar in Lancashire, England. On autopsy, a physician recovered not only a ball from a pistol but a portion of the wadding used to separate the ball from the gunpowder. The wadding was made of paper torn from a song sheet. Eighteen-year-old John Toms was later arrested with damning evidence in his pocket: a ripped song sheet matching the torn piece from the wadding. Toms was convicted and hanged on March 23, 1794. Although the matching wadding didn't constitute forensic ballistics in the purest sense of the word, it was a step in the right direction. Detectives were beginning to draw conclusions about a weapon based on its projectiles.[13]

The Frenchman Eugène François Vidocq of the security force Brigade de la Sûreté is credited with solving a case in 1822 when he ordered the removal of a bullet from a murder victim's body. He could rule out the husband as a suspect based on bullet size comparison. The bullet was too large to fit into the husband's dueling pistols. Vidocq then focused his attention on the deceased woman's lover, examined his firearm, and found a perfect fit. The lover confessed and was dispatched by guillotine.[14]

By 1831, comparison of a victim's wound track with the caliber of the weapon appears to have become a recognized investigative technique in Germany. An anthology of German criminal cases contains a proceeding in which the defense attorney complained to the court about the investigator not having done it.[15]

Henry Goddard, a member of the Bow Street Runners, London's first professional police force, obtained a confession for a staged burglary in 1835 based on his ballistic analysis. A burglar had allegedly shot at the butler, but missed, and then fled with jewelry and a silver plate. Goddard was able to extract the bullet from the headboard of the butler's bed and found a tiny imperfection, a little round pimple, on its surface. It came from a bullet mold and Goddard found a matching imperfection in the butler's own mold. The butler then confessed to staging the burglary.[16]

All of these early cases were examples of primitive firearm identification, in that investigators drew conclusions about a weapon or ammunition based on their projectiles, but none of them focused on striations. Lacassagne was the first to make the striation technique public. But how did Hammer know about the technique over fifty years earlier? If nothing else, Hammer's ballistic procedures raise the question of whether that kind of technique was commonly known and used in Germany. An exhaustive search of the German literature has not revealed any German publications about forensic ballistics prior to the Rieber assassination.[17] Occasional cases of an investigator consulting with a gunsmith in the mid-nineteenth century do appear in the German literature, but the issues involved were how recently the gun had been cleaned, filed, or fired, or from what distance it had been fired.[18]

Württemberg's state archives in Ludwigsburg, which house Württemberg's old criminal files, don't appear to contain any other cases prior to Rieber's murder involving an examination of striations. The finding aids mention only one other murder in which a gunshot was the cause of death. A load of pure birdshot was used, and the suspect weapon was a stolen rifle. Birdshot is small enough to make a forensic examination of any striations extremely difficult. The striations, if there were any, weren't mentioned at all in the investigator's summary of the case.[19]

In the first half of the nineteenth century, poisoning, strangling, and stabbing were far more popular methods of committing murder in Württemberg. This was most certainly due to the period gun controls. The law prohibited anyone other than a government officer, soldier, hunter, forester, or member of a shooting club from owning a firearm. Because shooting crimes were less common in Württemberg, publications focused on other investigative techniques.

There were two other good reasons why investigators hadn't developed the procedure prior to Lacassagne and both had to do with firearm technology. Period guns distorted the pattern of the striations. One factor was mechanical. Guns of the early nineteenth century were predominantly muzzle loading. The projectile had to be hammered down the bore of the rifle with a mallet. Bullets could pick up striations both on the way in, while being hammered into place, and on the way out, while being shot. A set of two superimposed striations hindered analysis. Both revolvers and breech-loading rifles were invented around the time of the Rieber murder but became popular only later in the nineteenth century. Those technologies load the ammunition from the back, not the front. So by 1888, Lacassagne was working with a technology far more conducive to striation comparison than Hammer was.

The second factor had to do with the propellant. Until smokeless nitrocellulose powder was developed in the 1880s, black powder was the only propellant available. The original "gun powder," a mixture of sulfur, charcoal, and saltpeter, burned both fast and dirty. Black powder fouled the bore with corrosive residues that required constant cleaning. If the rifling got coated with debris, it could keep the bullet from grazing the rifling, and thus hinder the formation of striations.[20]

So when Lacassagne performed his two autopsies in 1888, technology had just flung open the door to the development of forensic ballistics. He was the first to walk across the threshold and positively identify a murder weapon.

Given the state of firearm technology in 1835, what could Eduard Hammer find by test-firing? Something had allowed Eduard Hammer to stick his foot through the door well before Lacassagne and successfully eliminate a suspect weapon through ballistic fingerprinting. Was it possible that buckshot pellets, because they are smaller than bullets, could avoid getting scratched while being hammered into the bore? If so, and if the gun were clean, might some pellets pick up useful striations when fired?

Volker Schäfer, a firearms examiner with the state police in Baden-Württemberg, tested this theory in May 2015. He obtained a replica of an antique, muzzle-loading pistol with fine-groove rifling and invited the author to his laboratory, where he loaded the gun with two different com-

Buckshot with striations sufficient to classify them as having been fired from a weapon with finely grooved rifling. They were obtained by test-firing shot pellets at the state police facilities in Baden-Württemberg in an attempt to duplicate the conditions in the shooting of Mayor Rieber. (*Source:* Courtesy of Volker Schäfer, Landeskriminalamt Baden-Württemberg.)

binations of various sized buckshot, coupled with birdshot, and test-fired them. His results were similar to Hammer's. A few pellets picked up striations that were sufficient to classify the murder weapon as having a fine-grooved bore and to eliminate both smooth-bores and customary rifling in a suspect weapon.[21]

It was an unusual constellation of circumstances, then, that facilitated Hammer's feat. The murder involved a shooting, which was rare for its time in Württemberg. The murder weapon had a bore with unusual fine-grooved rifling. The rifle was clean enough to allow the projectiles to pick up striations. Finally, the murderer used shot instead of a bullet in his rifle, and that facilitated a clearer pattern of striations.

Based on the literature, Eduard Hammer, the investigating magistrate of the District Authority of Besigheim in the Kingdom of Württemberg, might have been the first to ever use the technique. His investigative file, at least, may constitute the first recorded instance of an attempt to identify an individual murder weapon based on comparisons of the striations on the projectile in a crime with a projectile from test-firing a suspect weapon. Hammer might also be the first documented detective to have *eliminated* an individual suspect weapon with forensic ballistics.

Had Hammer written an article about his technique, he might be considered the father of forensic ballistics today. He certainly would have had no personal objection against writing an academic publication; in fact, he had already published a journal article on judicial administration.[22]

But he was bound by ethics. Had he published something about his striation comparisons, it could have alerted the murderer to one critical fact: The detective knew the murder weapon was a rifle with fine-groove rifling. The rational response would have been for the murderer to ditch his rifle so that the detective could never find it and use it for a ballistic comparison. Hammer, then, had a professional duty to keep his technique a secret until the murderer was apprehended and the case solved. Unfortunately for Hammer, the assassin wasn't identified until after his death. He never had a chance to publish anything about his new technique.

Law enforcement officers sacrifice a great deal in their pursuit of public safety. They have to drop other commitments to testify in court; they need to be ready to answer the call of duty in the middle of the night. They sacrifice time with their families. They put their personal well-being and sometimes even their own lives on the line. Some officers suffer psychologically under the burden of a gruesome investigation and the public's demand that police quickly locate a killer.

And on occasion, they even sacrifice recognition for a breakthrough in forensic science.

Eduard Hammer's test-firing of Ludwig's rifle had one sad footnote. Somehow word of the investigator's interest in the rifle leaked out to the public. Like a corkscrew, gossip twisted the truth into barbed slander. Despite the evidence exonerating Ludwig, a rumor spread through town that he was the murderer and his rifle the murder weapon. Ludwig Schwarzwälder would suffer from public suspicion for the rest of his life.[23]

It would take another thirty-seven years to clear his name.

CHAPTER ELEVEN

Celestial Metronome

As it rounded the sun in late November 1835, Halley's Comet disappeared from view, coming out again at the beginning of 1836. It was now fading. But then, in late January 1836, something happened that has been observed only rarely in Halley's history. The comet experienced a "surge," a tremendous outburst of energy that increased its apparent size and brightness.[1]

Such surges had occurred during Halley's 1145 and 1066 visits, and perhaps in 607 as well. Each time, they appeared sixty-three to seventy-seven days following perihelion, or the closest pass to the sun. The 1836 surge kept Halley's Comet visible to the naked eye longer than originally predicted—until late March in the Southern Hemisphere.[2]

Inflated and luminescent, the comet hanging over San Antonio in February, and perhaps March as well, entered into folklore. There Texians had already captured the city and its fortress-like mission, the Alamo, in December. Santa Anna's Mexican troops arrived on February 23 and began a siege. Legend has it that the comet was visible during the siege and portended the fall of the Alamo. If Halley was still visible in the Northern Hemisphere, a norther during the night of February 25 probably veiled it. But as negotiations for surrender failed and the surrounded Texians waited for relief, the weather cleared. The comet might have been visible March 2–5.[3]

Clouds obscured the sky on that awful night of March 5–6. Even though the moon was up, it was veiled in an opaque haze.[4] The situation looked so hopeless for the men holding out in the Alamo that their commander, William Barret Travis, drew a line in the dirt and asked all of them who were willing to remain and die with him to step across the line. Everyone except a Frenchman named Louis Rose did. Later, starting at 1:00 A.M. on March 6, Santa Anna used the darkness of cloud cover to put his troops into place. He attacked just before dawn. In the end, Santa Anna killed every last Texian male—182 or 183 of them, excepting Travis's slave, Joe. Then the Mexican forces stacked up the corpses, poured oil on them, and set them afire. The dead included Davy Crockett and Jim Bowie.[5]

If comets really do portend disaster, it is hard to say for whom. The Alamo went badly for the Texians, but most of the rest of the short war would go badly for Mexico. The Alamo galvanized many Texians who previously felt neutral on the question of revolution. The romance of fighting to the last man increased support for the Texian rebellion in the United States. "Remember the Alamo!" became the battle cry of the revolution.[6]

On March 2, during the siege of the Alamo, a new Texian convention gathered at Washington-on-the-Bravos declared independence for the Republic of Texas. Its declaration reads somewhat like the American Declaration of Independence, invoking the right "to enjoy that constitutional liberty and republican government to which [Texians] had been habituated in the land of their birth, the United States of America."[7]

The Texians won the revolution in the eighteen-minute-long Battle of San Jacinto near present-day Houston at 3:30 A.M. on April 21, 1836, by attacking the Mexican army in its sleep. They killed 630 Mexicans and captured 730 against a loss of eight. Santa Anna was captured.[8] One of eight inscriptions on a battle monument erected a century later would emphasize the historical repercussions of this battle: "Measured by its results, San Jacinto was one of the decisive battles of the world. The freedom of Texas from Mexico won here led to annexation and to the Mexican War, resulting in the acquisition by the United States of the states of Texas, New Mexico, Arizona, Nevada, California, Utah, and parts of Colorado, Wyoming, Kansas, and Oklahoma. Almost one-third of the present area of the American nation, nearly a million square miles of territory, changed sovereignty."[9]

Some Texians insisted on Santa Anna's immediate execution, but the commander in chief of the Texan army, Sam Houston, and the president of the interim government of Texas, David G. Burnet, were too smart for that. Santa Anna was worth more to Texas alive than dead, Burnet insisted.[10] He forced Santa Anna to sign two treaties, one public and one secret. The first provided for prompt evacuation of the Mexican army from

Texas territory north of the Rio Grande. In the secret treaty, Santa Anna agreed to prepare his cabinet for recognition of the Government of Texas upon his return to Mexico. The secret treaty also set the Texan-Mexican boundary "not to extend beyond the [Rio Grande.]"[11]

When Sam Houston became the first president of the Republic of Texas in October 1836, one of his highest priorities was obtaining foreign recognition. When Santa Anna offered to meet with President Andrew Jackson to help arrange U.S. recognition, Houston was all too happy to send him. Santa Anna met with Jackson, sailed back to Mexico, and accomplished nothing. In fact, he repudiated the treaties once he set foot again on Mexican soil.[12]

Mexico had made a brilliant chess move while Santa Anna was still a prisoner in Texas. Just six days after the treaties were executed, Mexico City renounced Santa Anna as president and declared void all his actions as a captive.[13] Mexico did not recognize Texan independence.

The unsettled issue of the treaties' validity would continue to haunt the United States of America. In ten years time, President James K. Polk invoked the treaties, together with American blood spilled on the contested territory, as a ground for declaring war with Mexico.[14] Abraham Lincoln repudiated the treaties as a freshman congressman in his first full-length speech before the House of Representatives in 1848.[15]

In Arlington, Virginia, Robert E. Lee followed the war with interest. Dramatic battles of the Texas revolution had provided ripe fodder for the vibrant American penny press, the new flurry of one-cent-per-copy-come-read-all-about-it newspapers that focused on sensational news and targeted working-class readers. That reading material, coupled with a promotion to first lieutenant, buoyed Lee up and lessened his career frustrations. He decided to stay in the army.[16]

The Rieber assassin would become a volunteer soldier at Lee's side.

And the United States would eventually invade Mexico.

CHAPTER TWELVE

A Note in the Woods

All in all, a signpost deep in the forest was a strange place to find a clue.

In the late sixteenth century, a forestry superintendent named Caspar Pfeiffer built a cabin in the woods to offer a refuge to hunters and foresters. Up in the Stromberg mountain range, three-and-a-half miles from Bönnigheim's town center, the Pfeiffer cabin still offers benches and a roof to weary hikers. It's strategically located at the intersection of five forestry roads—narrow gravel paths used only by hikers, hunters, and forestry vehicles. A signpost stands at the intersection. It has several arms indicating which paths lead to the next towns.

A similar signpost stood there in the nineteenth century. Its arms were large, measuring almost one by three feet. White paint covered the arms, probably to provide a contrast to the dark lettering. On the white paint, two men found a clue in May 1836.[1]

Eduard Hammer had already terminated his daily investigation of the Rieber assassination. He had been able to eliminate all his possible suspects. Ludwig Schwarzwälder, the forester with the fine-grooved rifle, the young, pistol-shooting men in the churchyard, the forest ranger Foettinger, the vintner who'd make a drunken announcement, and the young man who'd traveled to Baden to start a new job all had good alibis. The suspects Mayor Rieber had suggested did too. Bönnigheim residents had fingered a few other people in the meantime, but Hammer had been able to eliminate them all as viable suspects.

As the investigation began to falter, someone—Hammer didn't note whether it was the city or a private donor—raised the reward for identification of the murderer to 1,000 *Gulden*, almost U.S. $22,000. But the new, generous carrot didn't result in any helpful bites.

"It is to my greatest regret," he wrote to the regional criminal court in Esslingen in May 1836, "that it so happened that a gruesome crime will remain unpunished." But he doubted the efficacy of continuing the investigation, he told the court. Motive is often the key to identifying a suspect, and in this case, the investigator had no idea what the motive could be. "The motive is based on such clandestine circumstances," Hammer wrote, but "that's precisely what's blocking sources and avenues of the investigation. In the meantime, I will not fail to investigate any facts that might justify reopening the investigation."[2]

Then the clue came in from the woods.

Hammer never realized the significance of the new lead because he investigated it from the wrong angle. In retrospect, it was one of the best leads in the case, precisely because it could have uncovered the motive. And the motive usually leads back to the murderer.

May is a delightful month in the Stromberg forest. Fluting blackbird songs and resonant two-note cuckoo calls filter through the foliage above

The Pfeiffer cabin in the Stromberg mountain range. (*Source:* Ann Marie Ackermann)

the soft, steady thrum of the insects. In 1836, a spacious stand of beech trees surrounded the Pfeiffer cabin, and by early May, the trees would have leafed out in an inviting spring green. The Pfeiffer cabin offered a pleasant destination for a day hike.

Two men had independently hit upon the same idea and had been strolling separately in the woods. But when they serendipitously ran into each other at the cabin, the case took a strange turn. They were first to notice a freshly penciled message on the signpost. On the white background of the arm pointing to Bönnigheim, someone had written three lines, although one word was unclear:

> *I need to tell you citizens something*
> *Your shoemaker . . . t . . . ger*
> *shot the mayor.*

When Hammer heard about the note in the woods, he traveled up to the Pfeiffer cabin to document the location and text. The detective dismantled the arm from the signpost for closer inspection, and when he examined it in detail, he could make out the word "Vötinger."[3]

A second arm contained two more lines:

> *In 1836, a shoemaker apprentice will travel*
> *to Heilbronn.*[4]

Twelve miles to the northeast, Heilbronn was the nearest large city, a port on the Neckar River. Local residents immigrating to America usually traveled overland to Heilbronn and from there by boat down the Neckar and Rhine to Amsterdam, where they boarded transatlantic ships.

Hammer's investigation now led him 537 feet down the mountain range to Bönnigheim. A quick check showed there wasn't any shoemaker in Bönnigheim with a name like "Vötinger," but a chance meeting with a forester cleared up the confusion. Bönnigheim's forest ranger, Foettinger—with the same German pronunciation as "Vötinger"—was nicknamed "Shoemaker." He had had that moniker for years, ever since he once had too much to drink and passed out in the neighboring town of Cleebronn. Someone had popped the drunk into a wheelbarrow and wheeled him back home to Bönnigheim. When asked what he was transporting in the wheelbarrow, the man pushing it answered, "A shoemaker." The name had stuck ever since.[5]

The forest ranger Ernst Philipp Foettinger had to have been the person meant in the note. And because Foettinger lived in the wing right behind Mayor Rieber's apartment, he was well positioned to shoot the city's top administrator and slip back home unseen.[6]

But for Magistrate Hammer, Foettinger's home was exactly where the lead fizzled out. He had already interrogated the forest ranger. Foettinger had been at home, with his family, at the time of the shooting and, to be more precise, in bed with his wife. Frau Foettinger and their daughter Heinrike had confirmed his statement. All three were at home when they heard the shot.[7]

Magistrate Hammer did not pursue the lead further, probably inferring that the note in the woods had been a prank. That was the biggest error in his investigation. He focused solely on the question of whether Foettinger was a viable suspect, and once he had ruled the "shoemaker" out, he let the lead drop.

Had he turned the question around, however, and asked if there was anybody out there who was angry enough with the forestry department, and with the forest ranger in particular, to pin a murder on him, his investigation might have taken a different course. A review of the forestry personnel files and recent job applications could have led him to the assassin. The timing, location, and content of the note all suggest the assassin wrote it.

Mayor Rieber's murderer was a hunter's apprentice and would have been intimately familiar with the forests of the Stromberg and Heuchelberg mountains. He most certainly knew the Pfeiffer cabin. As a hunter, he would have been allowed to purchase buckshot; he might have even made it himself.

He must have known the forest ranger Foettinger personally. The murderer's previous employment with the forestry department as a lumberjack would have acquainted him with the ranger. Because a forestry statute gave the forestry department direct control over all hunting within its district, the foresters played a supervisory role in the assassin's apprenticeship, even if they weren't the assassin's direct mentors. And it was the forest ranger who usually carried out the hunting duties in the royal forests. If there was any forester in the department who was mostly likely to have had contact with the young hunter, it was Foettinger.[8]

The assassin had recently applied for a lateral transfer as a game warden. Because a forestry statute required forest rangers to train new game wardens, it was likely that Foettinger had interviewed him. But the assassin didn't get the job. And that was the catalyst for the murder.[9]

The two men found the note in the woods only days after the assassin had left Württemberg for good, almost certainly traveling through Heilbronn, the Neckar port mentioned in the note. Had he received the job, he would have become Foettinger's apprentice, or "a shoemaker apprentice." Was the murderer giving a clue to his emigration? And might he have written the note as a final revenge against the forestry department and the man who should have hired him?

We will never know for sure who penciled those words, but the timing, location, and content contain intriguing parallels to the assassin's life.

Hammer wrote his last note to the file in 1837. It concerned a rumor that proved unsubstantiated. Then the case went as cold as the frozen grapes the vintners pressed in winter to make ice wine.[10]

In the meantime, the comb maker Frederick Rupp had been suffering ever since a groundless rumor began circulating through the streets and alleys of Bönnigheim. People said the young man, who had recently been discharged from royal military service and taken over his father's comb-making business, had pulled the trigger. But he hadn't.[11]

Frederick came from a family that was rich in children, not money. His father's estate was worth just a fraction of Mayor Rieber's. The parents had raised seven children in a modest house, where the father ran a workshop for producing combs for both people and horses. The family also farmed a vineyard on the side, pressed grapes in the fall, and produced some wine. By the time of the Rieber assassination, Frederick's father had already died, leaving his mother Elisabetha Gottliebin as the reigning matriarch.[12]

But reputation is everything in a small town, and Bönnigheim was no exception. With a population of only 2,244, all the residents were likely to have known each other. Anyone who got caught in the cogs of the rumor mill could expect to suffer lasting professional and social consequences.[13]

By the summer of 1836, Frederick's family had had enough. The Rupps decided to emigrate. One older brother was already married, settled in another town, and decided to stay. An older sister had already moved to America in 1832, married a Polish dyer, and was living in Philadelphia. But the rest—Elisabetha, Frederick, an older sister, and four younger siblings—renounced their Württemberg citizenship and appeared before the Bönnigheim city council in June 1836 to apply for a passport and the necessary permission to emigrate. Under Württemberg law, the city council had to approve all emigrations in advance. The family had a place to stay in America, according to the emigration documents. The sister in America had offered a temporary home.[14] Now all that remained was to sell off their possessions and arrange for their passage from Amsterdam to New York. And it wasn't cheap. Tickets cost at least €7,500 per person in today's values.[15]

One other person stood behind Frederick, and that was his fiancée, Caroline Luise Braun, a twenty-five-year-old butcher's daughter from the neighboring town of Vaihingen. Although forsaking her country and family of origin to move to the United States was probably not part of her dreams when she had first said "ja" to Frederick, she nevertheless appeared before her city council the same month to make the same application.[16]

Frederick's last public act in Bönnigheim was to marry Caroline Luise on July 17, 1836. Shortly thereafter, the family traveled down the Neckar and Rhine Rivers to Amsterdam and embarked on the *Petronella*, arriving in New York on November 15, 1836. The passenger list records the family's destination as Philadelphia.[17]

If the Rupps ever thought the residents of Bönnigheim would hang their heads in shame for driving them out of the country, they were wrong. If anything, their emigration only served to arouse further suspicions, a Bönnigheim forester noted in his memoirs. But like a corkscrew, fate twisted the significance of the Rupp family emigration 180 degrees. Had the Rupps never fled to America, the murder of Johann Heinrich Rieber would have never been solved.[18]

Bönnigheim's residents elected a new mayor in February 1836. When the notary public, Gottlieb Konrad Finckh, took the helm of the rudderless city administration, he did something to make sure the city would never forget the assassination. He hung his predecessor's bloody clothing, brown and crusted, in a display case in the city hall, to bear silent witness to an uncaught murderer. They would hang there for another thirty-six years before Mayor Finkh would have reason to take them down.[19]

Part Two

Exile in the United States: 1835-46

CHAPTER THIRTEEN

Hunter and Prey

Mayor Rieber was much easier to track than the usual prey. Deer and wild boar flitting through forest shadows could be hard to spot. As Gottlob Rueb raised his barrel and sighted, he would have found Rieber quite slow in comparison. The mayor was walking in an open courtyard and carried a lantern to boot.

But what made this hunt dangerous was that afterward, the hunter would become the prey, and a criminal investigator the predator. The menacing animals in this forest of houses and alleys were not bears, wolves, or lynx. It was other people, potential witnesses who could later describe him, who posed the biggest threat. But the huntsman Rueb had taken precautions. He was wearing a greatcoat and cap he could pull down over his face. Clinging to the cover of the shadows, he may have been the hunter, but he was exercising the caution of the hunted.[1]

This one shot would rectify a lifetime of career frustrations. Rueb had done what he could to correct them, but the man walking in the courtyard had ruined everything.

Gottlob Rueb was born in Stetten am Heuchelberg on December 30, 1804, as the youngest of nine children.[2] In 1835, Stetten was a small village of 986 people seven miles northwest of Bönnigheim. Although a busy nine-and-a-half-mile trade route connected the two towns, a low mountain in the middle made for slow travel. Both towns lay below a double mountain range, the Stromberg and Heuchelberg, just north of the Black Forest, stretching out like an upward thumb and four horizontal fingers pointing east. Bönnigheim lay at the tip of the index finger and Stetten am Heuchelberg at the far side of the thumb's knuckle. To get from one town to the other, a horse and buggy took three hours to cross the Zaber River valley and the heights of the Heuchelberg. Forests crowned the mountaintops, and now in October, cascading vineyards of red and yellow, orange and purple covered the slopes.[3]

Heuchelberg mountain range. Gottlob Rueb crossed it on the way home. (Ann Marie Ackermann)

Rueb's father Johannes, Stetten's schoolmaster, owned fields, gardens, a meadow, and a vineyard, but his salary was so meager that he belonged to the village's "nearly destitute lower class."[4] His annual salary was listed as only 60 *Gulden*, an equivalent of U.S. $1,338 (based on the values of the *Gulden* in 1837 and the dollar in 2015). Just how low that was can be seen in comparison with a period salary scale. In 1833, an annual salary of 240 *Gulden* (approximately U.S. $5,400, based on 1833 and 2015 values) was deemed insufficient to support a family. One major fringe benefit did help offset the teacher's miserable income: He and his family were allowed to live at the school.[5]

As a family, the Ruebs appeared to enjoy nature. Rueb's older brother became a forester and two of his sisters married foresters. Gottlob Rueb's own career choices of forester and hunter reflected the same inclination.[6]

Judging from his career choices, the boy also liked guns. At the time of the murder, Rueb was a huntsman's apprentice, but also wanted to become a game warden, a law enforcement position that allowed him to carry a rifle. Later, in the United States, he handled weapons in the armed forces. Perhaps it was fitting, then, that when he died, he was killed by one of the biggest guns in North America.[7]

U.S. military records describe Rueb as five feet eight inches tall, with dark hair, dark eyes, and a dark complexion. A former town spokesman of Stetten am Heuchelberg described him as handsome and with a strong physique.[8]

For the most part, the Rueb family appeared law-abiding. The father committed a horse-and-buggy version of a moving violation in 1816 when he drove through an animal enclosure. The municipal court designated the offense as "stupid driving" and fined the father two *Gulden*, a heavy fine in light of his meager annual income. Otherwise, there are no references to any unlawful acts in the Rueb family during Gottlob's childhood. A municipal court entry dated 1833 stated that public safety in Stetten was generally good. There had been no burglaries or thefts for a long time.[9]

Rueb may have had trouble finding gainful employment. His name doesn't appear in Stetten's archived list of active citizens, an indication that he wasn't working or paying taxes. By 1829 he found an apprenticeship with the regional forestry department as a *Forstwart*, or forest warden. It was an entry position with lumberjacking and timber management tasks. Forest wardens had a mediocre annual salary of 240 *Gulden*, so once he passed his qualifying exam, Rueb would be earning a lot more than his father. A myriad of fringe benefits supplemented the income. Forestry personnel received free room, board, and forest resources such as firewood.[10]

But in 1829, the wind shifted in Rueb's life, first fluttering the edge of his sails and then forcing a complete change of course. Gottlob Rueb was twenty-four. He was accused of severely wounding a man from a neighboring town. The Criminal Senate of Esslingen charged him with battery. On June 16, 1829, the court absolved him of criminal liability but made him pay the court costs. The file contains no information about the circumstances of the injury.[11]

While Rueb built up the muscled physique of a lumberjack, he developed the reputation of a lazy rascal in his own town. Stetten's mayor would later call him a "good for nothing." Rueb had continual problems on the job and "every couple months" asked his father to bail him out of debt.[12]

Between 1829 and the next court case in 1834, Gottlob Rueb made a sudden career move. He passed his qualifying exam as a forest warden in October 1832, but instead of settling into his career, he gave up the job almost immediately. Nothing in the records indicates why. By 1834, Stetten's court listed his occupation as *Jägerbursche* or huntsman in his last year of training. Forestry laws regulated a hunter's training and qualifications. Despite the apprenticeship nature of the new job, this lateral career move did not necessarily mean a step down. But once an apprentice became a full hunter with the forestry department, culling animals that damaged agriculture and silviculture in the fields and forests, he stood a good chance of earning more.[13]

But now Rueb's own father took legal action. Schoolmaster Johannes Rueb appeared before a city court in Stetten on March 3, 1834, to announce he couldn't pay his son's debts. The court entered a declaration that no one could lend money to the son without the father's consent and that the father would not assume any of Rueb's debts. The court indexed the entry as a declaration of Rueb's insolvency.[14]

Surely Rueb's father would have argued the court action was necessary to protect his own assets. But it was an unusual step, not lightly taken, because it tarnished the family's reputation. The father had publicly humiliated the son. Rueb, moreover, had reached an age at which most men were gainfully employed and married. He was neither. One can only speculate at the personal tragedy and character flaws that underpinned the father's decision to haul his son to court.

Rueb's financial situation worsened six months later. A creditor from the neighboring town of Maulbronn sued Gottlob in September 1834 and received a judgment of 5 *Gulden*, 33 *Kreuzer* against him. Rueb promised to pay the debts off by St. Martin's Day on November 11. The court records don't reflect whether the promise was kept.[15]

Over the course of the following year, Rueb's luck did not improve. There were two signs of career trouble. Despite the fact that his last year of hunting training had now stretched out to at least eighteen months, he still hadn't managed to become a licensed hunter. By October 1835, at the age of thirty-one, Gottlob Rueb attempted yet another lateral career move—but into another entry-level forestry position. Bönnigheim's forestry department had an opening for a game warden, and Rueb applied. Although the minimum salary amounted to a meager 43 *Gulden*, game wardens could supplement their income. In this position, he had the chance to earn commissions on the fines he collected. As the patrolmen of the forest, game wardens were responsible for policing poachers, lumber thieves, and other criminals. And with his previous forestry and hunting experience, he was more than qualified.[16]

Rueb applied for the position on October 5, 1835.[17]

But he didn't get the job.

And for that, he blamed Mayor Rieber. For reasons not specified in a renewed criminal investigation in 1872, Rueb concluded that the reason for his rejection was a bad job recommendation from Bönnigheim's mayor.[18]

For Gottlob Rueb, the rejection cut deep. Deep enough to make him want to kill.

Nothing in the investigative file indicates where in Bönnigheim Rueb hid on the night of October 21, 1835, waiting for Mayor Rieber to leave the Waldhorn. But fresh damage on the inside of the door and gate to Rieber's courtyard, caused by stray buckshot and found by the investigator the following morning, indicated that when he pulled the trigger, he was standing beyond the doorway, either in Mayor Rieber's courtyard next to the washhouse, or a few feet away in the palace courtyard, shooting through the fence. Some of the shot might have deflected from the fence into the gate.[19]

At least one thing went his way that night. Could there have been anything better than another shooting, just minutes before he himself planned to pull the trigger, to confuse the police investigation that was sure to follow? Some things you just can't plan. But for Rueb, things were falling into place.

When he raised the barrel of his rifle in the courtyard, Gottlob Rueb might have been aiming at more than the mayor: his father, the court, his creditors, the forestry department, and even Württemberg itself. He would ultimately turn his back on all of them. But his first actions were more immediate.

He pulled the trigger. Now he had to flee.

Rueb probably didn't hide by spending the night in one of Bönnigheim's inns. Checking the guest register of all the inns had long been a standard investigation technique. Even private residences were required to report overnight guests. It was an especially useful technique in a walled city, like Bönnigheim, where an offender could get trapped within the city walls. And that could have easily happened if the residents raised the hue and cry, and shut the city gates to trap him.[20]

The assassin's safest option would have been to quickly exit the city. And there was a safe exit. The man Jacob Wiedmann saw was headed in that direction.

The man's swift pace and selection of a route—taking him away from the crime scene through a narrow passageway between houses—were highly suspicious. And Wiedmann's estimate of the man's height matched Rueb's later military records in the United States. The man's route, at any rate, led away from the inns on the main street and toward one of the city's three exits.

If that man was Rueb, he had fled west into an alley immediately after pulling the trigger. After passing the washhouse on his left, he ducked into the passageway between two houses on the right. That would have made a good place to dismantle his rifle and hide it under his greatcoat. Gottlob then emerged onto an east-west alley, one block north of Rieber's house, called the Schlossergasse. Wiedmann said the man was walking as fast as possible without running as he passed him, heading north. That route led to a courtyard with just one exit on the other side: another narrow passage between two houses leading to a further courtyard. From there, the only possible route led to the west, onto a street, which led to an exit through the city walls.

Bönnigheim's city walls had two gates, the upper gate to the north and the lower gate to the south. But there was one other opening, and it would have remained open even if the residents had raised the hue and cry and slammed the city gates shut. Fifty yards to the north of the spot where

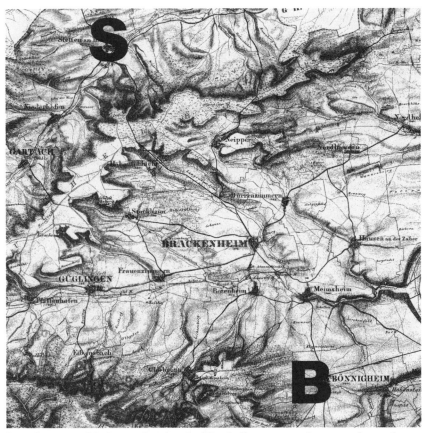

Period topographical map showing the Heuchelberg mountain range, the northwest tip of the Stromberg mountain range, and the Zaber valley in between. The *B* and *S* indicate Bönnigheim's and Stetten am Heuchelberg's respective locations. (*Source:* Detail from the Topographisches Atlas des Königreichs Württemberg, Blatt 9, Besigheim, 1844, courtesy of the Landesamt for Geoinformation und Landentwicklung Baden-Württemberg, Az.: 2851.2-D/8952; enhanced by Ann Marie Ackermann to show the locations of Bönnigheim and Stetten.)

Rueb's escape route led to the street, he could have turned west toward the castle square. Bönnigheim's medieval castle was integrated into the city wall, but just south of the castle there was a breach in the wall that opened to the countryside. A city map from 1832 shows the opening was large enough to permit traffic.[21] And for Rueb, that hole in the wall was in the direction of home. Stetten lay to the northwest.

If Rueb walked, he could have made it home before dawn. Although a trade route led from Bönnigheim, over the Heuchelberg mountain, to Stetten, Rueb might have considered the road too exposed and dangerous. He couldn't know how quickly the police would react to the shooting and if they would control the arteries leading away from Bönnigheim. But here he had an advantage. He was a huntsman's apprentice, knew the terrain, and was comfortable walking over the fields and through the woods at night. And once he was out in the countryside, people wouldn't have questioned what a person with his profession was doing out in the dark.[22]

The sky was clear and the moon was new. The stars offered some light, but it was Halley's Comet, suspended in the northern sky and swinging westward over the course of the night, that pointed the way home. And once home, all Gottlob could do was lie low and hope. Murder carried the death penalty, and his fate now depended on whether the investigator could catch him.[23]

CHAPTER FOURTEEN

Escape to America

Sometime that winter, after the grapevines had shed their leaves and the autumn mists were hanging heavy in the Stromberg and Heuchelberg mountains, Gottlob Rueb made a decision. There was one good way to escape the scrutiny of the investigating magistrate. That was to flee. But a neighboring European country might not be far enough. Twice in the nineteenth century, the Kingdom of Württemberg had extradited murderers, one from France, and the other from Prague. But there was a country with which Württemberg had no extradition treaty, and that was the United States of America. The two countries did not mutually recognize each other until 1842 and wouldn't bother to hash out an extradition treaty until 1853.[1]

In order to emigrate legally from Württemberg, Rueb would have had to apply for official permission at the city hall. One of the requirements for emigration approval was proof of sufficient funds to pay for the trip. Applications were made public to give creditors a chance to come forward before it was too late. And without that official approval, a person couldn't get a passport.[2]

Perhaps Rueb sensed that applying for a passport could arouse the investigator's suspicions. It already had for the Bönnigheim resident who traveled to Mannheim. Rueb didn't even try applying. Applications in the town of Stetten during the 1835–36 period are well preserved in the Baden-Württemberg state archives, and Rueb's name never appears in the record. Stetten's city archives also contain a separate list of each person who renounced his or her citizenship—a legal prerequisite for emigration. Rueb doesn't appear in any of those records either. That means he emigrated illegally.[3]

Decades later, when the prosecutor of Heilbronn, Germany, reopened the investigation into Mayor Rieber's assassination, the mayor of Stetten wrote a letter describing Gottlob's flight to America. He had disappeared overnight without warning. "Our files contain *nothing* on Gottlob Rueb's emigration," the mayor wrote. "I learned by inquiring that he left with a Johann Georg Kimmerle, who immigrated with his family to America, in April or May of 1836. There is *no* documentation on Rueb himself. The certificate for renunciation of citizenship [for Kimmerle] is dated April 7, 1836."[4] The story circulating around Stetten was that Rueb left because he couldn't find a game warden job, Stetten's mayor noted.[5]

Undocumented, illegal emigration was not unknown in Württemberg. Both debtors and criminals had reasons to flee the state. Criminals trying to escape active investigations in Europe were especially motivated to keep their mouths shut about the grounds for their emigration. Only rarely, perhaps in a letter back home, did they reveal their real reasons.[6]

Passenger ships of the period didn't usually sail in the winter, so Rueb had several months to prepare for the trip. For people in his region of Württemberg, the trip started in Heilbronn, the Neckar port mentioned on the signpost in the woods. From there, the emigrants traveled down the Neckar and Rhine Rivers to Holland for the ocean crossing.[7]

Johann Georg Kimmerle, with whom Rueb fled Württemberg, had been an innkeeper in Stetten. He applied for emigration on April 7, 1836, giving Ohio as his destination. Gottlob and Kimmerle do not appear on any 1836 ship passenger lists, so it is impossible to determine the exact moment of their arrival in the United States. It's possible that their ship's records were lost. But without an official passport, Rueb must have been traveling with forged documents and possibly under a false name, so it would be impossible to find him on a list anyway.

But arrive in America they did. A German-born tavern keeper named John G. Kimmerle appears in the 1850 census records in Montgomery Township, Ohio. But Philadelphia is where Gottlob Rueb next shows up in the documentary record. The records suggest he lived in the Old City/ Callowhill neighborhood, half a mile northeast of Independence Hall, where the Declaration of Independence was signed.[8]

Rueb abandoned forestry and found work as a baker. Until 1840, he measured flour and kneaded dough. For the large population of Württemberg immigrants in Philadelphia, the bakers most certainly made some regional specialties: savory cheese tarts with onion and caraway, plum cake, and anise-scented *Springerle* cookies.[9]

The dust of Philadelphia's city archives breathes a subtle tale of change. During his stay in Philadelphia, Rueb managed to make some changes. He stayed clear of the law. The court dockets and insolvency petitions at the Philadelphia City Archives don't contain a single entry under his name.[10]

But on December 29, 1837, something happened that caused him to stop firing ovens and start firing cannon. Britain invaded U.S. territory. The British military action was part of an undeclared war dubbed the "Patriot War," a Canadian attempt to throw off British rule. The conflict influenced American military policy for the next four years.

Grassroots discontent started the war. It took root in the structure of the government in Upper Canada (Ontario) and Lower Canada (Quebec). People felt corruption, nepotism, and patronage in the executive branch stifled the democratic voice of their representatives in the legislature.

Canadian democratic reformers called themselves "Patriots" and organized. Rising frustrations with the system led to armed skirmishes in both provinces by November 1837, which the British Army quickly put down. Several Patriots escaped and fled across the border to Buffalo, New York.

There, among U.S. citizens, they found fertile soil for recruitment. The Canadians invoked the idealism of the American Revolutionary War and their rhetorical arrows consistently hit the bull's-eye. Anti-British sentiments were already running high in the United States because of an economic recession. British banks had called in loans made to American banks, and Americans blamed Britain for the so-called Panic of 1837. And the Texas Revolution, which had just ended in 1836, left many young men in the United States flush with romantic visions: They saw themselves as democratic crusaders. As a result, hundreds of Americans volunteered to help fight a Canadian war for independence.[11]

On December 14, a Patriot group composed of Canadian and American volunteers occupied Navy Island, a Canadian island not far upstream from the Niagara Falls. The Patriots chartered the *Caroline*, an American steamboat, to shuttle provisions. On the night of December 29, 1837, the *Caroline* was moored by Fort Schlosser, about a mile above the falls, and well within U.S. waters. The British Navy rowed across the icy river that

Destruction of the American steamboat *Caroline*, ca. 1920. (*Source:* Library of Congress)

night and attacked the steamboat. In the ensuing fight, a stray shot killed an American bystander. The British put a match to the *Caroline* and set the burning ship adrift to break up and tumble over the falls. As orange balls of flame sank into the gurgling waters below, dissipating into puffs of steam and smoke, the United States was forced to make some policy changes.[12]

Word of the *Caroline*'s fate reached President Martin Van Buren on January 4, 1838. The report contained the erroneous information that Americans were on board the ship when it went over. They weren't. But the British intrusion onto U.S. territory was bad enough; the president had to react. By chance, he had invited Gen. Winfield Scott to dine with him that night. In his memoirs, Scott recalled how Van Buren pulled him aside from the presidential sideboard with the grim words, "Blood has been shed; you must go with all speed to the Niagara frontier. The Secretary of War . . . is now engaged in writing your instructions."[13]

General Scott had a threefold task: He had to keep Americans from violating neutrality laws by volunteering to fight a country against which the United States had not declared war, he had to intimidate the British from making another attack, and he had to chase the Canadian Patriots from U.S. soil. But there were no regular troops available on the Niagara frontier to help him. The U.S. Army consisted of only seven thousand men in 1838. Most were in Florida or the western frontier. Although Scott ordered extra detachments of army recruits on the way to New York, rhetoric and diplomacy were his only real weapons; he was certainly in no position to challenge the British on the basis of military strength. Scott succeeded. Although Patriots continued to trespass over the border along a front stretching from Vermont to Detroit, Scott was at least able to prevent a war with the British.[14]

But the situation highlighted the deficiency of the U.S. Army and the vulnerability of its northern border. The country reacted by mustering in more troops and by fortifying the Canadian border. That was the mood of the nation when Gottlob Rueb decided to shed his baker's apron for a dark blue coat, red-striped blue trousers, and a red worsted, eight-inch plume. It was the uniform of a private in a U.S. artillery regiment.[15]

Rueb enlisted in Company A of the 4th Artillery Regiment on January 4, 1840. On the intake form, the recruitment officer described Rueb as having dark hair, dark eyes, and a dark complexion. He entered "5'8"" for Rueb's height, which corresponded to Jacob Wiedmann's estimate. Wiedmann said the height of the man fleeing from the crime scene was half a head taller than his own five feet four inches. Rueb gave his age as twenty-nine. He lied. He was really thirty-five. When Rueb later enlisted in a Pennsylvania volunteer regiment, he remained consistent, providing an age corresponding to an 1810 birth year.[16] But documents from his estate proceedings years later leave no doubt he was indeed Gottlob Rueb, the son of the schoolmaster in Stetten am Heuchelberg in the Kingdom of Württemberg.[17]

As far as jobs went, this wasn't the greatest. A private's salary was low ($7 a month) and the desertion rate was high. Over half the enlisted men were foreigners and the rest of low social status. The well-educated, American-born officer class tended to deal a hard hand to the recruits; severe discipline was not uncommon.[18]

Rueb's company manned a Michigan frontier fort between a vast forest and Lake Huron: Fort Gratiot, north of Detroit, stood near the spot where Lake Huron meets the St. Clair River. There Rueb had to endure the austere, frigid Michigan winter, where hunters today gauge the temperature by checking whether their spit freezes before it hits the ground, where moisture crystallizes in their beards and teardrops harden on their faces. It was unlike anything he'd ever experienced in Württemberg's mild wine belt. Army weather readings in the Great Lakes region in the early nineteenth century showed a mean winter temperature of 19.77°F, four degrees colder than Norway's North Cape. The living conditions at Fort Gratiot were miserable: the hospital and barracks were damp and poorly ventilated. Every soldier stationed there could count on getting sick his first year there, according to a period medical report.[19]

Things improved a bit in the summer of 1841. Rueb's company was transferred to Madison Barracks at the easternmost corner of Lake Ontario, just below the Canadian border in New York. The facilities there were better and the death rate lower. In 1842, around the time the Webster-Ashburton Treaty resolved all the tensions between the United States and Great Britain on the Canadian border, the army ordered the 4th Regiment to defend the eastern seaboard. Rueb's company manned Fort Severn in Annapolis, at the current site of the U.S. Naval Academy. He was discharged in February 1845 and returned to Philadelphia.[20]

Rueb probably wouldn't have guessed that he would be reenlisting in the armed forces less than two years later.

In the meantime, the comb maker Frederick Rupp, the man Bönnigheim's rumor mill had painted as a murderer, made a new home. He and his bride settled in the Kensington district of what is now Philadelphia. Rupp tried his hand at inn keeping but wasn't successful. His name appears on a list of insolvents in 1840, in the wake of the recession caused by the Panic of 1837. Caroline gave birth to three children, and then they moved to Lancaster, Pennsylvania, where he switched careers and became a druggist. The family lived there for a while before relocating to Washington, D.C. It was there that Rupp would eventually break a record by cracking the oldest nineteenth-century German cold case ever to be solved.[21]

CHAPTER FIFTEEN

Changing Course

While Frederick Rupp was resettling in Pennsylvania, Robert E. Lee went through an identity crisis. Neither the Second Seminole War nor the Patriot War gave him any combat experience, what he needed to increase his chances for promotion. The army had a very different task for him in mind, a quieter, less conspicuous one, but one that influenced the nation's history nevertheless. He was to open the Midwest to commerce. And the key was the Mississippi River.

It is hard to imagine today what a vital role the Mississippi played in commerce back then. Before the era of modern roads and the railroad, the river and its tributaries linked the granaries of the Midwest to cotton of the South. Goods were transported in bulk on the river or they weren't transported at all.[1]

St. Louis was the hub for the Midwest commerce, and that was the problem. The currents had shifted, and starting in 1815, they deepened the Illinois side of the river and deposited sediment on the Missouri side. By the mid-1830s, a two-hundred-acre island, Duncan's Island, had risen out of the water, threatening to block the St. Louis harbor. St. Louis had already tried to fix the problem itself and failed.[2]

By 1837, Lee was begging the army to send him away from his desk job in Washington, D.C. St. Louis gave him what he wanted. Congress appropriated $50,000 to improve navigation on the Mississippi and the Army Corps of Engineers assigned Robert E. Lee to St. Louis. The task was threefold. Lee had to open the St. Louis harbor and create a navigable channel through or around two sets of rapids upstream.[3]

Between 1837 and 1840, Lee cut channels through the upper river rapids and built a dike in St. Louis. The dike led from the head of an island to the Illinois shore and deflected the current to the Missouri side. That washed out the sediment and deepened the St. Louis harbor. By 1840, the channel between the islands had deepened to the point that the largest steamboats could enter the harbor again. Lee also developed the reputation as a smart, dedicated, and hard worker in St. Louis, winning praise from both the mayor and the newspapers.[4]

Battling the "Father of the Waters" became a first for Lee in several ways. It was the first army project he directed, and that opened doors for him. As a Mississippi engineer, he mastered an assortment of jobs. He became a procurement officer, comptroller, technical expert, lobbyist, executive director, and leader of large groups of men.[5] "The opportunities that were to come to him in Mexico were created at Saint Louis," wrote one Lee biographer.[6]

Opening the river to navigation was more than just a personal accomplishment; it was a national one. St. Louis merchants celebrated the opening of the harbor, and with its confidence restored, a building boom swept through the city. The Army Corps of Engineers became a driving force in westward expansion.[7] As another biographer wrote, "Had Lee never become a hero of the Mexican War or commanding general of the Confederacy he would have deserved fame—and what is more, gratitude—for the two years he spent opening the Mississippi up at last. . . ."[8]

His tasks weren't easy ones. Lee lacked experience managing men and supplies. He had trouble motivating his workers, struggled with impatience, and took a harsh approach with his workforce and colleagues. But his leadership skills eventually evolved into the gentler approach he used so well during the Civil War.[9]

Leadership skills are something that comes from within, so it isn't surprising that Robert E. Lee went into a kind of identity crisis in St. Louis. It redefined his self-image.

During the winter months, when the weather conditions forced him to stop his work on the river, Lee had time for reflective thinking. His engineering accomplishments might have given him an idea of what he could accomplish, but didn't completely answer the question of who he was. Spurred by a recent interest in his forefathers, Lee wrote to his relatives and had them send copies of the Lee family tree and of the family coat of arms. He might not have understood all the heraldic symbolism, but his family roots tapped a long history of public service. If he ever wondered what sort of sap was coursing through his own veins, his ancestors' public record gave him plenty to ponder.[10]

The Lee dynasty in America began with the arrival of his great-great-great-grandfather, the Englishman Richard Lee, in Virginia as early as 1642. He became a justice, burgess (representative in the colonial legislature), secretary of the state for the colony, and member of the King's council. Two signers of the Declaration of Independence, seven governors or acting governors (one of whom was Robert E. Lee's own father), sixteen council members, seventeen burgesses, ten members of the state legislature, eight military commanders, six justices of the peace, two prosecuting attorneys, two diplomats, one member of the U.S. Cabinet, three members of the Constitutional Congress, four members of the U.S. Congress, and one federal judge had arisen from Richard's progeny by the time Robert E. Lee sat down to study his family tree.[11]

As early as 1659, the Virginia Lees had a coat of arms. It bore the inscription *Non incautus future* (not unmindful of the future), an idea represented by a squirrel, topping the crest next to a hazel branch and gathering a nut. The crest was identical to the arms of the Lee family of Shropshire in England, except for one small but significant change that gave the heraldry a uniquely American stamp. In the American version of the crest, the squirrel's color had changed from red, the color of the European squirrel, to gray, the color of the most common American squirrel. The Lee coat of arms survives today in the crest of Washington and Lee University, which is a combination of Washington and Lee heraldry. It retains the Lee motto, but the university replaced the squirrel with Washington's raven.[12]

Although later genealogical studies have not been able to establish a connection between the American Lees and the Shropshire Lees, Robert E. Lee believed, until the day he died, in the kinship. That kinship hinted of nobility and a sense of public responsibility. The Shropshire Lees traced their ancestry back to a high sheriff in the mid-fifteenth century. With somewhat less certainty, the Shropshire Lees had traced their ancestry further back to a man who accompanied William the Conqueror in 1066 and to a Lionel de Lee in the Third Crusade in 1183. A manuscript provided by Lee's cousin underscored the purported kinship. Even if Lee wasn't in fact related to the Shropshire Lee family, he believed he was related to conquerors and crusaders.[13]

That belief redefined his self-image. Lee matured on the Mississippi. He learned to face his obstacles with a calm poise. And his letters no longer reflected the same bitterness toward the army he had felt several years before.[14]

Following the Mississippi, the army assigned Lee to work on the fortifications in the New York harbor. This job, with intervals of administrative work in Washington, D.C., occupied him until 1846. From an engineering perspective, the work wasn't as interesting as the Mississippi River, but one task in 1844 turned out to be fortuitous. The chief engineer named him as one of the officers supervising final examinations at West Point in June. During this two-week period, Lee worked together with Maj. Gen. Winfield Scott, the commanding general of the army. Lee made a deep impression on Scott, who later called Lee the best soldier in Christendom for his rank.[15]

It was his ancestry that helped Robert E. Lee plot his course and the Mississippi that gave him experience. But it was Gen. Winfield Scott who, in the future, would blow the wind into Lee's sails. There was really only one obstacle in his way. Promotion during peacetime was rare, and Robert E. Lee's prospects for ascending much further in the army hierarchy didn't look all so promising.[16]

While he was working on the Mississippi, Lee received a promotion to captain. But he couldn't expect another promotion any time soon. However, war broke out in 1846, and Lee's next orders were to report to San Antonio, Texas, for service in Mexico.[17]

It was Texan statehood that ignited the Mexican-American War. Texas wasn't strong enough to survive as an independent nation and its first president, Sam Houston, knew it. It was thinly populated, financially weak, and its small army overtaxed. The new republic needed help. Citizens of the Lone Star Republic voted overwhelmingly for annexation to the United States—3,277–91—in 1836.[18]

But Texas's annexation overtures bristled with political complications. For the United States, annexation risked both war with Mexico and the balance of free and slave states. Between 1836 and 1845, the United States turned down Texas's hand in marriage, but at least twirled her in the dance of diplomatic recognition.[19]

When the two countries took their vows in July 1845, Mexico refused to forever hold its peace. The United States and Mexico spent the next three years battling over the bride they each claimed as their own. The ink wasn't yet dry on the Admission Act when Mexico broke off relations with the United States, renouncing the annexation as an act of war. It was not bluffing. The newly elected James K. Polk took a two-pronged response. He ordered troops, under the command of Gen. Zachary Taylor, who would follow Polk as U.S. president, to Corpus Christi, just south of the Nueces River. He also sent a diplomat on a special mission to Mexico City to work out a deal. Mexico refused to talk with him.[20]

Complicating the matter was the unresolved Texan-Mexican border. The United States contended it was at the Rio Grande, relying on the treaty Santa Anna signed after the Texas Revolution. But Mexico repudiated the treaty, insisting the old border remain at the Nueces River, 150 miles to the north, where New Spain had set it. In February 1846, President Polk forced the issue by ordering Taylor's troops south to the Rio Grande. In March, they entrenched themselves across the river from the Mexican city of Matamoros near the present city of Brownsville, but in April, Mexican cavalry slipped across the river and ambushed an American patrol, killing eleven U.S. soldiers.[21]

Polk, who had already planned to ask Congress for a declaration of war, exploited the skirmish to paint the war as a defensive measure. Mexico has "invaded our territory and shed blood on American soil," he told Congress. He requested a declaration of war on May 11 and Congress approved it on May 13. It then passed acts to increase the size of the regular army and authorized the president to raise fifty thousand volunteers from the various states.[22]

Like a railroad switch, the declaration of war changed the direction of two lives. It sent both an army captain and a German assassin into battle.

Robert E. Lee had been hoping for battle experience. It was the one thing he needed to rise in the ranks of the army.

Three months after the war started, he received orders to join Taylor's campaign in Mexico. While Taylor occupied Matamoros and marched south to Monterey, a second expedition under General Wool advanced further northwest. Assigned to the second expedition, Lee built bridges and repaired roads to facilitate the expedition's westward march. But after passing the border, battle experience seemed elusive. Wool's troops marched 365 miles into enemy territory and hadn't spotted a Mexican soldier since crossing the Rio Grande. Lee's most exciting adventure under Wool was a reconnaissance mission. Someone had reported advancing Mexican troops, and Lee offered to scout the area and rode twenty miles under the light of the full moon, following wagon trials to the purported Mexican camp. There he spotted white flecks on a hillside. They looked like army tents, but something made Lee creep up closer. They turned out to be a flock of sheep. Drovers taking the sheep to market had caused the wagon trails, not the Mexican Army. Lee questioned the drovers and found out the Mexican Army was on the other side of the mountains.[23]

Robert E. Lee, ca. 1846.
(*Source:* Library of Congress)

Back in the states, the commanding general of the U.S. Army, Winfield Scott, a great bear of a man whom many historians consider the ablest military commander of his time, planned a second Mexico campaign, and it was a daring one. He aimed to sail troops down to Veracruz, a Mexican port on the Gulf, and from there march westward to Mexico City, taking the same route Cortés did in 1519. The route would enable American troops to reach Mexico City much more quickly than Taylor could with his troops from the north. Scott hoped the capture of Mexico City, or at least the threat of capture, would offer the United States a better bargaining chip to negotiate peace with Mexico.

Scott's plan had one vulnerable point: a dangerous amphibious landing on the shores of Veracruz. The troops would be exposed to Mexican artillery during the landing. The American military had never tried the likes of it before and wouldn't again until D-Day. But Scott was willing to take the risk, planned the campaign, and ordered the construction of surfboats for the landing.[24]

While Lee was scouting the drovers and their sheep, Scott had already arrived at the border on the Gulf of Mexico to gather ships and supplies for his campaign. On January 16, 1847, Lee received orders to join him.[25]

Volunteers joined Scott as well. When Pennsylvania's governor received the declaration of war, he issued a call to the state militia. Companies enthusiastically started recruiting and drilling. Pennsylvania selected ten companies for the 1st Regiment of Pennsylvania Volunteers in late November 1846. Six hailed from Philadelphia.[26]

One of them was a German company. Gottlob Rueb, the former huntsman from Württemberg, joined it.

CHAPTER SIXTEEN

F-major Captain

Why would an immigrant take up arms and risk his life defending a foreign country—a country in which he doesn't claim citizenship?

One hallmark of the American army that battled Mexico between 1846
and 1848 was its multiculturalism. Between 40 and 47 percent of the regular army's recruits were foreign-born, mostly Irish and Germans. And
among the volunteers, enough Germans enlisted to form several companies composed almost solely of their countrymen. They experienced
some prejudice in the army—one German soldier said the "natives"
called him "sauerkraut" when they were friendly and "G—d—Dutch!"
when they weren't. But German immigrants enlisted anyway. In Cincinnati and Baltimore, they signed up in higher numbers than could be mustered. Pennsylvania raised two German companies, one more than could
be selected for service.[1]

Foreign adventure, personal glory on the battlefield, and the desire to
avenge the American deaths in Texas lured immigrants and native-born
Americans alike. In their minds, Texas had entered the stage as an under-
dog against a bullying Mexico. One historian's survey of soldiers' letters
and diaries during the war reveals more personal reasons for enlisting.
Wallets were still recovering from the Panic of 1837 and the army offered
good employment for their owners. The army was also a good place to
hide from creditors. Some men enlisted to escape domestic problems. For
immigrants, service offered an opportunity to learn English and American
culture. Some probably enlisted because they wanted U.S. citizenship and
thought service would look good on their record. And for one particular

immigrant, service in Mexico might have appeared like a good place to hide from the German law, just in case it should ever come looking.[2]

One aspect of nineteenth-century American culture in particular facilitated German enlistment. The popularity of state militias soared in the 1840s, and Pennsylvania made her militias even more attractive by paying militiamen. Immigrants formed their own militia companies and used them not only to drill, but to socialize and draw patronage from local immigrant groups. They offered a fertile recruiting ground for any captain seeking to form a volunteer company for the war.[3]

In the mid-1840s, Philadelphia boasted a German militia battalion consisting of four companies. Dressed in company uniforms, their members met every month in the Northern Military Hall on N. 3rd Street or in Philadelphia's armory to drill and practice target shooting. But they also contributed to the community. They participated in funeral marches and paraded on Washington's birthday. They splashed color and sound into the dreary Philadelphia winter by hosting annual society balls. For a few brief hours at a military ball, the German community's feet pivoted and glided to the rhythms of quadrilles, waltzes, and polkas. Although the stated purpose of the balls was fund-raising, the real reason for hosting them may have had more to do with giving the gentler sex a chance to twirl its bell-shaped skirts and breathe a pleasant coquetry into the companies' otherwise martial interactions.[4]

Occasionally the government called Philadelphia's German militia into service. Two companies fought in the Second Seminole War in Florida (1835–42). The all-German Washington Light Infantry helped put down the Nativist Riots that broke out in Philadelphia in May 1844. But that was nothing compared to what happened in 1846.[5]

On May 11, 1846, the day President Polk asked Congress for a declaration of war, news of General Taylor's battles on the Mexican border reached Philadelphia and electrified the city. One Philadelphian said the excitement reached its highest intensity on May 11 and 12. Shops shut down and groups of people were everywhere discussing the events. He found a nucleus of commotion in the mercantile community along Market, Front, 2nd and 3rd Streets, where people were reading the newspapers at every other door and gobbling up fresh accounts as the extras published them. Various companies of the state militia had already begun preparing for service and several captains called for nightly drills. The first one took place on the evening of May 11 in the state house yard. Drills continued the following day. Preparations were loud, and the people were ready.[6]

Between ten and fifteen thousand people attended a war meeting held the following day at the State House yard. Philadelphia residents resolved to protect and defend their country, no matter what circumstances might arise. The following week, eight to ten of Philadelphia's volunteer companies marched in review.[7]

Even though several companies began drilling right away, a German company, the Washington Light Infantry, was Philadelphia's first company ready for the field. Frederick William Binder, an adjutant major of Philadelphia's German battalion, stepped into the role of captain and prepared it for service. Like the huntsman Rueb, the thirty-six-year-old had something to hide. He had attended a Stuttgart boarding school in the Paulinen-Institut, an orthopedic clinic to treat the "crippled," especially the poor. Deformed spines, clubfeet, and contracture of the knee were the most common ailments. Years later, he said having received charity as a child made him more compassionate as an adult. Binder's patient records haven't survived, so it's impossible to determine what kind of disability he had.[8]

According to his obituary, Captain Binder sailed to the United States in 1837. Like Gottlob Rueb, he appears to have emigrated illegally from Württemberg. The German archives contain no record of his emigration.[9]

Whatever physical handicaps he might have had, Frederick Binder learned to overcome them. Once in Philadelphia, he became an innkeeper and was active in the early German state militia. When Polk's call for volunteers came in, Captain Binder was the busiest. His Washington Light Infantry was the first company in Philadelphia ready for the field. Binder's personality must have been part of the attraction. His company's English nickname was "the dashing infantry." One member of the Washington Light Infantry called Captain Binder estimable and patriotic. And if music is any indication, the captain bubbled with charisma. A lively quickstep in F-major, composed in Captain Binder's honor after his return from the war in 1848, bounces from the piano keys to nudge the listeners' hearts and feet. For Gottlob Rueb at least, Captain Binder was the Pied Piper. Along with eighty-three other Philadelphia Germans

Capt. Frederick W. Binder
(*Source: The Illustrated New Age* [Philadelphia], April 21, 1874)

in the Washington Light Infantry, Rueb, the long-sought assassin from Württemberg, signed up to fight with him.[10]

Preparing a company for war involved much more than drilling the men. Local women sewed uniforms, tents, and the company flag. The flag commanded the utmost respect. Once the women finished the banner, they usually presented it in a formal ceremony. The typical procedure was to have one lady give a speech, imploring the soldiers-to-be to defend their flag with their lives. One of the officers would accept the flag, assuring the women none of his soldiers would ever dishonor the women's handiwork. A toast to the women and a company dinner often followed the flag presentation.[11]

Nothing is recorded about the flag of the Washington Light Infantry, but it was probably similar to the flag of its sister company, the Washington National Guard, from whom it broke off in the 1830s when the latter became too large. A German newspaper described the latter's flag as blue silk with golden fringes and thirteen embroidered stars on each side. One side featured a flowering vine surrounding the text, "Deutsche Washington Guard," and the other the American eagle with the text, "Hail our new Country." German "women and maidens" sewed it, and they presented it in March 1836. The flag presentation to an all-German company from

Ohio took place in a German theater with the entire company present. German women, clad in white, exhorted the soldiers to fight in honor of both the German nation and their adopted homeland.[12]

Captain Binder and his company left Philadelphia on the morning of December 7, 1846, for the state rendezvous in Pittsburgh. Snow capped the roofs and fell heavily all that morning. Clad in their new blue uniforms, the Philadelphia companies left by train. A diverse crowd gathered to bid them farewell. One Philadelphian described a throng of both sexes and panoply of emotions: duty, friendship, envy, military pride, curiosity, and pain.[13]

Pittsburgh, the rendezvous point, plunged the volunteers into realities of military life. Some of the troops were quartered in a warehouse without heat. They also had to undergo physical examinations. Although army regulations required the recruits to completely disrobe—this allowed the examining physician to better assess disabilities, diseases, and check for the tattooed letters "D" or "HD" on a hip or arm, meaning deserter or habitual drunkard—the pressure to get volunteers sent off to Mexico was so great that one regiment of volunteers from an unspecified state went through the physicals fully clothed. If Captain Binder had any residual disability from his childhood, the superficiality of the exam may have allowed him to pass it.[14]

The doctors at least peered into the soldiers' mouths. The army required a set of strong front teeth. Soldiers needed them to load their muskets—they had to rip open the paper covering on the cartridges with their teeth.[15]

A lieutenant in the 3rd U.S. Artillery mustered the Washington Light Infantry on December 14. It became Company E of the 1st Regiment of the Pennsylvania Volunteers. On December 21, the regiment boarded steamboats to travel down the Ohio and Mississippi to New Orleans, from where it would sail to Mexico.[16]

Part Three

Heroism in Mexico: 1847

CHAPTER SEVENTEEN

Island of the Wolves

Gen. Winfield Scott's campaign, at first, was logistic. He gathered over ten thousand troops, some fifty ships, equipment, and supplies in the Gulf of Mexico for the assault on Veracruz. From December 1846 to February 1847, volunteer and regular soldiers, both from the United States and from Zachary Taylor's campaign in northern Mexico, swarmed like bees returning to their hives. They traveled across the gulf, where on a small island, Gottlob Rueb's and Robert E. Lee's courses would finally converge and run parallel.

For Rueb, the first leg of the journey was to Pittsburgh, and from there, he traveled by boat down the Ohio River. Floating ice gave way to cotton plantations as the steamboats carrying the first Pennsylvania regiment meandered south down the Ohio and Mississippi. For many of them, it was their first exposure to the South. One member of Rueb's regiment marveled in his memoirs over his first sight of orange groves and palm trees. When the steamboats approached New Orleans, he described flotillas of ducks and geese that stretched by the square mile. Flocks of pigeons—the now-extinct passenger pigeons—darkened the sky. But Rueb enjoyed none of the trip. His muster roll cards record an unspecified two-and-a-half month illness starting December 14.[1]

Rueb's misery only increased, as boat by boat, the regiment landed in New Orleans between December 28 and 31. Together with Louisiana and Mississippi volunteers, the Pennsylvanians pitched tents seven miles below the city at the battlefield where Andrew Jackson defeated the British in the Battle of New Orleans in 1815. There the regiments waited for ships to transport them to Mexico. It wasn't a nice place to be sick. The army ran out of food and the soldiers had to go hungry for a day. Then, ten days into 1847, the weather changed. A north wind pummeled the camp; rain and snow collected in icy puddles, flooded the tents, and dripped through tent roofs. "We had a rather cold time of it last night," wrote one private in Rueb's regiment. "No straw was provided us. Managed to get a few boards to lay in our tents, but had only one blanket apiece which is rather small allowance for a party just turned out of warm beds." Some of the soldiers moved into slaves' huts for the warmth.[2]

"Last night was one of the most unpleasant and disagreeable nights that I ever experienced in all the days of my life," wrote another private on January 11, "and, like the rest of my comrades, I shall never forget it, the longest day of my life, being half frozen to death. Our blankets and clothing on our backs were all frozen stiff and hard. Every fire-place was thronged with soldiers standing around to dry their blankets and clothing. . . ."[3]

Soaring pelicans and waterfowl greeted the Pennsylvania regiment when it embarked in mid-January and entered the Gulf of Mexico. En route to the next rendezvous point, a small island in the Gulf of Mexico, about 180 miles north of Veracruz, Rueb at least got out of the rain. But the conditions were just as pathetic. Storms continually raked the gulf, and in the rocking holds, almost all the sailors lost their fat-pork-and-bean-soup dinners. The ships stank and the water tasted "miserable."[4]

Rueb's ship, the *Russell Glover*, anchored at Lobos Island, about one-and-a-half miles in circumference, on February 1. A coral reef surrounding the island created a constant roar of surf. Lemon trees, India rubber, and corkwood thrived just beyond the white beaches, but thick underbrush of matted vines made it difficult to walk the island's interior. It was named for the "sea wolves," or seals, that frequented the island. Here the first few Pennsylvania companies rendezvoused with South Carolina and Louisiana men. With axes and spades, the soldiers cleared the ground to pitch their tents and create a parade ground. Although it was named after wolves, Lobos Island teemed with other wildlife. Rats, lizards, and sand crabs scurried by as soldiers worked. Ants bit the soldiers at night and left painful welts on their skin.[5]

Lobos posed other challenges for the ill Pennsylvania-German soldier. Heat seared the island. The men's faces and arms erupted in blisters after a few minutes of sun exposure. Temperatures climbed to 92°F in the shade, but quenching their thirst with water left a bad taste lingering in the men's mouths. They dug for water, but found it brackish; when they tried Mississippi water rowed in from the ship, they found it even worse because it had been stored in a sauerkraut barrel. All this time Rueb remained ill.[6]

Companies began practicing maneuvers. Captain Binder probably drilled his men in German. Well into the Civil War, German regiments conducted most of their business—drilling, orders, and correspondence—in German. They worked from German drill manuals, ate extra portions of sauerkraut, and sang German songs together. German soldiers even formed men's choruses in the Civil War.[7]

German companies, however, had a double duty. Not only did they try to maintain their native culture, they also used the war to prove their allegiance to their new land. Captain Binder made the first arrest in Scott's campaign when he was officer of the day on February 14. A small Mexican sloop lay near the mainland and sent three men in a small boat laden with fruit to Lobos Island. Captain Binder, suspicious they were spies posing as vendors, seized the boat and clamped them in irons the moment they beached. The crew from one of the American ships rowed over to the Mexican sloop and burned it. Binder was jubilant about having made the campaign's first arrest, and one private described him as a "gallant soldier and excellent man."[8]

General Scott and Robert E. Lee arrived one week later on the flagship *Massachusetts*, and for a while, Scott camped with Rueb's regiment. Cannons fired and bagpipes droned for Washington's birthday. Companies marched in a dress parade. The German company celebrated with a dinner, and the Germans drank to Washington, citing the words of Lee's father: "First in war, first in peace, and first in the hearts of his countrymen." They also toasted the army, the navy, the Commonwealth of Pennsylvania, President Polk, and various officers. The toast to Captain Binder praised his "warm and confiding heart" and predicted his Washington Light Infantry would never have cause to regret open conflict with the country's foes. The last toast was to the women they left home: "Our Wives and Sweethearts, and all Women in America—God bless them."[9]

Three days later, surfboats carried all the soldiers camping on Lobos Island to the waiting ships, and the soldiers sang "We Are All Bound for Mexico" as they embarked. Gottlob Rueb had finally recovered, just in time for the assault on Veracruz. On March 3, the flagship hoisted a signal, and all the ships weighed anchor to sail to Veracruz. There were so many ships the horizon looked like a wall of canvas. The largest United States naval armada to date was finally on its way.[10]

As the sailors hauled in the cables, the volunteers joined them in singing "We are now Bound for the Shores of Mexico, and there Uncle Sam's Soldiers we will Land, hi oh!"[11]

Capt. Robert Anderson had German privates in the 3rd Artillery who sang on the U.S.S. *Alabama* while under sail from Lobos Island to Veracruz. And as the *Henry's* bow sliced through the moonlit sea, Lt. Daniel Harvey Hill of the 4th Artillery also listened to soldiers singing. During one of their airs, a wave of unfamiliar grief swept over his heart, and he wondered about it in his diary: "We had songs from the soldiers last night with the moon softly shining upon us. One of these airs brought up associations that were painful. Why should I grieve for any thing when my sands are perhaps almost run?"[12]

General Scott, aboard the *Massachusetts*, probably didn't participate in any singing. He was putting the finishing touches on one of the most daring plans in military history.

CHAPTER EIGHTEEN

River of Gold, Fortress of White

Where there is gold, there will be pirates.

If Spanish Mexico hadn't been aware of that truism by the sixteenth century, it certainly discovered it by experience. If Mexico didn't exactly spill over with gold, it at least spawned rumors of gold. And that drew pirates.

Spain's expeditions to the New World triggered Mexico's fame for treasure. The first expedition to Mexico brought back small, handworked gold objects in 1517. To judge from the descriptions members of the second expedition in 1518 wrote, gold was as common as acorns. Native Americans fishing from canoes on the Grijalva River appeared to be using hooks of gold. Tribal chiefs presented the expedition leader with mounds of the stuff: golden armor, shoes, gaiters, breastplates, a jar, balls, a small golden statue, and a mask bordered with jewels. When natives bargained for the release of a prisoner the Spaniards had captured, they offered the Spanish the man's weight in gold. The expedition members thought Mexico might be the richest land in the world.[1]

The third expedition, the expedition of conquest led by Hernán Cortés, did nothing to tarnish Mexico's growing fame for precious metals. Cortés set up base near Veracruz, where Emperor Montezuma presented Cortés with heavy gold and silver wheels. It was from Veracruz that Cortés marched inland to conquer the Aztec Empire.[2]

New Spain, as Mexico was then called, became a wellspring of Spanish treasure. Gold and silver were carted overland to Veracruz, Mexico's first port, and there packed in ships destined for Mother Spain. Veracruz became a major gateway to the New World during the sixteenth and seventeenth centuries, a revolving door of the Spanish gold rush. Over the following centuries, a transatlantic river of silver and gold, flowing to the Spanish Crown, had its source at Veracruz.

And the pirates came.

French pirates captured some of Montezuma's treasure, en route to Spain, in 1521, and repeated the feat in 1523 by attacking two galleons Cortés sent to the motherland. Spain reacted by implementing a convoy system. Treasure-laden merchant ships sailed in flotillas accompanied by Spanish galleons for protection. The system worked so well that over the following 130 years, pirates captured Spanish bullion only twice on the high seas.[3]

That still left the ports as weak points the pirates could attack. In 1568, English privateers Francis Drake and John Hawkins sneaked into the Veracruz harbor disguised as Spaniards and took over an island, San Juan de Ulúa, a thousand yards offshore. An arriving Spanish flotilla ousted the pirates in a battle, but the incident made it clear Spain needed to do more to protect itself.

To defend its port, Spain erected defenses in Veracruz, not only along the city wall, but also on the island of San Juan de Ulúa. It built the castle of San Juan de Ulúa in the 1570s, and over the centuries reinforced and expanded it. The island castle served three functions. Its cannon thundered a sea defense against any incoming pirates. Its vast storage rooms safeguarded gold and silver while the treasures awaited shipment to Spain. And it sheltered the harbor from the strong north winds. San Juan de Ulúa became the most celebrated fortress of North America; for over three centuries, it served as Spain's foremost military stronghold in the Americas. And when Mexico won independence from Spain, San Juan de Ulúa became a symbol of Mexico's independence.[4]

By the time the Americans arrived in 1847, San Juan de Ulúa was still considered by many to be the strongest fort in North America. Covering eleven acres, the island castle boasted walls of coral and hard stone, four to five yards thick and sixty feet high, offering a favorite perch for pelicans. The walls, gleaming white in the sunshine like a warning beacon to incoming ships, formed a square surrounding storage rooms and cisterns large enough to hold over 93,000 cubic feet of fresh water. San Juan de Ulúa boasted 135 cannon, a garrison of 1,030 men, and a stockpile of more than a thousand thirteen-inch shells. Although the castle's armaments included some ancient Spanish cannon, most of the cannon were

The castle of San Juan de Ulúa with Veracruz in the background. (*Source:* Library of Congress)

modern. The French installed them there during their brief takeover of Veracruz in 1838. Its shells were rumored to be larger than anything the U.S. Army had. One West Point graduate called San Juan de Ulúa the most perfect fortification he'd even seen and its cannon the largest he'd ever encountered.[5]

General Scott also thought the castle was about the most dangerous he'd ever encountered. According to his intelligence, the Mexicans had expanded San Juan de Ulúa and doubled its armaments in the decade since the French occupation. "When we approached in 1847," Scott later noted in his memoirs, "the castle had the capacity to sink the entire American navy."[6]

When Commodore Perry asked a British officer whether the castle could be taken by a naval squadron, he replied that the castle "could blow to atoms all the navies of the world, before they could make an impression on its walls."[7]

Scott and his armada gave San Juan de Ulúa a wide berth and rendezvoused offshore about twelve miles south of Veracruz at Antón Lizardo. Scott wanted to survey the shoreline and select the best point for landing the army. Comm. David Conner, the navy's senior officer in the waters off Veracruz, invited Scott, his generals, and his staff onto the *Petrita*, a small steamer, for reconnaissance. Robert E. Lee went with them.[8]

They first viewed Collado Beach, two-and-a-half miles below Veracruz, and just out of range of San Juan de Ulúa, where Commodore Conner recommended the army land. Then they swung north to make a reconnaissance of the city and castle. When the *Petrita* came within a mile and a half of the island fortress, it spat shells and smoke, and its cannons thundered the wrath of Spain against pirates and the Mexican cry for independence. The *Petrita* was now so close that the Americans watching on the other ships feared the castle would shatter the steamer and send it to the bottom.[9]

The first shot was long. It flew across the bow and splashed down on the *Petrita*'s far side.

The second shot fell short.

The third, a shell, exploded directly above the steamer.

The *Petrita*'s crew veered her away and put as strong of a wake between the steamer and the castle as it could. San Juan de Ulúa fired eleven shells before the *Petrita* got out of range.[10]

Had the castle hit and sunk the *Petrita*, it would have changed American history within a short moment. It probably would have doomed the Veracruz campaign because its generals, Scott, Worth, Patterson, and Pillow, were all on board. The United States might have still won the Mexican-American War, but might not have won the vast stretch of land that now makes up the southwest United States.

But it would have also affected the course of the Civil War because among Scott's staff aboard the *Petrita* were several of its key players: Robert E. Lee, Joseph Johnston, P. G. T. Beauregard, and George Meade. "This operation I considered very foolish," wrote Meade in a letter home, "for, having on board all the general officers of the army, one shot, hitting the vessel and disabling it, would have left us a floating target to the enemy, and might have been the means of breaking up the expedition."[11]

San Juan de Ulúa's cannon fire was the first hostile fire Robert E. Lee had ever experienced. He managed to escape the castle's fire-whipped broadside.[12]

Gottlob Rueb would not.

CHAPTER NINETEEN

Amphibious Wager

What General Scott did next was unprecedented in American history. His goal was to take Veracruz and its castle, and from there march to Mexico City, following the same route Cortés once took, and force Mexico to surrender. But first he had to transfer over ten thousand troops from the ships to the beach, and he planned to land most of them in a single day.

Scott's landing of the American army on the beaches of Veracruz proved to be the largest amphibious assault in United States history until D-Day.[1]

He had ordered 141 lightweight, flat-bottomed, broad-beamed surfboats in advance. Designed by the navy and constructed by the army's quartermaster department in Philadelphia, each boat had to carry forty soldiers and a small naval crew to row it to shore. It was the first time the United States had constructed boats for an amphibious assault. Only sixty-five boats had arrived by the time of the assault, so Scott planned to land his troops in three waves of surfboat transfers.[2]

Because reconnaissance hadn't uncovered any defenses at Collado Beach, two-and-a-half miles south of Veracruz, Scott selected it as a landing site. Even though it lay beyond the range of San Juan de Ulúa, rowing the troops ashore would be a weak point in the expedition. The surfboats would leave the soldiers exposed and vulnerable. All the Mexicans had to do was to fire on the boats from trenches in the dunes while the Americans were all crammed together between the gunwales. Scott worried that the entire Mexican army, now alerted to his plans, might be hiding behind the dunes, ready to attack. He'd already received reports of a Mexican battery on shore to oppose his landing. All Scott could do was ask the navy to cover the beach with its cannon.[3]

By March 9, Scott was ready, and the day broke clear. "If we had had the choice of weather, we could not have selected a more propitious day," noted Raphael Semmes, a naval officer. "The sun shot forth his brilliant rays in a cloudless sky, and a gentle breeze from the south-east, which was favorable, and just sufficient for our purposes, rippled, without roughening, the sea."[4]

At 3:30 P.M., the crew of the flagship *Massachusetts* hoisted three flags in designated colors: red, yellow, and red-and-white, a signal to man the surfboats. General Worth's division was the first to go. Every soldier packed forty cartridges and two days' rations of food with him. Around 4:00 P.M., sailors lowered the surfboats on the lee side of the ships, and holding onto ropes, the soldiers clambered down the sides. The surfboats formed a line a mile long, where their crews waited for the signal to cast off.[5]

Tensions increased even before the first oars dipped into the water. Mexican cavalry appeared on the dunes. The American ship *Tampico* lobbed a shell in their direction, and the horsemen disappeared. The shot had no visible effect. As General Scott gave the signal to row ashore, the foremost question in every mind was of Mexican resistance. The *Massachusetts* fired a signal, hoisted a flag, and sixty-five surfboats pushed off. Seabirds squealed overhead, the surf pounded, and in the setting sun, the men's bristling bayonets and uniforms gleamed gold. On the waiting ships, navy and army alike watched their progress in tense silence. The navy aimed its cannon at the dunes, ready to shoot if the Mexicans opened fire on the surfboats. San Juan de Ulúa spat fire and coughed smoke, but was too far away to pose any real threat.[6]

What happened next was the last thing anyone expected. As the first boats approached the beach, the crews threw kedge anchors off the sterns to steady the small craft as they entered the breaking surf. The soldiers, 2,595 of them, leaped overboard into waist-high water, waded ashore, and planted the American flag on the dunes. Back on the ships, a cheer of a thousand throats rent the air and a dozen bands struck up the national anthem.[7]

The Mexicans didn't fire a single shot. When the army reached the top of the first dune, they discovered the Mexicans had fled.[8]

Landing of American forces under General Scott, at Veracruz, March 9, 1847. (*Source:* Library of Congress)

The surfboats returned to the ships to pick up the next wave of soldiers, the volunteers. Rueb came ashore with the second wave. "We rowed ashore," said Jeremiah Albee, a New York volunteer, "expecting any minute that we would be met with a hail of shot from the sand hills that slope gradually back from shore, and behind we thought were Santa Anna's men." But nothing happened and the volunteers landed safely. After the third wave, the surfboats ferried materiel—cannon, ammunition, tents, provisions, horses, and lumber—a task that continued throughout the following week. By 11:00 P.M., Scott had done the unprecedented: he had landed ten thousand troops in an amphibious landing without a single casualty. It would have been an impressive feat even for the army today.[9]

Mexico's failure to defend Collado Beach remains one of the greatest military mysteries of the war. It lost a chance to inflict heavy damage on the U.S. Army with little risk to itself. Mexican historians have been unable to provide a satisfactory explanation, according to Mexican-War scholar Jack Bauer.[10] William Harwar Parker, a young naval officer who participated in the landing, put it this way:

If the enemy will dispute the landing boldly it cannot be successfully accomplished. In the landing at Vera Cruz if the Mexicans had concealed themselves behind the sand hills until our boats were nearly in the surf, and had then come down and opened fire, it is my belief that half of the men would have been killed or wounded before reaching the beach. The gunboats could not have fired without endangering their friends, and the men in the boats crowded as they were would have been helpless. If there are no hills a moderately deep trench is all that is necessary for the shore party to shelter itself from the fire of gunboats. The idea is to keep under cover until the landing force gets about fifty yards from the shore and then let them have it with small arms and light artillery.[11]

Rueb, like the rest of the soldiers, spent the night sleeping on his arms under the night sky. It was cold, and the air sprinkled a heavy dew over the army. The next morning, his regiment forced down an unappetizing breakfast of moldy crackers, cold salt pork, and bad water. Then they marched. The army's goal was to encircle the city.[12]

A huge sandy plain surrounded Veracruz and its city walls. It rose gradually in elevation and ended in a series of dunes two miles inland. Those dunes, towering up to three hundred feet, stretched on another mile. Beyond the dunes loomed the mountains. On a clear day, the peak of Mexico's highest mountain, the Pico de Orizaba, floated above the horizon. To the southeast, a network of ponds and marshes dotted the landscape, draining into a stream and feeding the cisterns that gave Veracruz its water supply. Everywhere one looked, there were *zopilotes*, black vultures, plying lazy gyres in the thermals. So many thousands of them roosted in the city the rooftops looked like they were draped in mourning.[13]

While the soldiers trudged through knee-deep sand, temperatures reached 90°F–100°F in the shade, wrote James L. Freaner, a newspaper correspondent at Veracruz. The problem was the lack of shade. Dense chaparral, cactus, and small gnarled trees sporting five-inch thorns clothed the dunes, making passage difficult. The thorns snagged the troops' clothing and slashed their skin as they ascended the hills. When one German soldier stepped on one, the thorn sliced through his shoe.[14]

Feet blistered and the heat parched throats and tongues. One soldier lost his speech and another, stricken with sunstroke, wasn't expected to live. A captain fainted, was taken back to the ships, and had to be sent home. It was hard to walk ten steps without running into a collapsed soldier begging for water, one member of Rueb's regiment noted in his memoirs. The

Detail of a sketch of the assault on Veracruz made from behind the American lines by an American officer. (*Source:* John Darragh Wilkins Memorandum and Letters, Western Americana Collection, Beinecke Rare Book and Manuscript Library, Yale University.)

ground on which they lay pulsated with fleas, ticks, ants, and the occasional tarantula. San Juan de Ulúa kept up constant activity while the men marched, flinging shells and round shot at the troops. Bombs whistled overhead and went cracking and snapping through the chaparral. Despite its hardships, the 1st Regiment of the Pennsylvania Volunteers captured a hill, and on the following day, used their hands, bayonets, tin cups, and plates to dig trenches in the sand.[15]

General Scott landed the day after Gottlob Rueb did. He called a meeting with his staff to discuss strategy. Robert E. Lee, as the general's protégé, joined the discussion. The question was whether to take Veracruz by direct assault or by siege. The former would cost two to three thousand men, more men than Scott perhaps could afford. But the latter would take longer. Scott preferred the siege, and his staff concurred. The army set up siege lines.[16]

But the siege had its dangers, too. An invisible enemy festered in the ponds and marshes southeast of the city. Scott knew it was there, but science wasn't advanced enough in 1847 to pinpoint its cause. All Scott knew was that the *vomito*, the yellow fever of Veracruz, was poised to attack in March or April. When it did, it could also claim thousands of lives. Scott needed to move his troops out of the coastal range before the *vomito* started.[17]

The U.S. Army would not have much time to win its siege, and it was unclear whether the army's artillery was strong enough to do the job.

CHAPTER TWENTY

Roar of Tornadoes

The Mexican-American War catapulted Robert E. Lee's life in a different direction.

Almost twenty-two years had passed since he entered West Point, and at times he had been frustrated almost to the point of resigning from the army. Lee had advanced only to the rank of captain. One thing that could have helped him advance was still lacking: combat experience. His service in northern Mexico didn't offer that. General Wool never gave him a chance to prove himself.

But General Scott did. Scott remembered Lee from the two-week period they had worked together at West Point in 1844 and invited him to join his staff along with several outstanding officers. Ethan Allan Hitchcock was the inspector general. Also on the staff was an honor roll call of several young West Point–trained officers who would later distinguish themselves in the Civil War: P. G. T. Beauregard, George B. McClellan, Joseph Johnston, George Gordon Meade, and for a brief time, Ulysses S. Grant. But it was Lee whom Scott selected as a protégé.

Lee impressed Scott with his versatility during the Mexico City campaign: He had not only a good head for engineering and topography, but for reconnaissance and operations. Scott concluded Lee was the best soldier he'd ever seen in the field. He relied on Lee more than any other officer, and it was based on Lee's performance in the Mexico City campaign that Lee became Scott's preference for command of all the Union forces at the outbreak of the Civil War. Lee, in turn, learned strategies in Mexico he would employ years later in Virginia.[1]

General Scott needed to capture Veracruz to gain a foothold for his march to Mexico City, develop a base for supplies, and guard his rear. Although Scott's army couldn't know it at the time, its success with its Mexico City campaign would redraw the map of the United States and redefine the country. When the United States won the war, it acquired Texas, New Mexico, Arizona, Nevada, California, Utah, and parts of Colorado, Wyoming, Kansas, and Oklahoma.

For Gottlob Rueb, it was a chance to prove his allegiance to his new country.

To capture the city, Scott needed to breach the city walls with artillery. He tasked Lee with selecting the locations for the batteries and supervising their construction. Lee also reconnoitered the city walls, sometimes coming so close under the cloak of darkness he set the Mexican dogs barking. Once when he and P. G. T. Beauregard returned to the lines, following a narrow path through the chaparral, a suspicious American sentry challenged them, fired, and nearly killed Lee. The bullet passed between Lee's body and his left arm and singed his uniform. Had it deviated by only an inch, the bullet might have changed American history.[2]

Captain Lee broke ground for the batteries on March 17 about half a mile from the city walls. He constructed platforms and embrasures with sandbags to support and protect army cannon. But Scott knew the army artillery was probably too weak to do the job.

To get cannon heavy enough to breach the city walls, Scott and the U.S. Navy worked out a joint operation whose genius later won the undying admiration of military historians. They dismantled six monster navy cannon from the ships and hauled them three miles through the dunes to create what was assumed to be the heaviest battery ever mounted in a siege up to that time. Together, the army and navy used naval firepower to assault the city from the landward side. Robert E. Lee chose the naval battery's location, built it, and directed the fire, while the navy manned the cannon.[3]

Those cannon included three Paixhans, the first naval cannon designed to throw explosive shells. Each shell weighed sixty-eight pounds. The other three cannon fired thirty-two-pound solid shot. The white pine bottom of the surfboats was too heavy to handle their weight: Each of the six cannon weighed sixty-three hundredweight—6,300 pounds. On March 22, the same day the U.S. Army opened its batteries, the navy loaded its cannon onto its launches and hauled them ashore. Sailors placed them on skids, lashed them to the gunwales, and when they reached shore, set up gangway planks to roll the cannon onto the beach. They then placed the cannon on timber wheels to push them to the battery.[4]

That was the hard part. The hundreds of soldiers, both regulars and volunteers, helped push the monster cannon three miles through the dunes, through knee-deep sand and a knee-deep lagoon, over hills, but always keeping out of sight of the Mexican batteries. They worked through the night. A waxing half moon in the west offered some light, at least for the first half of the night. The sailors barked out nautical directions and frequent expletives. Rueb's regiment helped push the cannon into place.[5]

Robert E. Lee built the battery atop a dune seven hundred yards from the city, under the cover of darkness, hidden by the chaparral. The breastworks, made of sandbags, were eight feet high and ten feet deep. The Americans concealed the battery behind chaparral in the hope the Mexicans wouldn't discover it before it was scheduled to open fire on March 24. By 10:00 A.M. the cannon were in place. Robert E. Lee ordered the battery unmasked, and men dropped down in front of the cannon to clear the chaparral. Just as sailors sponged the last gun to get the sand out, Mexican shells came flying to the naval battery, a sure sign the Mexicans had discovered it.[6]

Mexican soldiers at seven forts along the city wall now swiveled their cannon to aim them at the naval battery. Their cross fire pelted the sandy terrain around the battery like iron hail. "For the first five minutes the air seemed to be full of missiles," Midshipman William Harwar Parker wrote. San Juan de Ulúa launched ten-inch shells. They sailed over the city toward the battery and pounded the ground.[7]

Now the naval battery opened. This was Robert E. Lee's first battle. He directed the fire at the Veracruz forts, then the city walls. Naval shells punched holes in the Mexican forts, sliced the city walls, and snapped off a Mexican flagstaff.

Mexican aim was good too. Parker heard a thud minutes after the naval battery opened. An incoming shell had taken off one of the sailors' heads. Mexican shells whizzed through the American embrasures, felling the sailors. One ripped a naval lieutenant's hat off. Another Mexican shell rolled across the sand, chasing a powder boy into a trench. He jumped out to escape the explosion, but fortunately, the shell didn't burst.

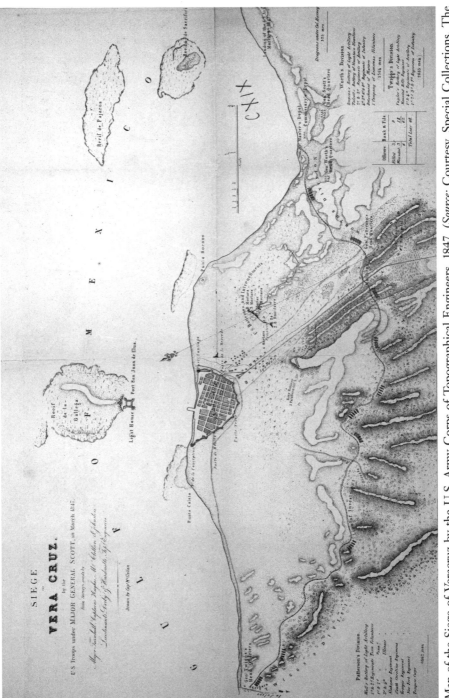

Map of the Siege of Veracruz by the U.S. Army Corps of Topographical Engineers, 1847. (*Source:* Courtesy, Special Collections, The University of Texas at Arlington Library, Arlington, Texas.)

Even more shells struck the sandbags and tore them open. A heavy cannonball dislodged a bag. The bag knocked a naval officer twenty feet. Over the course of the day, Mexican fire tore the embrasures to pieces.[8]

Robert E. Lee's older brother, Smith Lee, was a naval lieutenant and manned one of the Paixhan cannon. When he had a spare moment, Rob-

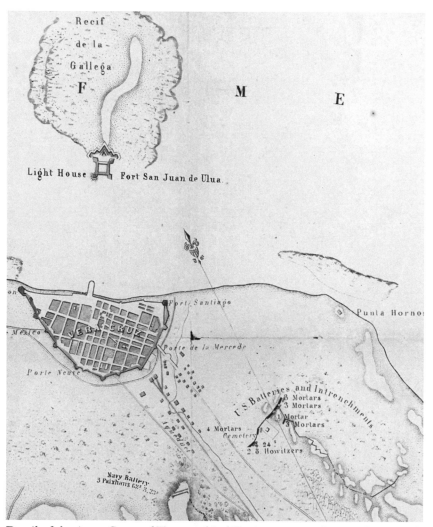

Detail of the Army Corps of Topographical Engineers map, showing San Juan de Ulúa on top and the naval battery at bottom center. (*Source:* Courtesy, Special Collections, The University of Texas at Arlington Library, Arlington, Texas.)

ert joined his brother. Thick smoke blurred the men's vision. It was the white of Smith's teeth that Lee saw whenever he looked at his brother.[9]

The battery ran out of ammunition by 4:00 P.M. Mexican fire slackened. The sailors left at sunset; a new captain with an incoming relief party and fresh ammunition replaced them. But Robert E. Lee and his engineers had to work through the night, refilling the sandbags and repairing the battery. It was a clear night and the starlight illuminated the city. "The castle of San Juan de [Ulúa], magnified out of proportion by the uncertain starlight, and looking ten times more somber and defiant than ever, appeared to enjoy unequal repose," one of the naval officers noted. Bombshells, with their lit fuses, carved brilliant arcs through sky before they exploded.[10]

Five sailors at the naval battery lost their lives that day. They were buried in the sand nearby. Some of the soldiers killed in action at the other batteries were brought in by horses to Malibran, an abandoned monastery near the line of investment.[11]

A member of the Tennessee cavalry described the scene at Malibran: "Some [soldiers] stop and appear serious for a moment, as they look at the mangled dead that lay under the arch of the buildings. One had a horrible appearance that struck them particular;—he was a stout, muscular man, of perhaps forty years of age. A cannon ball . . . had entered the embrasure, striking him fairly on the right breast, tearing a terrible hole through him, and taking his lungs through his back.—He was dead in an instant.—His countenance had an expression of mortal agony upon it;—his blear [*sic*] eyes gazed upward.—The wound was obscured with dirt and sand; his hands were clenched, and his bloody hair streamed back."[12]

Large trains of ammunition resupplied the batteries overnight. The naval battery was ready again by daylight on March 25. Many members of the 1st Pennsylvania Regiment took their places in a trench a mile behind the battery to protect it from enemy attempts to storm the American lines from the rear. Rueb's company took a forward position, right next to the naval battery, in trenches. The Germans' job was to protect Lee and the naval battery.[13]

The boatswain piped the sailors to arms with his shrill whistle and "grizzly bear" voice. Thus began the heaviest day of battle.[14]

Shells shrieked overhead, loud and discordant. Soldiers both felt and heard their horror. "Diabolical," wrote one man in his journal. "There is no earthly sound bearing the slightest resemblance. . . ." He could only

Naval battery at the Siege of Veracruz, ca. 1848. (*Source:* Library of Congress)

compare the sound to Milton's tale of the "harsh, thunder-grating of the hinges of the infernal gates."[15]

The shells roared like a tornado, said another soldier.[16]

Men could see the shells coming. Each thought the incoming bombs were about to hit his own head.[17]

Paixhans on both sides of the battle lines spat acrid smoke and sulfur. Bomb after bomb struck the embankments. They hurled barrels of sand and dirt over the men in the trenches. Soot blackened the men's bodies. Only by their voices could they tell each other apart.[18]

Cannon fire shook the earth. Church bells in Veracruz pealed as Paixhan shells pounded the ground.[19]

Two Mexican shells burst twenty-five yards behind the battery. They hit a keg and blew up 160 pounds of powder. The blast wiped out the battery's food and water supply. As the sun reached its zenith, tropical heat scorched the landscape. The men now thirsted and sweated with no chance to drink. They fainted at their guns.[20]

More shells screamed into the battery. They threw men off their feet, sliced a midshipman's throat, ripped off a sailor's head.[21]

From Rueb's trench, he might have been able to see the bombshell coming. San Juan de Ulúa fired one of its monster cannon, a cannon meant to sink enemy ships. In a deadly parabola, the shell shrieked toward the German volunteers.[22]

First Pennsylvania Pvt. Jacob Oswandel in Company A said it happened at noon. Another private in the same company, John Kreitzer, said it was later, in the afternoon. Rueb's muster roll card placed the event at the naval battery, as did Capt. James Nagle of Company B. A midshipman at the battery said it happened in a "company stationed near us." An army correspondent with the 1st Pennsylvania Volunteers said it happened in a trench.[23]

The bombshell bashed Gottlob Rueb in the chest.

He died instantly.[24]

The battle continued until the following morning, when Veracruz hoisted a white flag over the city. Fighting ceased while the two sides worked out the terms of surrender. By March 29, the U.S. Army assumed control of both the city and castle of San Juan de Ulúa. Scott marched inland before the outbreak of the *vomito*. Six months later Scott took Mexico

City in what has been called a campaign "unsurpassed in military annals," paving the way for a surrender that would increase United States territory by a third.[25]

But Gottlob Rueb from Stetten am Heuchelberg would not be among the conquering army. The murderer of Mayor Johann Heinrich Rieber was dead.

CHAPTER TWENTY-ONE

One Man Worth All of Mexico

Robert E. Lee's first battle was over. On March 27, he penned some of his feelings in a letter to his wife. The paper is now brittle and brown with age, spotted with what appears to be mildew. Pieces of the paper have broken off, so that a few words are missing. But the faded ink still reflects Lee's contemplation of the randomness with which fate deals out death on the battlefield. He told her of two men, aside from the sailors, killed on the American side during the siege and thanked God for sparing him and his brother Smith.[1]

Lee's comment about the only two men killed on the American side probably included Gottlob. Captain Vinton, the other man Lee named, was killed on March 22, before the naval battery opened. Gottlob was the only army death at the naval battery. Although other soldiers were killed at the other batteries and in skirmishes with the Mexicans, Lee wouldn't have experienced those deaths firsthand.[2]

Lee wrote a second letter on April 11 to his oldest son, Custis, working through his feelings about the man with a broken thigh who was laid in a trench for safety. Lee described the heat and how they had covered the man with brush as protection against the sun. They couldn't offer him fresh water because the unrelenting enemy fire made it impossible for them to leave the battery and fetch some. The barrage of the naval cannon shook the ground and must have been agony for him, but the man never complained. In the evening, when they finally had a chance to carry him away on a litter, an incoming Mexican shell killed him.

The man's death must have made a deep impression on Lee. "I doubt whether all Mexico is worth to us the life of that man," Lee told his son.[3]

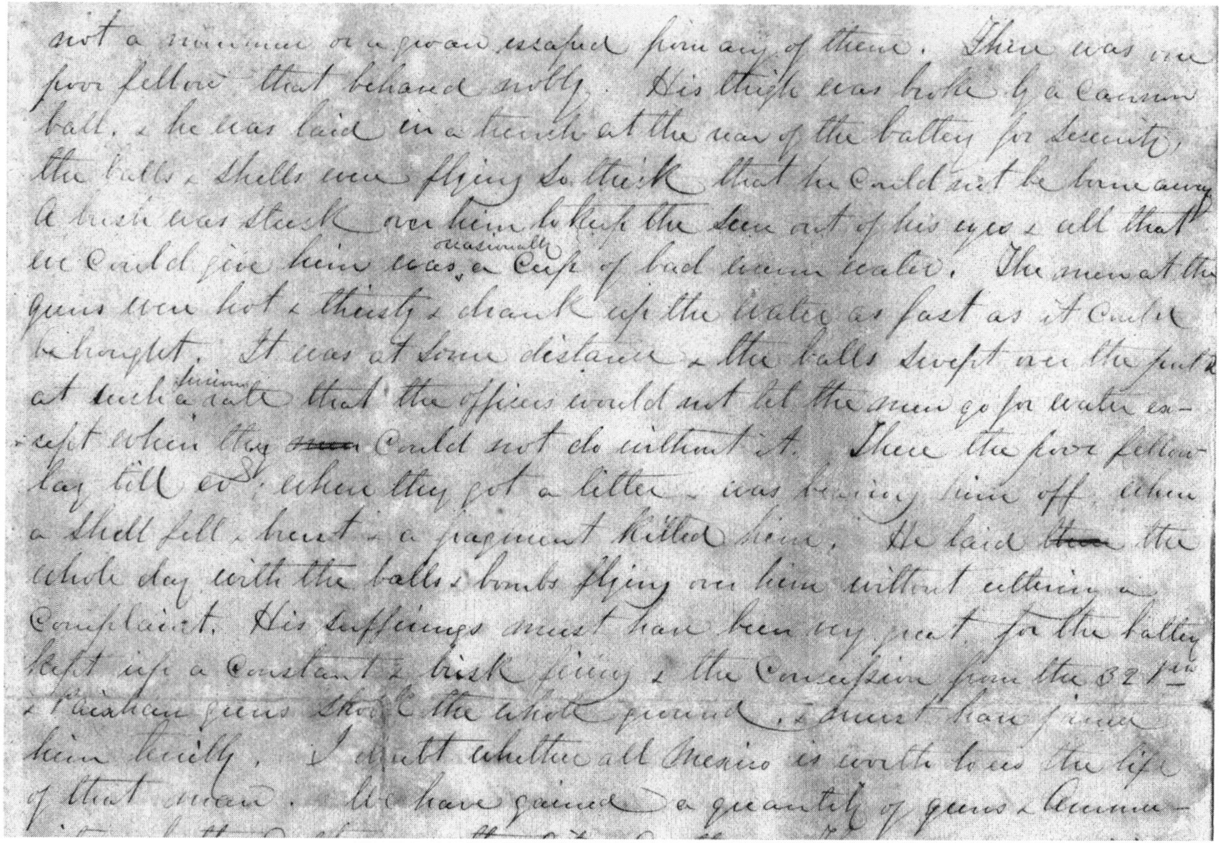

A midshipman who served at the naval battery also mentioned the man with the broken thigh. "One of our men had his leg broken, and while lying on the sand very near where I was standing, was hit again on the same limb, and had it again fractured."[4]

The man Lee thought was worth all of Mexico has been a discussion point in the literature. In his first war experience, Lee had to internalize the grit and gore that couldn't be illustrated on the West Point blackboards; he made his first acquaintance with battlefield death and suffering at Veracruz. Lee biographer Elizabeth Brown Pryor cites this letter to demonstrate Lee's concern for the plight of one single soldier, even though he was also enmeshed in the larger experiences of planning and directing warfare. A single death can make a larger impression than impersonal war statistics, she writes.[5]

Bernice-Marie Yates cites the letter to portray the depth and frequency of the correspondence between Lee and his fourteen-year-old son. That correspondence was Lee's method of educating him about war, humanity, and compassion. [6]

While he was in Mexico, Lee strove to mold his children's lives through his letters. One of his techniques was to give them examples by which to live. Lee viewed duty as the cornerstone of character, writes Elizabeth Brown Pryor, and as his children grew older, Lee became more fanatical about teaching them that. Lee didn't use the words *duty* or *courage* in his letter. Nevertheless, the man worth all of Mexico became Lee's object lesson when he tried to teach his son what they mean.[7]

Perhaps the most surprising part of the letter is that in the midst of the dust and din, blasts and bombs, and learning how to keep his cool under fire, Lee thought about more than his own safety and tactical decisions about where to direct the fire. The suffering of one man, tucked out of the way in a trench and under a bush for shade, still penetrated his consciousness.

But nobody has asked who that man was.

He had to have been a casualty at the naval battery because Lee mentions the thirty-two-pounders and Paixhan guns—the naval cannon. Military reports to the War Department list eight men killed in action at the battery during the three-day period it was open. Seven were sailors, and the eighth, Gottlob Rueb, was the only soldier. Other sources—ship logs, diaries, and letters—rule out the sailors. They all died different deaths, either in the hospital or from head wounds at their guns. Further sources point to only one man who died in the afternoon (or "evening," in Southern usage, as Lee put it in his letter) and in a trench. That man was Rueb. Appendix A contains a detailed discussion of the sources.[8]

Robert E. Lee couldn't have known Rueb was a murderer, or that the Kingdom of Württemberg wanted him for the crime of assassinating Bönnigheim's mayor. He probably didn't even know Rueb's name.

But it is a paradox of history that the perpetrator in one of Germany's most unusual cold cases became the man who so deeply impressed Robert E. Lee in his first battle.

Part Four

An International Solution: 1872

CHAPTER TWENTY-TWO

Post from America

By the time Frederick Rupp, the comb maker whom Bönnigheim's rumor mill had driven out of the country, made an unusual discovery in Washington, D.C., years had passed since the Mexican-American War. The vast swath of land the United States acquired in the war capsized the political balance between the North and South. Zachary Taylor, the hero of northern Mexico, became president, but during his brief administration—he died in office—he couldn't right the boat. His successors couldn't either.

The country erupted into a civil war. Robert E. Lee turned down General Scott's offer to take command of the Union Army. Unwilling to fight against his own state, he led the Army of Northern Virginia instead, and his surrender to Gen. Ulysses S. Grant at Appomattox was the nominal end of the Civil War. Lee became president of Washington College, now Washington and Lee University. In that position, he gained the North's respect for his resignation to defeat and support of reconstruction. By the early twentieth century, he came to be regarded as a national hero, especially in the South. Lee died in October 1870 and is buried in a chapel on the university campus.[1]

Captain Binder, along with a German bounty broker, worked with the Württemberg embassy in Philadelphia to prepare the documentation necessary for the administration of Rueb's estate in Württemberg. Two of Rueb's surviving older sisters inherited the land grant owing to him for his services during the war.[2]

Frederick Rupp moved with his family from Pennsylvania to Washington, D.C., by 1855. There he earned his living as a confectioner and by selling a medical ointment he'd developed. And it was there, in 1872, that he made a chance discovery in conversation that smote his conscience. He did some "discrete research," as he put it. But in the end, he felt obligated to send his findings to Bönnigheim.[3]

On April 29, 1872, he wrote the letter. It is now housed in the Württemberg state archives in Ludwigsburg. The paper, once white, has now

First page of Frederick Rupp's 1872 letter to Bönnigheim. (*Source:* Investigative file; courtesy of the Landesarchiv Baden-Württemberg, Staatsarchiv Ludwigsburg.)

yellowed with age, but the black ink is still legible. One corner contains a brown stain and the other a blue-penciled numerical notation from the archives. The text of the letter is in German, penned in the looping letters of the late medieval German cursive.

Washington, D.C. 29 April 1872

To the highly honored, praiseworthy Mayor
And city council in Bönnigheim, District Authority of Besigheim
Kingdom of Württemberg!
Most Honorable Gentlemen!

I consider it my duty to inform you that after many years and some discrete research, I have finally learned who the heinous murderer of our highly esteemed but unfortunate Mayor Rieber was. [Rieber] was, as far as I remember, shot by a heinous murderer in the autumn of 1835, in the night at 9:45 PM, as he came home from his brother's inn, the Waldhorn, where he had eaten—he lived next to the palace—while he was opening his door. They offered a huge reward for arresting the murderer, but the entire investigation was fruitless, and as far as I can still remember, several upright citizens, who were innocent, as it now appears, came under suspicion. In order to remove that suspicion from those miserable families, I see it as my sacred duty to report everything to you exactly as I discovered it recently by coincidence. I was namely in the company of people who were discussing all sorts of things, among them murder stories, which unfortunately occur quite often in this country, and so I told the sad story of the murder of our deceased Mayor Rieber, and when I mentioned it, one of my friends said, "I knew the murderer of your mayor. He told me everything in Philadelphia back then when he arrived from Europe. Then he became a soldier here and had to go to Mexico, and was killed in action under General Taylor." The name of this wretch was allegedly Gottlieb Rieb. He was born in Stetten am Heuchelberg, District Autority of Brackenheim. The reason for this terrible deed was apparently that the said G. Rieb had submitted an application at the time to become a game warden with the Royal Forestry Department, but he was rejected because he believed that Mayor Rieber was against him and that's why he didn't get the job and thus committed this terrible, bloody deed out of hatred. That's what I heard. Now, would you be so good as to see if the said Gottlieb Rieb applied for such a job with the Royal Forestry Department at that time, and when he immigrated to America. That would confirm, to a certain extent, whether he could really be the murderer, so that the black deed will rest on the real murderer and his family and not on innocent people. With respect to the murderer, I believe that the righteous judge already passed sentence on him long ago, a sentence no one can escape. If this person is really the heinous murderer, then as the saying goes, no thread can be spun so fine that that the sun [doesn't] finally shine on it.[4] But sometimes it happens too late for the criminal to be punished in this world. Yet God is just, and His ways are not our ways, and no man can escape His righteous judgment, and if it's not temporal, then it's eternal. In the hope that you will soon inform me of this very important matter, I remain obediently yours and hope that you remember me in friendship.

My name is August Freidrich W. Rupp, born in Bönnigheim, District Authority of Oberamt Besigheim, Kingdom of Württemberg, on 4 May 1811. Our family left our memorable homeland on 17 July 1836 to seek our luck in America. We landed successfully on 11 November of the same year, after we completed a long, but thank God, safe sea journey. The loving God has blessed me abundantly. We are healthy and have our livelihood. My family consists of eight living children and eight children who have already departed from us; four of the children are already married. Thank God they are all doing well. Because I don't believe friends will remember us after so many years, I ask you to pass on my greetings to any, still living, who might.

P.S. If Mayor Fink is still living, a thousand greetings to him and his family from me, as well as to Herr Marsteller.

My address is as follows:

A. Fredr. Rupp

No. 812 O St. between 8 & 9

Washington, D.C. America[5]

Bönnigheim's former comb maker posted the letter. Now all he could do was wait to see how Bönnigheim reacted.

CHAPTER TWENTY-THREE

New Investigation and Case Closure

When it first arrived, its outward appearances gave no indication that this letter would solve a thirty-seven-year-old cold case. Addressed to the "Office of the Honorable Mayor of Bönnigheim," the envelope bore black and red postmarks, dated May 1 and May 2, from Washington, D.C., and New York. A return address was missing. Although the year was illegible, Bönnigheim's postmaster Gottlieb Eberhard wouldn't have cared. The bald, white-bearded, and bespectacled sixty-one-year-old flipped the envelope over, and with two muffled thuds, stamped the back side with his own postmark: "Bönnigheim 17.5.1872." He probably had no premonition. As small as the town was, even Bönnigheim had its emigrants who corresponded from America.[1]

The letter needed to go to the city hall in the town center. History never recorded the name of the person who delivered this letter, but a forestry assistant described the letter's reception in his memoirs. It detonated like a bomb.[2]

Mayor Gottlieb Konrad Finckh was Mayor Rieber's successor. As soon as Mayor Finckh took over the rudderless city administration in 1836, he hung his predecessor's bloody clothing in a display case in the city hall as a reminder that the murder had not yet been solved. Over the following thirty-six years, people visiting the hall were confronted with the view of the bloody garments, now brown and crusted with age. When the letter from America arrived in 1872, the clothing still hung there.

Finckh had now been in office for thirty-six years and enjoyed the reputation of possessing an "extraordinarily calm" disposition. He was known to have lost his composure only once, and it was because of this letter.[3]

The mayor slit open the envelope, took out the four pages, and with surprise, read them. *Gottlieb Rieb*, the letter said. That was the name of Bönnigheim's long-sought murderer. From the town of Stetten am Heuchelberg, nine-and-a-half miles away.

But the former comb maker Frederick Rupp had written the letter, and that presented a bit of a problem. Wasn't he once a suspect, if not in the eyes of Magistrate Hammer, in the mind of the public? If the letter were true, it meant the pendulum of fate had catapulted the town scapegoat into the town hero. Rupp would have solved the case, after almost four decades, and in the United States of all places. But anyone can make up a story like that. Might Rupp have just invented this story to clear his name as an old man?

What made the letter intriguing was that Rupp offered a way to corroborate the truth of his statement. This "Gottlieb Rieb" had apparently applied for a job at the Forestry Department shortly before the murder. Since Rupp had never worked for the Forestry Department, he had no way of knowing this detail. He had never been privy to any information in its internal personnel files. If the forestry department still had a record of the application, it would mean comb maker Rupp was telling the truth because it reflected knowledge only the perpetrator would have.

Letter in hand, the mayor stormed out of his office, wound his way down the grand staircase, and marched over to the Forestry Department. A young forestry assistant named Carl Adolf Stock was there when Mayor Finckh arrived. Finckh was "very excited," Stock later wrote in his memoirs. The mayor demanded that the foresters read the letter and search the old files. They should look for any reference to the job application in 1835.[4]

It was Stock himself who found it. The tall, slender man, in later years depicted with a long, drooping mustache, rifled through old business report protocols. There he found a memorandum by the former head forester, Baron Friedrich Carl Eduard von Sternenfels, documenting a job application on October 5, 1835, by a hunter's apprentice with a similar name. The Forestry Department had decided not to hire him because after it inquired into the applicant's reputation, it discovered he was an "unstable, slovenly person."[5]

"One could hardly doubt," wrote Stock in his memoirs, "that this report [from Rupp] was true." He regretted that the forester Ludwig Schwarzwälder had already died the year before. People had falsely accused him of the murder when they learned of Magistrate Hammer's special interest in his rifle, and Schwarzwälder never lived to see the day that Frederick Rupp's letter vindicated him.[6]

Mayor Finckh wanted to be extra sure about Rupp's proposed solution and wrote a letter to the mayor of Stetten am Heuchelberg, the town of Gottlob Rueb's birth, to request more information about Bönnigheim's new suspect. Finckh first received a letter in response from Schwaigern, a town neighboring Stetten. The letter, from a former town official in Stetten, confirmed the huntsman Rueb's reputation and clarified the discrepancy in his name. And the author emphasized one phrase describing Rueb's character by centering it on a line all by itself:

Venerated friend!

Your correspondence regarding the discovery of the murderer of your predecessor was as interesting as it was surprising. That the criminal was allegedly the hunter Gottlob—not Gottlieb—Rueb, a son of the deceased, honest, and worthy schoolmaster Rueb in Stetten, really astounded me. I don't know this man very well because I first became a spokesman in Stetten in 1838, while Rueb had already immigrated to America three years before. This was after he had caused his valiant father distress of all types, and a multitude of grief and worry, through his reckless and—I believe I may put it this way—slovenly conduct. He never deigned to keep his job as a hunter's apprentice or game warden and every few months became a burden to his good father. Overall, Gottlob Rueb, an otherwise handsome man with a strong physique, had the reputation of a

good-for-nothing.

I actually never heard of any pranks attributed to him. The reason for his emigration was that because of his bad reputation, he could no longer find a job as a game warden in his fatherland. Whether he was capable of committing the serious crime of this murder I can't say, because I never knew his godfather well. But I am well aware of the fact that Rueb died in the 1840s in the Mexican War. As payment from the United States for his services in the war, he was granted 100 acres of land, and I acted as an intermediary with one of his nephews, the son of the deceased forester of the Baron von Degenfeld, Mezler, who moved to Stebbach. The nephew's father paid the sister—formerly of Stetten but now deceased—of the soldier killed in action an appropriate sum of money for her portion of her inheritance of those 100 acres of land. I can't offer you any further information, but I hope, by the way, that the report you received will exculpate innocent third parties from suspicion of their participation in this severe crime.

In friendship to you and your wife,

Schwaigern, 26 May 1872

Notary Public

Schuster[7]

A letter from the mayor of Stetten in early June confirmed Rueb's emigration in 1836: "Our files contain *nothing* on Gottlob Rueb's emigration. I learned by inquiring that he left with a Johann Georg Kimmerle, who immigrated with his family to America, in April or May of 1836. There is *no* documentation on Rueb himself. The certificate [of Kimmerle's] renunciation of citizenship is dated April 7, 1836."[8]

On May 22, the relatively new Public Prosecutor's Office of Heilbronn reopened the Rieber murder case. A package of legislation enacted in 1868–69 had reorganized Württemberg's criminal justice system and created this office, which still exists today. Rieber's assassination was one of the first murder cases it handled. The head prosecuting attorney, Ernst von Hochstetter, retrieved the old file from the archives, collected the correspondence from Bönnigheim, and analyzed the evidence.[9]

Of particular importance to the Heilbronn prosecutors was Stock's discovery in the forestry archives. In a memorandum to the file, the prosecutor noted the documentation of Gottlob Rueb's application to the Forestry Department in October 1835 and the grounds for his rejection.[10]

In August 1872, the prosecutor finally closed the case as solved. Thirty-seven years had passed since the murder. Magistrate Hammer, the investigator, had died in the interim. Wars had been fought; new national identities molded. And Halley's Comet, which had dominated the night sky during the murder and investigation, was now only a few months from aphelion, the farthest point from the sun.[11]

The prosecutor checked off a preprinted form on the cover of the file. The cover listed the handwritten name of the defendant and the charges: "Charges against Rueb, Gottlieb from Stetten, Administrative District of Brackenheim, former huntsman's apprentice, for the murder of Mayor Rieber in Bönnigheim." At the bottom, there was a section called "case resolution" with four options the prosecutor could check off. He selected one called "through satisfactory explanation" and recorded the date: August 7, 1872.[12]

Hochstetter may not have been aware of it, but with the stroke of his pen, the Heilbronn prosecutor's office had just broken two German records. No other nineteenth-century German prosecutor's office had ever closed a murder case based on a clue uncovered in the United States apart from a confession from an immigrant. And no other nineteenth-century German murder was solved after such a long period of time.

Rueb had now been formally named as Johann Heinrich Rieber's murderer. His fate in the Mexican-American War at the naval battery prevented any further investigation or prosecution. The Germans weren't aware of Robert E. Lee's connection to Rueb's death and probably wouldn't have cared if they did. That was a matter for American historians, who likewise never knew the background of the one volunteer killed at the naval battery. It was a fluke of history that connected one of Germany's most unusual murder cases to the Civil War hero's first battle and his poignant letter back home.

With the case now officially closed as resolved, the prosecutor's office forwarded the file to the state archives for storage.

Unpaid Debt: 2017

Two hundred *Gulden*. . . .

That amounted to nearly $5,000.[1]

The reward for information leading to the identification of the murderer hadn't been entirely forgotten. The former comb maker Frederick Rupp mentioned it in his letter to Bönnigheim: "They offered a huge reward. . . ." But Rupp got one fact wrong. The reward was not for arresting the murderer, but for information leading to the murderer's *identification*. And the wording of Bönnigheim's city council minutes never specified the murderer still had to be alive. Once the prosecutor closed the case in 1872, naming Gottlob Rueb as the murderer, Rupp became the first person in thirty-seven years with a valid claim to the reward.

Did Bönnigheim ever pay it? Nothing in the investigative file indicates it did, but the reward would be a matter for the city administration, not the prosecutor's office. The city council minutes would be a better place to look.

Bönnigheim's city council minutes for 1872–73 are also silent on the matter, but one must proceed with caution. A bomb destroyed most of Bönnigheim's archives toward the end of World War II. If you want to confirm the reward was paid, you'd be advised to double-check elsewhere.

In the assumption that newspapers would publish an article about the payment for a reward for solving a thirty-seven-year-old murder, I checked the local German papers for 1872–73. One newspaper, from Ludwigsburg, carried an article about Rupp's information having solved Mayor's Rieber's murder, but it mentioned nothing about the reward. No further articles on the case appeared. Issues of the Heilbronn newspaper that carried an article about the murder in 1835 (discussed in chapter 13) are missing for the critical years 1872–73. The Stuttgart newspaper, which also ran an article about Rieber's murder in 1835, was silent about the case resolution and reward thirty-seven years later.[2]

Might a Washington, D.C., newspaper have covered the story if one of its residents received a reward from Germany for solving a nearly four-decades-old crime? To rule out that possibility, I hired a retired Washington, D.C., archivist to search the papers for me. She could find no newspaper that mentioned Rupp in connection with the murder or the reward.

It appears Bönnigheim never paid the reward. If it didn't, what was the reason? The investigative file contains a good explanation. In the course of his 1835 investigation, Magistrate Hammer took Bönnigheim's original city council minutes offering the reward and filed them in his investigative file. He used the minutes as a basis of a press release containing his call for witnesses (see chapter 15). When the Heilbronn prosecutor's office reopened the Rieber murder case, it retrieved Hammer's original investigative file from the archives and incorporated it into its own. Then the file got archived again—as a criminal case in the state archives, but not as Bönnigheim city records.

There were certainly Bönnigheim residents still alive in 1872 who remembered the reward. But before the city council could justify paying out such a hefty sum, it probably needed the original documentation of the city's offering the reward. That documentation was missing from Bönnigheim's archives, and it's quite likely that by 1872, no one knew where to find it.

In 2014, I brought the results of my research to Kornelius Bamberger, Bönnigheim's current mayor (*Bürgermeister*). The aspect of the case that interested him the most was that his predecessor had been murdered and the reward for information leading to the murderer's identification had, by all appearances, never been paid. He did not see the city as legally obligated to pay the reward—after the passage of 180 years, the 1835 city council resolution was no longer enforceable. But on the other hand, he thought that recognizing Frederick Rupp and his descendants in some manner was the proper and diplomatic thing to do.

My Washington, D.C., researcher is also a genealogist, and she located two of Frederick Rupp's great-great-grandchildren still living in the United States. Bürgermeister Bamberger decided to offer these descendants a

Bönnigheim's mayor, Kornelius Bamberger, next to a monument the city erected in 2015 to the memory of the murder victim, Johann Heinrich Rieber. (*Source:* Courtesy of Inge Hermann.)

posthumous reward of €200 instead of 200 *Gulden*. At the annual meeting of Bönnigheim's historical society in March 2015, Bürgermeister Bamberger outlined his intention to invite the descendants to Bönnigheim and present the reward. Representatives of two local banks who were present announced they would contribute to the reward, raising it to €1,000.

Bürgermeister Bamberger and I drafted letters to the descendants, summarizing the story, and enclosing a copy of an article I'd previously published about the Rieber case in German, together with a translation. We invited them to travel to Bönnigheim for a formal reception and presentation of the reward, and I offered to pay for their flights and three nights in a hotel. Bürgermeister Bamberger had the German consulate in the United States deliver the letters.

A year later, as of September 2016, the city of Bönnigheim has yet to hear back from Frederick Rupp's descendants. We fear that despite the diplomatic courier's stamp of authority, the descendants might have taken the letters as junk mail or a fraud. Bürgermeister Bamberger's next step will probably be to send the €200 per an escrow agent. The banks' contribution will remain outstanding but can be presented if the descendants come to Bönnigheim.

It's my hope that the publication of this book will convince Frederick Rupp's descendants that neither this story nor the reward is a hoax. It is to them that I address my final words.

Bönnigheim was devastated by the murder of its mayor 180 years ago, and your great-great-grandfather earned his place not only in the town's history by identifying the murderer, but in Germany history by breaking a couple of criminal justice records.

Frederick Rupp's gravestone in Washington, D.C. (*Source:* Courtesy of Michael McCormick.)

But the town did your ancestor wrong, not just once, but twice. The townsfolk falsely suspected him of the murder, and their flagrant back-fence gossip drove him and his family from Württemberg to the United States. And when he finally solved the case, he not only proved his own innocence, but that of several Bönnigheim residents who had once been suspects. He solved Bönnigheim's greatest unsolved mystery, and the town failed to give him the reward due.

The town of Bönnigheim, nestled away among the vineyards of the Neckar valley in the northern part of Baden-Württemberg, recognizes its old errors now. If you decide to return to your great-great-grandfather's birthplace, you will be welcomed as the descendant of a town hero.

I hope you will consider it.

Sources Indicating Lee Wrote His Letter
about Gottlob Rueb

Before evaluating the primary sources on the identity of the object of Lee's admiration in his letter, one must first clarify discrepancies in the historical record about both the date and time of Rueb's death and the spelling of his name.

Date of Gottlob Rueb's death. Although his muster roll cards list his death as occurring on March 26,[1] all the other sources place Rueb's death on March 25. These include General Scott's list of the killed, wounded, and missing to the War Department and the diaries of four soldiers in Rueb's regiment.[2] The newspaper report of John of York, an embedded journalist in the regiment, also places the death on March 25.[3] A further newspaper article—a published letter from a midshipman—mentions the death of a volunteer at the battery while he was serving at the battery. That midshipman served at the battery from 5:00 P.M. on March 24 through March 25 under Captain Mayo, but not on March 26.[4] The March 26 entries on Gottlob Rueb's muster roll cards probably stemmed from a clerical error; no other primary source places Rueb's death on March 26.

Time of Rueb's death. One private in Gottlob's company wrote that Rueb died "at noon"; another stated he was killed in the "afternoon."[5] That Robert E. Lee placed the death of the man he admired in the evening does not preclude Rueb because in Southern usage, "evening" includes the afternoon.[6]

Spelling of Rueb's name. There are enough discrepancies in the spelling of Gottlob Rueb's name to confuse the reader and broach the question of whether the private who was killed at the naval battery was the German named Gottlob Rueb from Stetten am Heuchelberg in Württemberg.

Scott's report, for instance, lists the private killed at the battery as "Goth-lib Reip" and places him in the wrong company (G).[7] Oswandel calls him "Rupe," the muster roll cards list him alternately as "Reeb" and "Rueb," and a published list of Pennsylvania volunteers uses "Gottlieb" instead of "Gottlob" and confuses his first name with his last name by indexing him under "Gottlieb, Rueb."[8] A newspaper report calls him "Raap."[9] The muster roll cards also provide an age that doesn't correspond to Gottlob's birth date in Stetten, which only adds to the confusion.

Despite the name confusion, it is certain that the one soldier who died at the naval battery was Gottlob Rueb. Rueb's estate records, both in Germany and the United States, clarify that the private who died at the naval battery was the same Gottlob Rueb from Stetten am Heuchelberg

Gottlob Rueb's muster roll card with a record of his death at the naval battery. (*Source:* National Archives, digital image courtesy of Fold3.com.) The March 26 date of death is probably a clerical error. All the other primary sources place Rueb's death on March 25.

whom the Public Prosecutor's Office of Heilbronn later concluded had murdered Mayor Rieber. Following his death, his two surviving sisters in Württemberg hired an agent to assist them in making a claim for his land bounty, granted to volunteers as compensation for their service in the war. Notarized documents from Germany in the U.S. National Archives identify the soldier killed at the battery as *Gottlieb* Friedrich Rueb, born on December 30, 1804, in Stetten am Heuchelberg in Württemberg, and son of Johannes Rueb, the schoolmaster in Stetten, but the rest of the documents, including those written by the decedent's sisters, use the name *Gottlob*.[10] An additional letter from a former German schoolteacher who taught near Stetten and later moved to Philadelphia also identifies the soldier as "Gottlob Rueb or Rub, Comp. E, Captain Binder," the son of Stetten's schoolteacher.[11]

In Germany, the records of Rueb's estate proceedings also record that he was from Stetten and died in the Mexican War. They contain a letter from the Württemberg Consulate in Philadelphia, referring to testimony from Captain Binder, who said Gottlob Rueb was the first man in his company who was shot and killed.[12] Those records further solidify the deceased soldier's identity.

Deaths at the Naval Battery on March 24–25. Eight men in all were killed at the naval battery during the Siege of Veracruz. The army's report of casualties at the Siege of Veracruz listed only one soldier, a volunteer, killed at the naval battery, namely Gottlob Rueb, on March 25, 1847.[13] The other deaths were naval personnel. Captain Aulick's report for March 24 included the following men, with their ranks and ships:

Wm. Marcus, seaman, *Mississippi*
Jno. Williams, quarter gunner, *Raritan*
Jno. Harrington, boatswain's mate, *St. Mary's*
Daniel McGinnis, landsman, *St. Mary's*
Jno. Fookey [Tookey?], seaman, *Potomac*.[14]

Captain Mayo's report for March 25 listed two men killed at the naval battery but doesn't list their ships.

Midshipman T. B. Shubrick
John Williamson, seaman.[15]

Sources describing the deaths of these men rule out the naval casualties as the man Lee praised in his letter and further point to Rueb. Lee wrote of a man killed in the "evening" or afternoon, either in a trench or while being carried out of the trench, after having broken a thigh. The man had lain in the trench nearly all day, injured, during a period of heavy fire.[16]

It is relatively simple to eliminate the five sailors killed on March 24. The logbook for the USS *Potomac* states that one of them, John Tookey, was left wounded at the hospital.[17] Subsequent log entries don't mention his death, so Tookey must have died at the hospital. One private wrote in his memoirs that four sailors were killed a short time after the battery opened at 10:00 A.M. on March 24; another wrote four sailors were killed "outright" that day.[18] Yet another participant puts the deaths of three of them at about an hour after the battery opened, or at about 11:00 A.M.[19] These four deaths would account for Marcus, Williams, Harrington, and McGinnis. That they were killed in the morning, not the afternoon, would also rule them out along with Tookey.

Additional details from the logbooks indicate the sailors were killed at their guns, not in or at a trench. William Marcus, according to the USS *Mississippi*'s logbook, was killed "doing his duty," which suggests he was at the guns.[20] The USS *St. Mary*'s log explicitly states both Harrington and McGinness [McGinnis] were killed at their guns.[21] Unfortunately, the USS *Raritan*'s log is missing for that period, so it is impossible to find information about John Williams's death there.[22] An embedded journalist at Veracruz reported that every man who was killed at the naval battery on March 24 was struck on the head. The Mexicans shot at them every time they poked their heads up above the parapet.[23]

That would indicate that the man about whom Lee wrote died on March 25. Further information also points to the 25th. The heaviest fire was on the 25th,[24] which corresponds to Lee's description. Fire had slackened on both sides during the afternoon of the 24th, in part due to a norther, and in part due to ammunition running out on the American side.[25]

Turning to March 25, we can easily eliminate Midshipman Shubrick. A number of sources describe how he was hit while, or directly after, sighting his cannon.[26] John Williamson is more difficult to rule out because nothing about the manner of his death is mentioned in the logbooks, nor could I find direct information in any newspapers or other eyewitness accounts. Indirectly, however, one eyewitness account rules out Williamson. Writing about the incoming cannonballs on March 25, one naval officer said that "now and then, one would come whistling through the embrasures, taking off some poor fellow's head."[27] The writer implied it happened more than once. If more than one man was killed at the embrasure that day, the second would have to have been Williamson.

Additional information also points to Gottlob Rueb as the man in Lee's letter. Rueb was the only man killed in action at the battery whom we can place at or near a trench at the time of his death.[28] He is also the only one known to have been killed in the afternoon.[29] A published letter from a midshipman who served at the naval battery from 5:00 P.M. on March 24 through March 25 also mentions a man whose leg was broken twice.[30] That man may have been the same man with the broken thigh Lee wrote about. The midshipman's period of service at the battery overlapped Gottlob's. The combination of details both ruling out the sailors and putting Gottlob at the right time and place makes it likely Robert E. Lee wrote the passage in question about the long-sought murderer from Württemberg.

One must, however, proceed with caution. A major difficulty in researching the naval battery is the less-than-optimal state of record keeping by the navy of that time. The navy did not maintain any system similar to the army's muster roll cards; none of the sailors listed as casualties above can be found in the records regarding enlisted men in the navy for that time period.[31] In addition, the logbook entries don't match the navy's official casualty reports. According to the midshipman's letter, March 25 saw two navy casualties, Shubrick and "one man from the Albany." John Williamson's death isn't mentioned in the USS *Albany*'s logbook. Instead, it mentions the death of another sailor, Richard Simms, who wasn't listed in the casualty reports at all. Because that entry was made on the evening of March 26 and mentions the sailors returning to the ship with Simms's body at 5:45 P.M. that day, it's possible that Simms died during the early morning conflict of March 26, before the cease-fire.[32]

A sailor serving on the USS *Mississippi* during the siege wrote that his ship lost three men at the Siege of Veracruz—Shubrick, Marcus, and one other man whose name he couldn't remember.[33] Because the official casualty lists include only two men killed in action at the battery from the USS *Mississippi*, there might be another one missing. The sailor's letter doesn't indicate whether the third sailor was killed at the battery or elsewhere. These records of additional deaths, coupled with the lack of specific details about the deaths we know about, add an element of uncertainty to the conclusion. As the Mexican-American War historian K. Jack Bauer pointed out, the naval casualties in the Mexican-American War have never been accurately ascertained.[34] However, the historical record, as it now exists, supports Gottlob Rueb as the best candidate for the object of Lee's admiration.

Additional History of Pennsylvania's German Company in the Mexican-American War

Even before the Mexican-American War, the government occasionally called Philadelphia's German militia into service. Two companies fought in the Second Seminole War in Florida (1835–42). When the Nativist Riots broke out in Philadelphia in May 1844, the city called up the state militia. Fueled by anti-immigrant and anti-Catholic sentiments, Nativist mobs ransacked Irish homes and burned Catholic churches. Philadelphia's sheriff called up the state militia, whose commander sent one German company, the Washington Light Infantry, to protect St. John the Evangelist Church near 13th and Market streets, one block east of Philadelphia's current city hall. The company's officers had left the company there by St. John's when the situation grew precarious. When rioters tried to set fire to the church, Württemberg-born Sgt. John F. Ballier—who later became a Civil War general—stepped up to command the company. Strong winds whipped the city during the riots, kicking up dust clouds around the city and threatening to spread fires to other buildings. The German community later credited Ballier's cold-blooded determination with saving both the church and the surrounding property.[1]

It was this company, the Washington Light Infantry, that served in the war as Philadelphia's German company, Company E of Pennsylvania's 1st Regiment. Following the Siege of Veracruz, the company advanced with Scott's army toward Mexico City. It participated in the battle of Cerro Gordo in April 1847 without incurring any casualties.[2]

Scott's forces occupied the fortress San Carlos de Perote later that month en route to Mexico City. The 1st Pennsylvania Regiment arrived at the fortress on May 8 and was assigned to garrison it. Duties included protecting the army's supply line from Veracruz to Mexico City, escorting prisoners, skirmishing, and chasing guerrillas. The companies drilled, and one member of Company C praised the Washington Light Infantry for its good aim in target shooting. Captain Binder led a detail composed of five men from each company to scout the area.[3]

The fortress served as an American hospital for the rest of the war. Many men suffered from diarrhea and dehydration, which sometimes proved fatal.[4]

In August, while still stationed at Perote, Captain Binder became gravely ill for three weeks.[5] According to a later pension claim, Binder suffered from a severe "inflammation of the brain" or a sunstroke.[6] Captain Binder himself described his affliction as a pain in the frontal region of the left side of his head that continued throughout his service and for a year thereafter. While at Perote, he became delirious and had to be hospitalized.[7] The colonel of Pennsylvania's first regiment feared for Captain Binder's recovery and testified that Binder never fully recovered from the stroke. His health was "shaken" and "impaired" thereafter.[8]

On September 17, 1847, thirty of Captain Binder's men were court-martialed for disobedience of an order. Each forfeited $5 of their pay as punishment. A Prussian officer attached to the U.S. Army noted that Colonel Wynkoop, who commanded the Perote garrison, lost control over his volunteer troops during this period. They regularly engaged in a myriad of property crimes, including the robbery of Mexican women on the open streets of Perote, theft in their own quarters, burglary, and theft in the Mexican church. The court-martials might have been part of a crackdown from above, although the other companies stationed at that time don't reflect a large number of court-martials on that date.[9]

The Washington Light Infantry participated in the battle of Huamantla on October 9, 1847, but the Mexicans had fled before the 1st Pennsylvania had approached close enough to see action. The company suffered no casualties. That battle was the last significant engagement of the war. From a total of ninety-seven men who served in Captain Binder's German company, twenty-two died in service, mostly from illness. Rueb was the only man killed in action. One sergeant disappeared mysteriously in late 1847 and was presumed murdered; another drowned inexplicably in a millpond.[10]

Captain Binder returned with his company to Pittsburgh on July 15, 1848, and to Philadelphia nine days later. They were mustered out on August 5. Philadelphia's German newspaper reported the Washington Light Infantry's general good appearance and the company's praise for its captain. Philadelphia celebrated their return with a parade, a series of banquets, ringing church bells, music, and banners. Captain Binder led the parade, decorated with wreaths. Stores closed and people lined the street to throw wreaths to the marching soldiers. "Captain Binder's Quick Step," composed to celebrate the company's homecoming, must have been played at the festivities.[11]

Philadelphia hosted a large banquet for the Washington Light Infantry in the Military Hall on August 3. Three hundred people attended. Col. Francis M. Wynkoop spoke and said that the Germans' conduct during the war changed his mind about immigrants' devotion to their adopted country. Lt. Col. Samuel W. Black spoke about the Siege of Veracruz and mentioned Rueb's death. His words were "heart-rending," according to the local German newspaper.[12]

One of Captain Binder's last war-related duties was to facilitate Rueb's international estate proceedings. He made an official statement about Rueb's death at the Württemberg Consulate in Philadelphia. Perhaps to offer some comfort and extra information for his family, Binder noted that Gottlob was the first man killed in action in the company (he was actually the only man in the company who was killed in action).

Binder continued to participate in the local militia, which was called out to quell Philadelphia's October 1849 race riot. He was compensated for his service as the acting quartermaster for the 1st division of the Pennsylvania Volunteers during that riot. He also served as the captain of the watch for the old district of Kensington.[13]

Afterwards, Frederick W. Binder's fortunes took a nosedive. In October 1850, he was arrested and held on bail for the attempted murder of an acting special police officer. The incident occurred at a German ball held at the Northern Military Headquarters in Northern Liberties. The officer intervened in a fight over a female. Someone turned out the lights, and in the dark, the officer received three serious knife wounds in his left side. The officer accused Binder of stabbing him. Evidentiary issues involved in a later habeas corpus hearing focused on witness prejudice against Captain

Binder. The wounded police officer later died. Murder charges against Binder, however, were dropped in February 1851.[14]

Around the same time, in the early 1850s, Captain Binder was struck by a paralysis of his left side. He was able to continue working, however. The 1860 census shows him as an attorney at law, and IRS tax lists for the early 1860s as a liquor retailer. In the late 1850s, he also served as an alderman and police magistrate for Philadelphia's 15th ward.[15]

By 1865, Captain Binder had become the proprietor of a large beer saloon in Philadelphia at Sixth and Arch streets. In April 1865, a man entered the saloon, knocked Binder down, and kicked him. Binder was injured so severely his doctor didn't expect him to live, but he managed to pull through. The man was caught and charged with assault and battery with intent to kill.[16]

Toward the end of his life, Binder sought to receive a military pension on the basis of his paralysis, arguing that it resulted from his sunstroke during the Mexican-American War. The army was dubious. The reviewing medical examiner did not see a medical connection between the sunstroke and a paralysis ensuing several years later. Binder's vague answers led the examiner to suspect malingering. Nowhere does Captain Binder's pension claim file mention his childhood as a patient in Stuttgart's orthopedic clinic or what role his childhood disability might have played in the captain's later medical condition. Binder died in January 1876.[17]

Several members of the Washington Light Infantry distinguished themselves as officers in the Civil War. John F. Ballier, the sergeant who took command of the Washington Light Infantry in the absence of his commanding officers during Philadelphia's 1844 riots, served not only as a private in Captain Binder's company during the Mexican-American War, but as an acting assistant quartermaster for Pennsylvania's 1st Regiment. From April to August 1861, he helped organize Pennsylvania's 21st Regiment Infantry, in which he served as colonel. Following the 21st Regiment's dissolution, Ballier organized a new regiment out of the old regiment's ranks and added new recruits. Once again, he served as colonel. The resulting 98th Regiment of Pennsylvania was almost exclusively German. Ballier was wounded at Salem Heights and Fort Stevens. Abraham Lincoln promoted him to brevet brigadier general on July 13, 1864.[18]

After returning from the war, Ballier wrote the chapter on the 98th Regiment for Samuel Bates's seminal *History of Pennsylvania Volunteers*,

1861–5; he also served as a member of a court-martial in Washington, D.C. Following the Lincoln assassination, President Johnson appointed Ballier as day inspector at Philadelphia's customs house. Ballier was also one of the founders of Philadelphia's Canstatter Volksfest-Verein, an organization that still survives, and from 1873 served as its vice president.[19]

Although Ballier had trained as a baker in Germany and continued that occupation in Philadelphia, one overlooked aspect of his biography might explain his military success. For his secondary schooling, starting in 1832, he attended a military school in Stuttgart founded by one of his relatives. It was there that General Ballier first trained in military strategy.[20]

John Koltes, a 2nd sergeant under Captain Binder during the Mexican-American War, commanded Philadelphia's Home Guard, organized in April 1861, as captain. Germans served in the Home Guard as well. The men's choir, the *Maennerchor,* joined as a body. Koltes organized the group as a rifle company and prepared it for active service. He then served as colonel of the 73rd Pennsylvania Volunteer Infantry from September 1861 until he was killed in action at 2nd Bull Run in August 1862.[21]

Adam Kramer, a 1st corporal in the Washington Light Infantry during the Mexican-American War, joined the 15th Pennsylvania Cavalry, where he rose from a private to the captain of Company M. Following the war, he continued serving in the regular army and retired as a major of the 6th U.S. Cavalry in January 1897.[22]

Henry Hohnstein, who served alongside Ballier as a private in the Washington Light Infantry in Mexico, became a 1st lieutenant in Company I of Ballier's 98th Regiment. He served in that position until his death in December 1861.[23]

Charles Angeroth, another private in Binder's company, became lieutenant colonel of the 27th Pennsylvania Infantry in 1861 and colonel of the 2nd Pennsylvania Heavy Artillery in 1862.[24]

At least one other member of the Washington Light Infantry enlisted in the Civil War. William Kohler was a private in companies C and D of Ballier's 98th Regiment. Henry Simon, another one of Binder's privates, reportedly served in the 2nd U.S. Artillery during the Civil War, but that information remains unconfirmed.[25]

Notes

PREFACE

1. None of the cases I found in the following German anthologies of historical crimes were solved in America or after such a long period of time: Pflieger, *Die Geschichte(n) der württembergischen Staatsanwaltschaften*; Müller, *Verurteilt*; Müller, *Um Kopf und Kragen*; Feuerbach, *Aktenmäßige Darstellung*; Hitzig, *Annalen*, 73 vols.; Hitzig and Häring, *Der neue Pitaval*, 36 vols. History records one German murder case that was solved after the murderer confessed in a letter sent from the United States. Schultz and Heck, *Ensinger Bilderbogen*, 121–22.

2. The dearth of statistics on Germans who immigrated to the United States in order to escape criminal prosecution or detection in Germany is due to the infrequency with which such grounds were recorded in governmental files. Schmal, "Verpflanzt, aber nicht entwurzelt," 107. Obviously, the criminals had reasons to keep quiet about their backgrounds. There exists at least one recorded case in which a murderer fled to America and later sent a letter in which he confessed. Schultz and Heck, *Ensinger Bilderbogen*, 121–22.

3. Kemp, "Battle of San Jacinto."

4. McCaffrey, *Army of Manifest Destiny*, 29.

5. Ibid.

6. Orr and Miller, "Introduction," xviii, xix.

7. Zeh, *An Immigrant Soldier*, 4. Zeh was referring to Company E of the 1st Regiment of the Pennsylvania Volunteers. Almost all the names of its recruits are of German origin; Hackenburg, *Pennsylvania in the War with Mexico*, 132–142. The captain himself was a German immigrant from Stuttgart. Konsulat Philadelphia, HStAS.

8. Orr and Miller, "Introduction," xviii–xixnn15–18.

9. The first is Zeh, *An Immigrant Soldier*. See Orr and Miller, "Introduction," xviii.

10. Unless otherwise indicated, all translations from the German are mine. Because the text contains several similar German names that can be confusing for an American reader, I will refer to some Germans by their names and professions after introducing them. To make it easier to read, I've used the anglicized version of the assassin's name, as it appears in the American records.

Research in German archives can be frustrated by damage incurred during World War II. In Bönnigheim, for instance, a bomb destroyed the city hall and its archives on April 7, 1945. With that bomb, the city's memory of Mayor Rieber's personal appearance evaporated; any mayoral portrait left hanging in the city hall went up in flames. My survey of older residents in Bönnigheim to tap their memories of portraits in the city hall proved fruitless.

Likewise, a bomb destroyed the archives in Stuttgart that held the personnel records for the lower-entry forestry jobs; all the forestry information in this narrative is based on the personnel records for high-level jobs and on a memoir.

For that reason, gaps appear in the historical record. I haven't bothered to mention those gaps in the narrative. But what has been mentioned is documented in the German archives.

1. A NAMELESS HERO

1. "Letter from a Midshipman," *Newark Daily Advertiser*, Apr. 17, 1847.
2. John of York, "Army Correspondence," *North American*, Apr. 27, 1847.
3. Robert E. Lee to George Washington Custis Lee, Apr. 11, 1847, DeButts-Ely family papers, VHS.

2. CRIME SCENE BÖNNIGHEIM, 1835

1. Hahn, *Rede*, 9, WLB; SR V:99 and VI:107 (1828–45), AEKB; Kurz et al., *Die wechselvolle Geschichte*, 297.
2. Kurz et al., *Die wechselvolle Geschichte*, 162, 297, 363; Hahn, *Rede*, 9, WLB; Privat-Inventarium, 3, SAB.
3. Dalkowski, "Die Retter des Abendbrots"; Friederike Rieber, WS, PB 189; Karl Friedrich Rieber, WS, PB 106.
4. Hammer, Rieber autopsy report, PB 34b; Privat-Inventarium, 14, SAB. No other physical description of Mayor Rieber survives. Tank bombardment during France's occupation at the end of World War II set Bönnigheim's city hall aflame on April 7, 1945, destroying both the building and any mayoral portrait that might have been hanging on the wall. Older Bönnigheim residents still remember the old town hall, but no one recalls a portrait of Mayor Rieber that could provide a basis for a physical description today.
5. Karl Friedrich Rieber, WS, PB 14; Christian Ludwig Schwarzwälder, WS, PB 16; Schmidlin, *Handbuch*, §40 [statute prescribing forester's clothing].
6. Kurz et al., *Die wechselvolle Geschichte*, 144, 158. Sophie von La Roche's novel is called "The History of Lady Sophie von Sternheim" in English.
7. Christian Ludwig Schwarzwälder, WS, PB 16–17b; Meighörner, *"Was ich als Frau dafür halte,"* 78.
8. Becker, *Kriminalität*, 40; Bronner, *Weinbau*, 67 [wine varieties in Bönnigheim].
9. Hammer, crime scene sketch, investigative file; Andreas Nellmann, WS, PB 2–2b; Friederike Rieber, WS, PB 106; Ernst Philipp Foettinger, WS, PB 91b].

10. Johann Heinrich Rieber, witness statement, PB 9b; Hammer, memoranda and various witness statements regarding the second shooting, PB 4b–44.

11. "Augsburg," *Allgemeiner Zeitung von und für Bayern* 23 Oct. 1835, http://books.google.de/books?id=v-5DAAAAcAAJ&pg=PA1185&lpg=PA1185&dq=Allgemeine+Zeitung+%2223.+Oktober+1835%22&source=bl&ots=XFQPZ5mCx1&sig=3f1rflhCvI9furOymhOUqw6JgWI&hl=de&sa=X&ei=aGBSU027KrSToQW7hYCwCw&ved=0CD0Q6AEwAQ#v=onepage&q=Allgemeine%20Zeitung%20%2223.%20Oktober%201835%22&f=false.

12. Schaaf, *Comet*, 179; Rollwagen, "Halley." The 1759 return was closer to the earth but wasn't as well positioned for the Northern Hemisphere. Watson, "Halley's Comet," 210, 214; Eppenauer, *Ueber den Kometen*, 9. With the exception of October 18, 1835, which had variable weather (*"meistens heiter"*), Württemberg's weather had been miserable. "Stuttgarter Witterungs Beobachtungen," *Schwäbische Chronik*, Oct. 6, 9, 13, 16, 18, 23, 24, 1835.

13. Hammer, crime scene sketch, investigative file; Johann Heinrich Rieber, WS, PB 8b–9; Hammer, memorandum, PB 4b. "Washhouse" was a nickname because the building housed a water tank.

14. Andreas Nellmann, WS, PB 2b; Johann Heinrich Rieber, WS, PB 8b–9.

3. PORTENTS OF REBELLION

1. Robert E. Lee to Andrew Talcott, Oct. 21, 1835, Talcott Papers, MSS1T1434 b 165, VHS, quoted in E. M. Thomas, *Robert E. Lee*, 83.

2. Freeman, *R. E. Lee*, 14–17, 31.

3. Ibid., 30–85, 94–132; E. M. Thomas, *Robert E. Lee*, 32–75.

4. Freeman, *R. E. Lee*, 133–34; E. M. Thomas, *Robert E. Lee*, 81–82.

5. E. M. Thomas, *Robert E. Lee*, 81–83; Robert E. Lee to Mary Custis Lee, Aug. 21, 1835, Mss HM 20561, Huntington Library, San Marino, California, quoted in Cuthbert, "To Molly," 271 [quote].

6. E. M. Thomas, *Robert E. Lee*, 83–89; Freeman, *R. E. Lee*, 108, 133–34.

7. Long, *Memoirs*, 31.

8. Freeman, *R. E. Lee*, 82.

9. Robert E. Lee to Andrew Talcott, Feb. 2, 1837, Talcott Papers, MSS1T1434 b 190, VHS, quoted in Freeman, *Robert E. Lee*, 84.

10. Robert E. Lee to Andrew Talcott, May 23, 1836, Talcott Papers, MSS1T1434 b 182, VHS; Gwynne, *Empire*, 25.

11. Campbell, *Gone to Texas*, 110–22, 127–37.

12. Gammel, *Laws of Texas*, 510.

4. A TOWN REACTS

1. Michael Borwarth, WS, PB 158b–159.

2. Louise Hepperle, WS, PB 4b–5b; Catherine Maier, WS, PB 13–13b; Heinrich Böhringer, WS, PB 80b–81.

3. Ernst Phillipp Foettinger and Luise Foettinger, WS, PB 91b–95b.

4. Hammer, crime scene sketch, investigative file; Juliane Stölzle, WS, PB 45–47b.

5. Hammer, crime scene sketch, investigative file; Juliane Stölzle, WS, PB 45–47b.

6. Friedrich Kachel, WS, PB 11–11b; crime scene sketch, investigative file.

7. Christof Wenz, WS, PB 50b–53b.

8. Christian Ludwig Schwarzwälder, WS, PB 16–17b; Eduard Vischer, WS, RB 17b–18b.

9. Fischer, *Behandlung*, 413–1028, in particular, 652 §590.

10. Hammer, memorandum, PB 7b, PB 19; Rieber autopsy report, PB 33b–39.

11. *Oberamt* in German.

12. Hammer, memorandum, PB 19; Johann Andreas Nellmann, WS, PB 2–3b.

13. Johann Andreas Nellmann, WS, PB 2–3b; Karl Friedrich Rieber, WS, PB 13b–14; Friederike Rieber, WS, PB 105b; Hahn, *Rede*, 10.

14. Nellmann to Oberamt Besigheim, Oct. 21, 1835, investigative file.

15. Christof Wenz, WS, PB 50b–53b; Königliches statistisch-topographisches Bureau, *Besigheim*, 137; Hammer, memoranda, PB, 1, 10b; Ehrensperger, *Besigheimer Häuserbuch*, 32–33; Schulz, "Aus der Geschichte," 163.

16. Christian Ludwig Schwarzwälder, WS, PB 16–17b; Johann Andreas Nellmann, WS, PB 2–3b; Böhringer, Chirurgischer Bericht, Oct. 21, 1835, investigative file.

17. Heinrich Böhringer, WS, PB 80b–81.

18. Ibid.

19. Wörner and Zipperlin to Oberamtsgericht, Oct. 21, 1835, 11:00 P.M., investigative file; Hammer, memorandum, PB 1b.

20. Eduard Vischer, WS, PB 17b–18b; Michael Borwarth, WS, PB 158b–159.

21. Hammer, memorandum, PB 4.

22. Wörner to Oberamtsgericht, Oct. 22, 1835, 4:00 A.M.; Hammer, memorandum, PB 3b–4.

23. Hammer, memorandum, PB 66.

5. THE DETECTIVE'S HOURGLASS

1. Hammer, memoranda, PB, 1, 10b.

2. Hammer, memoranda, PB, 1; Gross, *Handbuch*, 109, 125–26. Gross wrote that a good scribe was critical to a criminal investigation. That the handwriting in Hammer's protocol book is different from the handwriting in his correspondence indicates that Hammer also used a scribe to record his interrogations.

3. *Oberamtsrichter* in German.

4. Gundert, *Rede*, 5–6, 9–11; Hammer, "Ueber den Zustand der Rechtspflege," 311–28; Brandt, *Parlamentarismus*, 134; *Königlich-Württembergisches Hof- und Staatshandbuch*, 40.

5. Hauff to Oberamtsgericht, Oct. 22, 1835, 5:00 A.M., investigative file; Wörner and Zipperlin to Oberamtsgericht, Oct. 21, 1835, 11:00 P.M., investigative file; Wörner to Oberamtsgericht, Oct. 22, 1835, 4:00 A.M.; Hammer, memorandum, PB 1–1b.

6. "Witterungsbeobachtungen," *Schwäbische Chronik*, Oct. 28, 1835; Hammer, memorandum, PB 2; Ehrensperger, *Besigheimer Häuserbuch*, 33. The two city council members who assisted Eduard Hammer in the investigation were Georg Adam Michael Voelter and Gottfried Zipperlin.

7. Andreas Nellman, WS, PB 2–2b.

8. Hammer, memorandum, PB 3b–4b.

9. Louise Hepperle, WS, PB 4b–5b.

10. These are German size numbers for shot used to kill foxes or badgers.

11. In German, 3 *Fuß* 9 *Zoll* and 3 *Schuh* 7 *Zoll*, respectively. Hammer, memorandum, PB 6–6b.

12. Hammer, memorandum, PB 6b–7.

13. Hammer, memoranda, PB 5b–8, 33b.

14. Hammer, memorandum, PB 8b.

15. Johann Heinrich Rieber, WS, PB 8b–10b.

16. Hammer, memorandum, PB 10.

17. Georg Jacob Kurz, WS PB 12b–13; Catherine Maier, WS, PB 13–13b; Karl Friedrich Rieber, WS, PB 13b–14; Christian Ludwig Schwarzwälder, WS, PB 16–17; Eduard Vischer, WS, PB 18–18b.

18. One *Quint* in German.

19. Hammer, memorandum, PB 19–19b.

20. Hammer, memorandum, PB 8.

21. Fischer, *Uebersicht*, 317; Horn, Nasse, and Wagner, *Universal-Register*, 176; Tortora, *Human Anatomy*, 565, 577.

22. Fischer, *Uebersicht*, 318.

23. Laennec, *Treatise*, 504; Hammer, memorandum, PB 8b; Hahn, *Rede*, 10.

24. Fischer, *Behandlung*, 941.

25. Hahn, *Rede*, 10; Franck, *Württembergisches Gesangbuch*, 355.

26. Hahn, *Rede*, 10.

27. Wörner to Oberamtsgericht, Oct. 23, 1835, 5:00 A.M., investigative file.

6. QUEEN OF THE CAROLINA

1. Sauer, *Im Namen des Königs*, 14; Schild, "Geschichte des Verfahrens," 198; Kappler, *Handbuch*, 537; Payne-James and Stark, "Clinical Forensic Medicine," 4. Württemberg enacted the Carolina in 1551.

2. CCC Art. 22, 62, and 67 (1532) [partial English translation available in Langbein, *Prosecuting Crime in the Renaissance*, 261–308]; Langbein, *Torture*, 4–5, 145n4; Schild, "'*Von peinlicher Frag*,'" 50.

3. Schild, "'*Von peinlicher Frag*,'" 59–84.

4. Peters, *Folter*, 127.

5. Mittermaier, *Beweise*, 410, §54.

6. Strafprozessordnung [Code of Criminal Procedure] §§338–339, Regierungsblatt für das Königreich Württemberg 33 (July 14, 1843).

7. Kesper-Biermann, *Einheit und Recht*, 43.

8. Hammer, memorandum, PB 20–20b, 26–27.

9. Christoph Friedrich Hepperle, WS, PB 27b–28.

10. Juliane Bleil, WS, PB 28b–29.

11. Casper Bleil, WS, PB 32b–33b.

12. Christiana Siegel, WS, PB 74b–75.

13. Hammer, memorandum, PB 20–20b.

14. Christian Wachter, WS, PB 20b–26; crime scene sketch, investigative file.

7. Buckshot in the Scales of Justice

1. Hammer, memorandum, PB 38b–39; Groß, *Leichenschau*, 34, 37.
2. Groß, *Leichenschau*, 20–37.
3. Hauff and Jung, memorandum, Nov. 11, 1835, investigative file; Hammer, memorandum, PB 34b–38.
4. Hammer, memoranda, PB 19a, 44b.
5. Hammer, memoranda, PB 19, 26–28; 41.
6. Hammer, memoranda, PB 41b, 43–44; Oberamtsgericht Besigheim, court order, Feb. 17, 1836, investigative file.
7. Hammer, memorandum, PB 41–41b.
8. Hammer, memorandum, PB 41b. Conversions from *Quints* and *Grans* are based on von Hippel, *Maß und Gewicht*, 84, 197.
9. A saddler who examined the wadding much later in the investigation questioned whether it was made of deer hair. He thought it might have been hair from a calf. Because homemade deer hair wadding in rifles was rare, the saddler considered the possibility that the wadding might have had another origin. Magistrate Hammer noted that someone had recently moved out of the Kavaliersbau in which Mayor Rieber lived, raising the possibility that the wadding was a piece of upholster from furniture that had fallen out during the move. The origin of the wadding was never precisely determined. Hammer, memorandum, PB 149–149b.

8. Like Cain Will You Wander

1. *Königlich-Württembergisches Hof- und Staatshandbuch* (1835), 167.
2. Quellmalz, "Christoph Ulrich Hahn," 176–211; Hahn, *Beschreibung*; Haumer, "1863," 1340.
3. Quellmalz, "Christoph Ulrich Hahn," 182.
4. Kurz et al., *Die wechselvolle Geschichte*, 299; Haumer, "1863," 3, figure 1.
5. "Witterungs-Beobachtungen," *Schwäbische Chronik*, Oct. 28, 1835 [weather report; 7° Réaumur]; AEBK, SR 5:107 [date of funeral].
6. Hahn, *Rede*, 1–2.
7. Ibid., 4–5.
8. Ibid., 6–7.
9. Ibid., 7–8.
10. La Roche to Hirzel, July 26, 1771, in La Roche, *"Ich bin mehr Herz,"* 140 [Schwaigern, a town next to Stetten am Heuchelberg, was three hours from Bönnigheim].
11. Stock, "Auszüge," 305.

9. Witness!

1. Oberamtsgericht Besigheim to Criminal Senat Esslingen, Dec. 7, 1835, 8n"#," investigative file; Hammer, memorandum, PB 45.
2. Hammer, memorandum, PB 19b–20b; Carl Gartmann, WS, PB 48b–50b, 108b–109b; Rosina Gartmann, WA, PB151–151b; Ludwig Schweiher, WS, PB 56b–57.

3. Jakob Hofmann, WS, PB 57–59; crime scene sketch, investigative file.

4. Conversions from *Fuss* and *Zoll* are based on von Hippel, *Maß und Gewicht*, 196–97.

5. Jacob Wiedmann, WS, PB 62–64b; Hammer, crime scene sketch, investigative file.

6. Jacob Wiemann [father], WS, PB 67–68b; Juliane Sommer, WS, PB 69b–70b; Jacob Wiedmann [son], written oath, PB 70b–71; Johann Friedrich Brenner, WS, PB 70b–71; Christian Altmann, WS, PB 71b–72; Friedrich von Hoven, WS, PB 72b; Conrad Krapf, WS, PB 73–73b; Christian Müller, WS, PB 73b–74b; Christiane Siegel, WS, PB 74b–75; Catherine Siegel, 76–76b.

7. Gross, *Handbuch*, 384.

8. Ibid.

9. Schmidlin, *Handbuch*, §163(d), §163n4½; *Fabrikation und Verkauf*, StALB.

10. Hammer, memorandum, PB 34–34b.

11. Friederike Rieber, WS, PB 105b–107.

12. Hammer, memorandum, PB 42b; Gendarme Stations-Commandant Bofinger, WS, PB 77–78; Jacob Andreas Hilligard, WS, PB 79b–80.

13. Ferdinand Krafft, WS, PB 59b–60; Johannes Maier, WS, PB 83b–85; Gottlieb Bihl, WS, PB 82–83b; Friedrich Meuer, WS, PB 87–89.

14. Johann Michael Deterle, WS, PB 78–79b.

15. Hammer, memorandum, PB 91b; Ernst Phillipp Foettinger and Luise Foettinger, WS, PB 91b–95b; Heinrike Foettinger, WS, PB 116–116b.

16. Hammer, memoranda, Dec. 6, 1835, 11–11b, investigative file, and PB 98; Gottfried Kölle, WS, PB 98b–100.

17. Gottfried Kölle, WS, PB 98b–100; Christiane Elisabethe Kölle, WS, PB 100–100b [quote].

18. Hammer, memorandum, WS, PB 101; Johannes Scherle, WS, PB 107b–108b; Carl Gartmann, WS, PB 108b–109b; Johanna Haug, WS, PB 109b–110b; Jacob Friedrich Haug, WS, PB 110b–111.

19. Hammer, memoranda, Dec. 6, 1835, investigative file, and PB 11–11b, 15–15b.

20. Hammer, memorandum, PB 102–102b; Bönnigheim City Council, Auszug Stadtraths-Protokolls II, Blatt 260.12, §289, Oct. 22, 1835, and Auszug Stadtraths-Protokolls II, Blatt 262, §290, Oct. 28, 1835, investigative file [city council protocols documenting the decision to offer the rewards].

21. *Heilbronner Intelligenz-Blatt*, Nov. 5, 1835.

22. Friedrich Bleil, WS, Nov. 8, 1835, investigative file; Hammer, memorandum, Dec. 6, 1835, investigative file, and PB 10b–11.

23. Oberamtsgericht Besigheim to Oberamtsgericht Brackenheim, Nov. 7, 1835, and handwritten answer on the same page, Nov. [8?], 1835, investigative file.

10. THE BIRTH OF FORENSIC BALLISTICS

1. Oberamtsgericht Besigheim to Criminal-Senat Esslingen, Dec. 7, 1835, 6b, investigative file.

2. Gross, *Handbuch*, 379.

3. Hammer, memorandum, PB 104–105.

4. Hammer, memorandum, PB 119b–120; Hartmann, *Populäres Handbuch*, 644.

5. Hammer, memorandum, PB 119b–120; Frevert, *Die kasernierte Nation*, 157; Schmidlin, *Handbuch*, 163–64, §111n1; *Verhandlung in der Versammlung*, 172.

6. Hammer, memoranda, PB 119b–120, 146b.

7. Hammer, memorandum, PB 120b–121.

8. Ibid.

9. Eduard Vischer, WS, PB 161b–164; Ludwig Schwarzwälder, WS, PB 16–18b, 164–165b; Oberamtsgericht Besigheim to Criminal Senat Esslingen, Dec. 7, 1835, investigative file.

10. Volker Schäfer, e-mail message to author, Apr. 15, 2015.

11. Lacassagne, "De la déformation," 70. For more literature on the history of forensic ballistics, see Starr, *Killer of Little Shepherds*, 46–47; Thorwald, *Jahrhundert der Detektive*, 488–93; Block, *Science vs Crime*, 65–81.

12. Lacassagne, "De la déformation"; Steele, "Ballistics," 1–29.

13. McCrery, *Silent Witnesses*, 51.

14. Wagner, *Science of Sherlock Holmes*, 63–65, 119–20.

15. Hitzig, "Notwehr, Erfüllungs-Eid," *Annalen* 15 (1833): 157–72.

16. Wagner, *Science of Sherlock Holmes*, 120–22. Some sources assert the crime was murder, but Wagner claims Goddard's own memoirs describe the crime as a staged burglary.

17. It's notable that a 1930 German review of the forensic ballistics literature doesn't mention an article as early as Hammer's time, even while defending German and American claims to competency in the field against French assertions of supremacy. Kraft, "Kritisches zur gerichtlichen Schußuntersuchung." Prior to 1835, no discussion of ballistic fingerprinting procedures appears in period anthologies of criminal cases such as Feuerbach, *Aktenmäßige Darstellung*, or Hitzig, *Annalen*.

18. Examples include Goltdammer, *Archiv*, 551; Schäffer, *Archiv*, 170–71; Glaser and Nowak, "Strafsache," 301.

19. Kreisgerichtshof/Landgericht Ellwangen, Findbuch, E 341 I, StALB; Kreisgerichtshof Tübingen, Findbuch, E331, StALB; Kreisgerichtshof Ulm, Findbuch, E 350, StALB; Kreisgerichtshof Esslingen (1817–70), Findbuch, E 319, StALB; Oberjustizkollegium, Findbuch, D 70, StALB [The cause of death isn't always listed in the finding aids, however]; Verfahren gegen: Friedrich Preiffer, Bericht an den Criminal-Senat, Feb. 4–6, 1823, StALB.

20. Heard, *Handbook*, 11, 81–82, 161.

21. Although the caliber of the murder weapon wasn't known, and thus impossible to replicate in the test-firing, a similar ratio of the pellet size to the caliber would suffice to simulate Hammer's results. Hence, Schäfer tried several different pellet sizes. Volker Schäfer, in discussion with the author, May 2015.

22. Hammer, "Ueber den Zustand."

23. Stock, "Auszüge," 305–6.

11. CELESTIAL METRONOME

1. Lloyd, "An Account of an Observatory," 190; Herschel, *Astronomical Observations*, 401.

2. Schaaf, *Comet*, 179.

3. Campbell, *Gone to Texas*, 139, 143–45; Schaaf, *Comet*, 180.

4. Peña, *With Santa Anna*, 46.

5. Ibid., 46; Campbell, *Gone to Texas*, 145–77; Greenberg, *A Wicked War*, 9.

6. Campbell, *Gone to Texas*, 146–47.

7. Texas Declaration of Independence, para. 3.

8. Campbell, *Gone to Texas*, 156–57.

9. Kemp, "Battle of San Jacinto."

10. Campbell, *Gone to Texas*, 160.

11. Campbell, *Gone to Texas*, 148, 158–60; Treaty of Velasco (Public), Republic of Texas-Mexico, art. 3; Treaty of Velasco (Private), Republic of Texas-Mexico, art. 3–4.

12. Campbell, *Gone to Texas*, 162–63.

13. Greenberg, *A Wicked War*, 10; "Treaties of Velasco."

14. James K. Polk, *Congressional Globe*, 29th Cong., 1st sess. 783–84 (1846), http://memory.loc.gov/cgi-bin/ampage?collId=llcg&fileName=016/llcg016.db&recNum=830.

15. Abraham Lincoln, *Congressional Globe*, 30th Cong., 1st sess. 154–56(1848), http://memory.loc.gov/cgi-bin/ampage?collId=llcg&fileName=019/llcg019.db&recNum=205; Greenberg, *A Wicked War*, 245–48.

16. Greenberg, *A Wicked War*, 9; Larry Schweikart, "Penny Press," in Tucker et al., *Encyclopedia of the Mexican-American War*, 2:499–500; Freeman, *R. E. Lee*, 135.

12. A NOTE IN THE WOODS

1. Kurz et al., *Die wechselvolle Geschichte*, 420; Hammer, memorandum, July 28, 1836, investigative file.

2. Eduard Hammer to Criminal Senat, May 27, 1836, investigative file.

3. Hammer and Finckh, memoranda to file, July 28, 30, 1836, investigative file.

4. Hammer, memorandum, July 28, 1836, investigative file. See also Pierer, *Universal-Lexikon*, 8:287 [*Gesell* can mean "comrade," but in context with a trade, such as a shoemaker, it means "apprentice"].

5. Hammer, memorandum, July 28, 1836, investigative file.

6. Eduard Hammer, memorandum, July 28, 1836, and crime scene sketch, investigative file.

7. Ernst Phillip Foettinger, WS, PB 91b–93b; Luise Foettinger, WS, PB 94–95b; Heinrike Foettinger, WS, PB 116–116b.

8. Schmidlin, *Handbuch*, 49 §22, 29 §182.

9. Ibid., 47–48 §20 [forest rangers' [*Forstwarth Unterförster*] supervision of game wardens].

10. Eduard Hammer, memorandum, Mar. 7, 1837, investigative file.

11. Stock, "Auszüge," 305, HGB; Auswanderungen/1836, StALB.

12. Nachlass von Georg Michael Rupp, SAB; Güter-Buch, Theil 3, SAB.

13. *Königlich Württembergisches Hof- und Staatshandbuch* (1835) 167.

14. ER III163 and FR I 397a, AEKB; Auswanderungen/1836, StALB.

15. Gürth, *Alte Heimat*, 71. The Rupp family sold their house and vineyard in 1836. Güter-Buch, 735b–737b, SAB.

16. FR I 397a, AEKB; Auswanderungen/1836, StALB.

17. FR I 397a, AEKB; Passenger list, *Petronella* (Amsterdam–New York), Nov. 15, 1836, Passenger Lists of Vessels Arriving at New York, 1820–97, NA.

18. Stock, "Auszüge," 305, HGB.

19. Ibid.; Elisabeth Zipperlen to Kreisarchivpfleger Willy Müller, Nov. 22, 1955, Nachlass Elisabeth Zipperlen, Ordner "Berühmte Söhne," Abteilung "Stadtschultheiß Heinrich Rieber," SAB [Mayor Rieber's bloody clothing remained on display in the city hall until at least 1900].

13. Hunter and Prey

1. Jacob Wiedmann, WS, PB 62b–63.

2. Familienblätter 1638–1807, s.v. "Rüb, Johannes," AEKSaH; Schuster to Finckh, May 26, 1872. Gottlob's birth records contain a misspelling that would follow him to the grave. According to the church records, he was baptized *Gottlieb* Friedrich Rüb, but a former town spokesman of Stetten later clarified for the prosecutor investigating the case that the first name was really Gottlob. The Stetten municipal court case uses both first names to describe the same person. His military records in the United States reflect both first names as well as several spelling variations of his last name.

3. *Königlich Württembergisches Hof- und Staatshandbuch* (1835) 175; Sophie von La Roche to Johann Caspar Hirzel, July 26, 1771, in Sophie von La Roche, *"Ich bin mehr Herz,"* 140 [Schwaigern, the town next to Stetten am Heuchelberg, was three hours from Bönnigheim].

4. Clement, *Schwaigern*, 306.

5. Steuerbuch VIII, 67, 72, 77, 74b, 75, 80, SAS-SAH; Clement, *Schwaigern*, 304–6, 314; "Förstliche Notizen über Württemberg," *Allgemeine Forst- und Jagdzeitung*, Dec. 27, 1833, https://books.google.de/books?id=FptPAAAAcAAJ&printsec=frontcover&source=gbs_ge_summary_r&cad=0#v=onepage&q&f=false.

6. Familienblätter 1638–1807, s.v. "Rüb, Johannes," AEKSaH.

7. Königliches Finanz-Ministerium , *Instruktionen für die königlichen Forstwarthe*, 3, §1; Schmidlin, *Handbuch*, 135–36, §81 [forestry personnel were allowed to shoot at armed poachers who did not give themselves up]; Linck, "Der Wolf von Cleebronn," 2:19 [game wardens used rifles to track and shoot a wolf].

8. Rub, Gottlob, Descriptive and Historical Register, NA; Schuster to Finckh, May 26, 1872, investigative file.

9. Gerichtsprotokoll 1807–16, B: 264, 316b, SAS-SAH; Ruggerichtsprotokoll 1821–1912, B: 318, 94, SAS-SAH.

10. Verzeichnis der aktiven Gemeinde-Bürger (1828), B513, SAS-SAH; Königliches Finanz-Ministerium, *Instruktionen*, 7–8, §18; Schuler et al., *Zur Geschichte des Forstberufs*, 11, 25, 63; "Förstliche Notize über Württemberg," *Allgemeine Forst- und Jagd-Zeitung*, Dec. 27, 1833 [see n. 8].

11. Untersuchungs-Sache gegen den Forstwart Gottlob Friedrich Rüb, SAS-SAH.

12. Schuster to Finckh, May 26, 1972, investigative file.

13. Gwinner, *Die königlich Württembergischen Forstdienst-Prüfungen*, 43–44; Untersuchungs-Sache gegen den Forstwart Gottlob Friedrich Rüb, SAS-SAH.

14. Gerichtsprotokoll 1834–38, B: 268, 8b and index, SAS-SAH.

15. Schuldklagprotokoll, B: 301, Sept. 20, 1834, SAS-SAH.

16. Schuler et al., *Zur Geschichte des Forstberufs*, 11, 25, 42; Königliches Finanz-Ministerium, *Instruktionen*, 3–7, §§1–12.

17. Finckh to Hofstetter, June 26, 1872, investigative file.

18. Rupp to mayor and city council of Bönnigheim, Apr. 29, 1872, investigative file. The reasons for the rejection are not specified in the file.

19. Hammer, memorandum, PB 5b–6b.

20. Bösken, *Das Ende*, 33.

21. Kurz et al., *Die wechselvolle Geschichte*, 107; Bau von Dohlen, StAB.

22. Clement, *Schwaigern*, 75–76.

23. CCC, art. 137.

14. Escape to America

1. Kriminalsenat Tübingen: Strafsache gegen Johann Georg Fischer, StALB; Kriminalsenat Ulm: Strafsache gegen Philipp Jakob Speidel, StALB; U.S. Department of State, Office of the Historian, "A Guide to the United States' History of Recognition, Diplomatic, and Consular Relations, by Country, since 1776: Württemberg," http://history.state.gov/countries/wurttemberg.

2. Gürth, *Alte Heimat*, 70–72.

3. Oberamt Brackenheim: Auswanderungen, Stetten Bd. 1 (1807–50), StALB; Oberamt Brackenheim: Auswanderungsverzeichnis, StALB; Bürgerrechtsverzeichnis-Urkunden, SAS-SAH.

4. Kümmerle to Finckh, June 4, 1872, investigative file [emphasis in original; "Johann Georg Kümmerle" in the letter, but in his emigration application, the name "Kimmerle" was used].

5. Schuster to Finckh, May 26, 1972, investigative file.

6. Gürth, *Alte Heimat*, 71; Brunner, *Nach Amerika*, 57; Schmal, "Verpflanzt, " 107.

7. Brunner, *Nach Amerika*, 47; Stierle, "Die Auswanderer," 43.

8. Auswanderungen, Stetten Bd. 1 (Apr. 7, 1836), StALB; Kimmerle, John G., Seventh Census, NA; Bounty Land Files, NA. Several years later, two men later made sworn statements to facilitate Gottlob's estate proceedings. Because they were asked to clarify Gottlob's marital status while he lived in Philadelphia, it is likely they were either Gottlob's landlords or neighbors. Both had addresses from the north end of the Old City district near Vine Street. The witnesses lived near Alderman Erety at N. 3rd and Vine Streets. *McElroy's Philadelphia City Directory* (1847), s.v. "Erety." The directory places one witness, Godfrey Goekeler, also a baker, at 96 Crown. Crown Street no longer exists under that name, but part of it survives as N. Lawrence Street. The other witness, John Herman, lived on either 4th or Vine. Gottlob wasn't counted in the 1840 census because he was on the frontier. He doesn't appear in any Philadelphia directories, which probably means he was renting a room.

9. Descriptive and Historical Register of Enlistments in the U.S. Army, NA; Records of the Adjutant General's Office, NA.

10. The sources consulted at the Philadelphia City Archives are listed in the bibliography.

11. Peskin, *Winfield Scott*, 101; McLaughlin, *Patriot War*, 1–2, 181–82.

12. Peskin, *Winfield Scott*, 103.

13. Scott, *Memoirs*, 306–7.

14. Peskin, *Winfield Scott*, 103–11; Scott, *Memoirs*, 308–17.

15. Conway and Jamroz, *Fort Wayne*, 7; Adjutant General's Office, *Regulations for the Uniform*, 25–26; Urwin, *United States Infantry*, 58.

16. Rub, Gottlob, Descriptive and Historical Register, NA. The recruitment officer spelled Rueb as Rub, a common variation. The commanding officer of Company A was Brevet Maj. John L. Gardner. "Stations of the Companies of the Fourth Regiment of Artillery," *Army and Navy Chronicle*, Aug. 20, 1835, http://babel.hathi trust.org/cgi/pt?id=nyp.33433009345665;view=1up;seq=304; Burdsall, *Diary*, 91, College of William and Mary Digital Archive.

17. Steinbeis, Paper C, Bounty Land Files, NA; Friedrich Gentner to Adjutant General, 1848, Letters Received by the Office of the Adjutant General, NA.

18. Peskin, *Winfield Scott*, 121.

19. Forry, *Climate*, 114, 131–33 [temperatures provided for Green Bay, Wisconsin; no temperatures were provided for Michigan].

20. "Military Intelligence," *Army and Navy Chronicle*, Sept. 2, 1841, http://babel .hathitrust.org/cgi/pt?id=nyp.33433009300744;view=1up;seq=31; "The Army," *Niles National Register*, Dec. 4, 1841, https://books.google.de/books?id=RFc5AQAAMAAJ &pg=RA1-PA211&lpg=RA1-PA211&dq=U.S.+Army+Register+1841+%22Mad ison+Barracks%22&source=bl&ots=ZYnzLWo1bn&sig=lfp8htRjr5kJ8pJxyuxXs oiq3M&hl=en&sa=X&ei=4F50VcXzOMayswHS44DACw&ved=oCCwQ6AEw Ag#v=onepage&q=U.S.%20Army%20Register%201841%20%22Madison%20 Barracks%22&f=false; Forry, *Climate*, 135–39; Dyer, "Fourth Regiment of Artillery," 846–47; Descriptive and Historical Register of Enlistments in the U.S. Army, NA.

21. Death certificate for Caroline Elizabeth Brown, Aug. 26, 1927, No. 273215, Washington, D.C., Archives [showing family living in Philadelphia area in 1837]; *Hospital Tickets*, s.v. "Benjamin Rupp, private," July 6, 1867, 159, NA [showing Rupp family still living in Philadelphia area as late as 1844]; Fiatkowsky family, *Seventh Census of the United States*, NA [birth of son Edward indicates the Fiatkowsky family was still living in Maryland in 1841]; "List of Insolvents," *Public Ledger* (Philadelphia), Apr. 4, 1840, 1 [Frederick Rupp in Kensington, later to become a part of Philadelphia]; Rupp family, *Seventh Census of the United States*, NA [showing Rupp family in Lancaster and Frederick Rupp working as a druggist]; Rupp family, *Eighth Census of the United States*, NA [Rupp family now living in Washington, D.C.].

15. Changing Course

1. Korda, *Clouds of Glory*, 80–96.

2. Moody et al., *Lewis and Clark's Observations*, 46; Pryor, *Reading the Man*, 111; Freeman, *R. E. Lee*, 90, 145.

3. Freeman, *R. E. Lee*, 138; Pryor, *Reading the Man*, 109, 116–18.

4. Thomas, *Robert E. Lee*, 90–91, 97; Pryor, *Reading the Man*, 114–15; Freeman, *R. E. Lee*, 151, 154–55, 179–83.

5. Freeman, *R. E. Lee*, 138; Pryor, *Reading the Man*, 109, 116–18.

6. Freeman, *R. E. Lee*, 182.

7. Freeman, *R. E. Lee*, 152; Pryor, *Reading the Man*, 111.

8. Korda, *Clouds of Glory*, 88.

9. Pryor, *Reading the Man*, 118; Crocker, *Robert E. Lee*, 29.

10. Freeman, *R. E. Lee*, 159.

11. Ibid., 159, 164–67.

12. Korda, *Clouds of Glory*, 3; Norris, *Westmoreland County*, 174; Washington and Lee University, General Commencement Information (2015), http://www.wlu.edu /commencement/general-commencement-information.

13. Freeman, *R. E. Lee*, 160; Korda, *Clouds of Glory*, 3.

14. Freeman, *R. E. Lee*, 160, 182.

15. Ibid., 192; Bullitt, "Lee and Scott," 446.

16. Thomas, *Robert E. Lee*, 94.

17. Freeman, *R. E. Lee*, 202.

18. Tucker et al., *The Encyclopedia of the Mexican-American War*, s.v. "Manifest Destiny"; Greenberg, *A Wicked War*, 10; Campbell, *Gone to Texas*, 161, 182–83.

19. Tucker et al., *The Encyclopedia of the Mexican-American War*, s.v. "Texas."

20. Campbell, *Gone to Texas*, 185–86; Greenberg, *A Wicked War*, 76–79; Winders, *Mr. Polk's Army*, 8; Tucker et al., *The Encyclopedia of the Mexican-American War*, s.v. "Slidell, John."

21. Winders, *Mr. Polk's Army*, 8–9.

22. Ibid., 9–10.

23. Freeman, *R. E. Lee*, 201–16.

24. Peskin, *Winfield Scott*, 141–42.

25. Freeman, *R. E. Lee*, 217–18.

26. Hackenburg, *Pennsylvania in the War*, 2–4.

16. F-major Captain

1. Weigley, *History*, 168; McCaffrey, *Army of Manifest Destiny*, 29; Zeh, "Erinnerungen," 57 [quote]; Foos, *Short, Offhand, Killing Affair*, 42–43.

The two German companies from Philadelphia were Capt. Frederick Binder's Washington Light Infantry, which eventually served as Company E in the 1st Regiment of the Pennsylvania Volunteers, and Capt. Arnold Seyberg's (sometimes spelled Syberg) Steuben Fusiliers. Harrisburg's German newspaper categorized both companies as German. "General-Befehl, No. 8: Hauptquartier, Philadelphia, December 3, 1846," *Pennsylvanische Staats-Zeitung*, Dec. 9, 1846; "Companien von Pennsylvanien," *Pennsylvanische Staats-Zeitung*, Feb. 24, 1847; "Pennsylvanische Volunteers," *Pennsylvanische Staats-Zeitung*, July 8, 1846. See also Hackenburg, *Pennsylvania in the War*, 5–8, 317; Zeh, "Erinnerungen," 57 (Zeh describes one of the Philadelphia companies in Pennsylvania's 1st Regiment as "exclusively German").

2. McCaffrey, *Army of Manifest Destiny*, 30–34.

3. Foos, *Short, Offhand, Killing Affair*, 42–43.

4. These companies were the 1st company of the Washington National Guard, the 2nd company of the Washington National Guard (which changed its name

sometime prior to 1844 to the Washington Light Infantry), the Washington Jäger Compagnie, and the Washington Volantair Compagnie. "Bekanntmachungen: Be-taillonsbefehl," *Philadelphia Demokrat* (diverse articles and advertisements between 1844 and 1846). The sources for dances popular in Philadelphia from 1843 to 1846 are the *Philadelphia Demokrat*, Feb. 14, 1844 [German waltzes], and Erwin, Journal, Oct. 9, 1843, Feb. 10–11, 1845, July 13–14, 1846, BMCOC.

5. Undated, untitled clipping from an unidentified German newspaper (clipping damaged and identifying information missing) regarding two Philadelphia German companies in the Seminole War, JFBP, JHML; "General John F. Ballier" (undated clipping from an unidentified German newspaper regarding Ballier's role in the Nativist Riots), JFBP, JHML; Rosengarten, *German Soldier*, 253; Schrag, "Nativist Riots;" Erwin, Journal, May 7–8, 1844 (winds during the riots).

6. Erwin, Journal, May 12, 1846.

7. Ibid., May 13, 18, 1846.

8. Young, *Memorial History*, 173; obituary of Captain Binder, *Philadelphia Inquirer*, Jan. 24, 1876; "Bekanntmachungen: Betaillons-Befehl," *Philadelphia Demokrat*, Jan. 9, 1844; Binder to von Hügel, May 25, 1859, Konsulat Philadelphia: Bewerbungen, HStAS; Stadler and Wilken, *Pädagogik bei Körperbehinderung*, 35–36; *Zweiter Jahres-Bericht über die Armen-Anstalt für Verkrümmte im Paulinen-Institute zu Stuttgart* (surviving copy in Aufnahme von Staatspfleglingen, StALB).

9. Obituary of Captain Binder, *Philadelphia Inquirer*, Jan. 24, 1876.

10. *McElroy's Philadelphia City Directory* (1845), s.v. "Binder, Frederick W."; Binder, F. W., Seventh Census (1850), NA; Rosengarten, *German Soldier*, 216; Scharf, *History of Philadelphia*, 679; "History of General John F. Ballier," para. 3, JFBP, JHML; "From Harrisburg—Progress of the Volunteers," *Monroe Democrat*, Dec. 25, 1846, http://www.libraryweb.org/~digitized/newspapers/monroe_democrat/vol.XIX.pdf; Viereck, *Capt. F. W. Binder's Quick Step*; Hackenburg, *Pennsylvania in the War*, 132–42.

11. McCaffrey, *Army of Manifest Destiny*, 21–22.

12. Undated, untitled clipping from an unidentified German newspaper (clipping damaged and identifying information missing), JFBP, JHML; Rattermann, "General August Moor," 486n25.

13. Hackenburg, *Pennsylvania in the War*, 132, 143; Erwin, Journal, Dec. 7, 9, 1846.

14. Oswandel, *Notes*, 15; McCaffrey, *Army of Manifest Destiny*, 24; Henderson, *Hints*, 79–80, 99–100.

15. McCaffrey, *Army of Manifest Destiny*, 24.

16. Hackenburg, *Pennsylvania in the War*, 132; Oswandel, *Notes*, 22–30.

17. Island of the Wolves

1. Oswandel, *Notes*, 22–27; NA, Washington, D.C., Compiled Service Records, Gottlob Reeb or Rueb, Private, Dec. 14, 1846 to Feb. 28, 1847.

2. Hackenburg, *Pennsylvania in the War*, 13; Oswandel, *Notes*, 34–40; Peskin, *Volunteers*, 19 [quote].

3. Oswandel, *Notes*, 39.

4. Ibid., 42, 44, 53 [miserable water]; Sargent, *Gathering Laurels*, 4.

5. Oswandel, *Notes*, 42; C. Brown to Emma Brown, Feb. 22, 1847, Alex and Chauncey Brown Mexican War letters, UTASC; Sargent, *Gathering Laurels*, 4; Hartman, *A Private's Own Journal*, 6; Peskin, *Volunteers*, 29–32; Hiney, Mexican American War Diary, Jan. 29, 1847, SBPC; "The Island of Lobos," Niles' National Register, Mar. 13, 1847, http://www.history.vt.edu/MxAmWar/Newspapers/Niles/Nilesf 1847MarApr.htm#NR72.021March131847Descriptionof; Moore, *Scott's Campaign*, 1; Winders, *Mr. Polk's Army*, 173.

6. "The Island of Lobos," Niles' National Register, Mar. 13, 1847.

7. Helbich, "German Immigrants," 172–73.

8. Peskin, *Volunteers*, 30; Kitchen, *Record*, 22–23 [gallant soldier and excellent man]; Hiney, War Diary, Feb. 14, 1847. The army later tried the three Mexicans and acquitted them. "Collection of troops and transports at Lobos Island for the demonstration on Veracruz," Niles' National Register, Mar. 27, 1847, http://www .history.vt.edu/MxAmWar/Newspapers/Niles/Nilesf1847MarApr.htm#NR72.059 March271827collectionof.

9. Hiney, War Diary, Feb. 21, 1847, SBPC; Peskin, *Volunteers*, 33–34; Oswandel, *Notes*, 59; Kreitzer, Journal, HSP; Freeman, *R. E. Lee*, 221–22; John of York, "Army Correspondence Island of Lobos," *North American* (Philadelphia), Mar. 23, 1847 [toasts].

10. Oswandel, *Notes*, 60 [song]; Eye-Witness, "The Capture of Vera Cruz," 1; Peskin, *Winfield Scott*, 150.

11. Oswandel, *Notes*, 63; NA, Washington, D.C., Compiled Service Records, Gottlob Reeb or Rueb, Dec. 14, 1846 to Feb. 28, 1847.

12. Anderson, *Mexican War*, 68, 71; Hughes and Johnson, *A Fighter*, 65 [aboard the *Henry*], 69; D. H. Hill Diary, #00882, SHC, Mar. 3, 1847 [quote].

18. River of Gold, Fortress of White

1. Thomas, *Rivers of Gold*, 417, 419–20.

2. Ibid., 425.

3. Montero, "Guerra, Navagación y Piratería," 141–42; Goodman, *Spanish Naval Power*, 3–4.

4. *Complete History of the Late Mexican War*, 69; Pérez-Mallaína, *Spain's Men*, 11.

5. *Complete History of the Late Mexican War*, 70; Peskin, *Winfield Scott*, 150; Grone and Grone, *Briefe über Nord-Amerika*, 30; World Monuments Fund, "San Juan de Ulúa Fort," https://www.wmf.org/project/san-juan-de-ul%C3%BAa-fort; Bauer, *Surfboats*, 83; Dana, *Monterrey Is Ours!*, 198; "The Town . . . Castle of San Juan de Ulua, " Mexican War Articles, BRBML.

6. Freeman, *R. E. Lee*, 227; Winfield Scott, *Memoirs*, 422.

7. "The Town . . . Castle of San Juan de Ulua," Mexican War Articles, BRBML.

8. Scott, *Memoirs*, 413–14; Clark Jr. and Moseley, "D-Day Veracruz," 108.

9. Freeman, *R. E. Lee*, 223; Blackwood, *To Mexico with Scott*, 113.

10. Freeman, *R. E. Lee*, 223; Bauer, *Surfboats*, 77.

11. Freeman, *R. E. Lee*, 223, Peskin, *Scott*, 150; Meade, *Life and Letters*, 187.

12. Freeman, *R. E. Lee*, 223.

19. Amphibious Wager

1. Bauer, *Mexican War,* 244; Tucker et al., *Encyclopedia of the Mexican-American War,* s.v. "Veracruz, Landing at and Siege of"; Clark and Moseley, "D-Day Veracruz," 107. Bauer places the number of troops at just above 8,600, but most sources place it at ten thousand, e.g., Peskin, *Winfield Scott,* 151.

2. Clark and Moseley, "D-Day Veracruz," 107–8; Bauer, *Surfboats,* 236.

3. Bauer, *Mexican War,* 241; McCaffrey, *Army of Manifest Destiny,* 166; Hitchcock, *Fifty Years,* 390.

4. Semmes, *Service Afloat,* 126.

5. Clark and Moseley, "D-Day Veracruz," 110; Oswandel, *Notes,* 83; Wm. G. Temple, "Memoir of the Landing of the United States Troops at Vera Cruz in 1847," in Conner, *Home Squadron,* 77.

6. Bauer, *Surfboats,* 81; Eye-Witness, "The Capture of Vera Cruz," 2; Semmes, *Service Afloat,* 127; Mansfield, *The Mexican War,* 168.

7. Bauer, *Surfboats,* 82; Parker, *Recollections,* 93; Semmes, *Service Afloat,* 128.

8. Bauer, *Surfboats,* 82.

9. Jeremiah Albee, "When Uncle Sam Lay Siege to Vera Cruz in 1847," *Oakland Tribune,* Aug. 23, 1914.

10. Bauer, *Surfboats,* 82.

11. Parker, *Recollections,* 95–96 [quote]; Bauer, *Mexican War,* 244.

12. Hughes and Johnson, *A Fighter,* 74; Oswandel, *Notes,* 74.

13. Bauer, *Mexican War,* 245; Clary, *Eagles and Empire,* 293–94; Mayer, *Mexico,* 3–4.

14. Reilly, *War,* 105; Oswandel, *Notes,* 71–73; Zeh, *Immigrant Soldier,* 13.

15. Oswandel, *Notes,* 71–73; Kreitzer, *Journal,* 32–33, HSP; Smith, *Company "A,"* 20; Winders, *Polk's Army,* 173; Kitchen, *Record,* 30.

16. Peskin, *Scott,* 153–55; Bauer, *Mexican War,* 246–47.

17. Bauer, *Mexican War,* 205, 246–47.

20. Roar of Tornadoes

1. Pryor, *Reading the Man,* 160–61; Peskin, *Winfield Scott,* 155, 243; Freeman, *R. E. Lee,* 295–99, 432.

2. Pryor, *Reading the Man,* 161; Freeman, *R. E. Lee,* 228–29.

3. Freeman, *R. E. Lee,* 228–29; Bauer, *Mexican War,* 247; Eye-Witness, "Capture of Vera Cruz," 3, Wm. G. Temple, "Memoir," in Conner, *Home Squadron,* 47n4.

4. Hatch, *Heroes of Annapolis,* 81; Wm. G. Temple, "Memoir," in Conner, *Home Squadron,* 47n4, 69–70; Bauer, *Mexican War,* 250.

5. Parker, *Naval Officer,* 103–4; Pryor, *Reading the Man,* 162; Oswandel, *Notes,* 89; Freeman, *R. E. Lee,* 229; Jones, *Life and Letters,* ch. 3; Sargent, *Gathering Laurels,* 7.

6. Parker, *Naval Officer,* 105; Pryor, *Reading the Man,* 161–62; Freeman, *R. E. Lee,* 230; Peskin, *Volunteers,* 57.

7. Parker, *Naval Officer,* 108; Oswandel, *Notes,* 89–90.

8. Parker, *Naval Officer,* 108–9; Furber, *Twelve Months Volunteer,* 526; Allan McLane to Louis McLane, Apr. 3, 1847, Louis McLane Correspondence, LOC;

"From Vera Cruz," *New Hampshire Gazette*, Apr. 20, 1847; Henry Eld Papers, Mar. 24, 1847, LOC.

9. Freeman, *R. E. Lee*, 231.

10. Ibid., 232; Pryor, *Reading the Man*, 162; Semmes, *Campaign*, 25 [quote].

11. United States Congress, 30th Cong., 2d sess., House Executive Document No. 1, Mar. 25, 1847, 1182–85; Clark and Moseley, "D-Day Veracruz," 109; Furber, *Twelve Months Volunteer*, 526.

12. Furber, *Twelve Months Volunteer*, 533.

13. Freeman, *R. E. Lee*, 232; Parker, *Naval Officer*, 106; Grant, *Personal Memoirs*, 52; "Letter from a Midshipman on board the U.S. Steamer Mississippi," *Newark Daily Advertiser*, Apr. 17, 1847; Hiney, Mexican American War Diary, Mar. 24, 1847; Kitchen, *Wyoming Artillerists*, 30; Kendall, *Dispatches*, 176.

14. Semmes, *Service Afloat*, 138.

15. Ballentine, *Autobiography*, 155.

16. Kendall, *Dispatches*, 163.

17. Ibid.

18. Hitchcock, *Fifty Years*, 244; Frost, *Mexican War*, 136.

19. Eye-Witness, "Capture of Veracruz," 4; Clark, *Notorious "Bull" Nelson*, 17.

20. "Letter from a Midshipman," *Newark Daily Advertiser*, Apr. 17, 1847; McWilliams, "A Westmoreland Guard in Mexico," 222; Allan McLane to Louis McLane, Apr. 3, 1847, McLane Correspondence, LOC.

21. "Letter from a Midshipman," *Newark Daily Advertiser*, Apr. 17, 1847; Parker, *Naval Officer*, 111; Semmes, *Service Afloat*, 139.

22. Oswandel, *Notes*, 92; Kreitzer, Journal, Mar. 25, 1847, HSP. The shell came from the castle.

23. Oswandel, *Notes*, 92; Kreitzer, Journal, Mar. 25, 1847, HSP; NA, Washington, D.C., Compiled Service Records, Gottlob Reeb or Rueb, Private, three muster roll cards dated Mar. 26, 1847; Nagle, Diary, Mar. 25, 1847, BUDL; "Letter from a Midshipman," *Newark Daily Advertiser*, Apr. 17, 1847 [quote]; John of York, "Army Correspondence from our own Correspondent; History of the Siege, Incidents, Movements and Descriptions; Camp before Vera Cruz; March 25—night," *North American*, Apr. 27, 1847.

24. John of York, "Army Correspondence," *North American*, Apr. 27, 1847.

25. Peskin, *Scott*, 191.

21. One Man Worth All of Mexico

1. Robert E. Lee to Mary Custis Lee, Mar. 27, 1847, George Bolling Lee papers, Mss.L5114c16, VHS [quote]; Freeman, *R. E. Lee*, 231.

2. United States Congress, 30th Cong., 1st sess., Senate Executive Document No. 1 (1847), 253.

3. Robert E. Lee to George Washington Custis Lee, Apr. 11, 1847, DeButts-Ely family papers, VHS.

4. "Letter from a Midshipman," *Newark Daily Advertiser*, Apr. 17, 1847.

5. Pryor, *Reading the Man*, 173.

6. Yates, *Perfect Gentleman*, 92–94.

7. Thomas, *Robert E. Lee*, 120; Pryor, *Reading the Man*, 105.

8. United States Congress, 30th Cong., 2d sess., House Executive Document No. 1 (1847), 1182–85; 30th Cong., 1st sess., Senate Executive Document No. 1 (1848), 253 [lists of those killed in action at the naval battery].

22. POST FROM AMERICA

1. Connelly, *Marble Man*, 3–4.

2. Nachlassteilung, StALB; Friedrich Gentner to Adjutant General, Sept. 14, 1858, Letters Received by the Office of the Adjutant General, NA; Bounty Land Files, NA. The bounty brokers facilitated payment of military bounties for the heirs of deceased volunteers in other countries. Rueb's sisters in Württemberg hired Friedrich Gentner to facilitate payment of Rueb's bounty.

3. Rupp family, Eighth Census, NA; *Evening Star*, May 28, 1855; *Critic-Record*, Aug. 16, 1873; Rupp to Stadtschultheiß und Stadtrath in Bönnigheim, Apr. 29, 1872, investigative file.

4. The German proverb should read: "No thread can be spun so fine that the sun *doesn't* finally shine on it." Samuel Singer, *Lexikon*, 74. Rupp left out the word "doesn't" and I added it to his letter so that the proverb makes sense in context.

5. Rupp to Stadtschultheiß und Stadtrath in Bönnigheim, Apr. 29, 1872, investigative file.

23. NEW INVESTIGATION AND CASE CLOSURE

1. Rupp to Stadtschultheiß und Stadtrath in Bönnigheim, Apr. 29, 1872, investigative file; Kurz et al., *Die wechselvolle Geschichte*, 373.

2. Stock, "Auszüge," 305, HGB.

3. Kurz et al., *Die wechselvolle Geschichte*, 363; Stock, "Auszüge," 305 [quote].

4. Stock, "Auszüge," 305, HGB.

5. Ibid., 306; Finckh to Hofstetter, June 26, 1872, investigative file. Stock's grandson, an artist, made several sculptures, paintings, and sketches of Stock in his later years. My description is based on those images. *Der junge Künstler I: Berlin von 1932/1933 bis 1938* [art exhibition catalogue], http://wolfgang-stock-werkverzeichnis.de/pdf/01_Der_junge_Kuenstler_I.pdf.

6. Stock, "Auszüge," 306, HGB.

7. Schuster to Mayor Finckh, May 26, 1972, investigative file [emphasis on "good-for-nothing" by centering it on its own line in the original]. The documents Schuster helped prepare for the heirs' bounty claim are archived in Bounty Land Files, NA.

8. Kümmerle to Finckh, June 4, 1872, investigative file [emphasis in original; Johann Georg Kümmerle in the original letter, but in the emigration application the name Kimmerle was used].

9. Hochstetter, memoranda, May 27 and 28, 1872, investigative file; Pflieger, *Geschichte(n)*, 97–99, 112.

10. Staatsanwaltschaft Heilbronn, memorandum, Aug. 7, 1872, investigative file.

11. Gundert, *Rede*, WLB; Richardson, "An Attempt," 22.

12. File cover, investigative file.

EPILOGUE

1. According to the *Deutsche Bundesbank*, 200 *Gulden* in 1835 amounted to U.S. $4,653 in 2015 values.

2. "Bönnigheim," *Ludwigsburger Tagblatt*, May 23, 1872. The Stuttgart newspaper in question is the *Schwäbische Chronik*. It published an article about Rieber's murder in 1835. "Besigheim," *Schwäbische Chronik*, Oct. 25, 1835.

APPENDIX A

1. NA, Washington, D.C., Compiled Service Records, Gottlob Reeb or Rueb, Private. Three muster roll cards place the date on Mar. 26, 1847.

2. Winfield Scott, "Report of killed, wounded, and missing . . . ," Apr. 6, 1847, United States Congress, 30th Cong., 1st sess., Senate Executive Document No. 1, 253; Oswandel, *Notes*, 92; Nagle, Diary, Mar. 25, 1847, BUDL; Kreitzer, Journal, Mar. 25, 1847, HSP; Schultz, Journal, Mar. 25, 1847, PSA.

3. John of York, "Army Correspondence," *North American*, Apr. 27, 1847.

4. "Letter from a Midshipman," *Newark Daily Advertiser*, Apr. 17, 1847.

5. Oswandel, *Notes*, 92; Kreitzer, Journal, Mar. 25, 1847.

6. Robert E. Lee to George Washington Custis Lee, Apr. 11, 1847, DeButts-Ely collection of Lee family papers, Mss1 L51c VHS; *Merriam-Webster's Collegiate Dictionary*, 11th ed. (Springfield, MA: Merriam-Webster, 2012) s.v. "evening."

7. United States Congress, 30th Cong., 1st sess., Senate Executive Document No. 1 (1848), 253. Because no one else in Pennsylvania's 1st Regiment had a similar name, Gottlob must have been meant. See Hackenburg, *Pennsylvania in the War*, 390–91.

8. Oswandel, *Notes*, 92; NA, Washington, D.C., Compiled Service Records, Gottlob Reeb/Rueb, Private, Mar. 26, 1847; Montgomery, *Pennsylvania Archives*, 317. The use of alternative first names of Gottlob and Gottlieb is also reflected in the German records; see ch. 12, n. 2. He was baptized Gottlieb Friedrich Rüb, but went by Gottlob in other records. Rueb is the anglicized variation of Rüb.

9. John of York, "Army Correspondence," *North American*, Apr. 27, 1847.

10. Steinbeis, Feb. 26, 1849, Bounty Land Files [English translation in Paper C], NA.

11. Friedrich Gentner to Adjutant General, 1848, Letters Received by the Office of the Adjutant General, NA.

12. Friedrich Klett to Schultheißenamt Stetten am Heuchelberg, Dec. 18, 1848, Nachlassteilung, StALB.

13. Winfield Scott, "Report of Killed, Wounded, and Missing . . . ," Apr. 6, 1847, United States Congress, 30th Cong., 1st sess., Senate Executive Document No. 1, 253 [spelled "Gothilp Reip"].

14. J. H. Aulick, "List of Killed," United States Congress, 2d sess., House Executive Document No. 1, 1182–83.

15. "Report of Captain Mayo," Mar. 26, 1847, United States Congress, 30th Cong., 2d sess., House Executive Document No. 1, 1183–84.

16. Robert E. Lee to George Washington Custis Lee, Apr. 11, 1847, DeButts-Ely collection of Lee family papers, LOC.

17. *Potomac* (Mar. 12, 1847–July 31, 1848), Vol. 14 of 40, Logs of U.S. Naval Ships, NA, Mar. 25, 1847.

18. Furber, *Twelve Months Volunteer,* 526; Oswandel, *Notes,* 90.

19. Allan McLane to Louis McLane, Apr. 3, 1847, McLane Correspondence, LOC.

20. *Mississippi* (Mar. 5, 1847–Mar. 12, 1848), Vol. 3 of 23, Logs of U.S. Naval Ships, NA, Mar. 24, 1847.

21. *St. Mary's* (Dec. 13, 1844–Apr. 30, 1847), Vol. 1 of 32, Logs of U.S. Naval Ships, NA, Mar. 25, 1847.

22. Likewise, the Records Regarding Enlisted Men Who Served in the Navy, 1842–85, Bureau of Navigation, Records of the Bureau of Naval Personnel, NA, RG 24, contained no information about these men.

23. "Capture of Veracruz," *Commercial Advertiser,* Apr. 16, 1847.

24. Semmes, *Service Afloat,* 138.

25. Bauer, *Mexican War,* 250; Freeman, *R. E. Lee,* 232.

26. Henry Eid to "Father," Mar. 27, 1847, LOC; Oswandel, *Notes,* 90; "Letter from a Midshipman," *Newark Daily Advertiser,* Apr. 17, 1847; "Capture of Veracruz," *Commercial Advertiser,* Apr. 16, 1847.

27. Semmes, *Service Afloat,* 139.

28. John of York, "Army Correspondence," *North American,* Apr. 27, 1847.

29. Kreitzer, Journal, Mar. 25, 1847; Oswandel, *Notes,* 92.

30. "Letter from a Midshipman," *Newark Daily Advertiser,* Apr. 17, 1847.

31. Records Regarding Enlisted Men Who Served in the Navy, 1842–85, NA. The following records were checked: Box 110, Harkness James to Harrington, John for James Harrington; Box 170, McGinley, Andrew to McGrath, William for James or Daniel McGinnis; Box 180, Manning, Michael to Marsell, Simon for William Marchus or Marcus; Box 276, Todd, James to Trafzer, Ernest, A for John Toohey or Tookey; Boxes 294, Williams, Elmore to Williams, John, and 295, Williams, John to Willis, James, for John Williams or John Williamson.

32. "Letter from a Midshipman," *Newark Daily Advertiser,* Apr. 17, 1847; *Albany* (1846–Aug. 1847), Vol. 1 of 33, Logs of U.S. Naval Ships, NA, Mar. 26, 1847, 4–6 P.M.

33. Henry Hickson, "Letter from an 'Old Salt': Naval Vessels Employed in the War with Mexico," *Vedette,* May 15, 1880.

34. Bauer, *Mexican War,* 399n9.

APPENDIX B

1. Undated, untitled clipping from an unidentified German newspaper (clipping damaged and identifying information missing) regarding two Philadelphia German companies in the Seminole War, JFBP, JHML; "General John F. Ballier" (undated clipping from an unidentified German newspaper regarding Ballier's role in the Nativist Riots), JFBP, JHML; Rosengarten, *German Soldier,* 253; Schrag, "Nativist Riots"; Erwin, Journal, May 7–8, 1844 [winds during the riots].

2. Hackenburg, *Pennsylvania in the War,* 132–42.

3. Ibid., 132; Bauer, *Mexican War,* 272–74; Oswandel, *Notes,* 173, 177, 184; Nagle, Diary, May 8–Oct. 6, 1847, June 5, 1847 [Binder's detail], BUDL.

4. Tucker et al., *Encyclopedia*, vol. 2, s.v. "Perote Castle"; Oswandel, *Notes*, 171, 178.

5. Hackenburg, *Pennsylvania in the War*, 134; Oswandel, *Notes*, 239 [Binder's company remained at Perote in August].

6. Affidavit by Wilson Jewell, Sept. 23, 1865, correspondence from William F. Small, Feb. 7, 1853, and Thomas Bunting, July 11, 1853, in Soldier's Certificate No. 7739 (File No. 2995), Frederick W. Binder, NA.

7. Report of medical examination by Ja. H. Oliver, June 2, 1865, in Soldier's Certificate No. 7739 (File No. 2995), Frederick W. Binder, NA.

8. Affidavit by Francis M. Wynkoop, Feb. 12, 1853, in Soldier's Certificate No. 7739 (File No. 2995), Frederick W. Binder, NA.

9. Hackenburg, *Pennsylvania in the War*, 97–169; Nagle, Diary, Sept. 18 and 23, 1847, BUDL; Grone and Grone, *Briefe über Nord-Amerika*, 62–63.

10. Hackenburg, *Pennsylvania in the War*, 72, 132–42.

11. "Vermischte Nachrichten: Pittsburgh–Rückkehr Ankunft der Freiwilligen," *Philadelphia Demokrat*, July 22, 1848; "Willkommen unsern heimgekehrten Freiwilligen!" *Philadelphia Demokrat*, July 25, 1848; "Stadt-Neuigkeiten," *Philadelphia Demokrat*, July 26, and Aug. 2, 3, and 4, 1848; Viereck, *Captain F. W. Binder's Quick Step*.

12. "Stadt-Neuigkeiten," *Philadelphia Demokrat*, Aug. 7, 1848; "Colonel Wynkoop: Another Richmond in the Field," *Jeffersonian Republican*, Aug. 24, 1848, http://chroniclingamerica.loc.gov/lccn/sn86053954/1848–08–24/ed-1/seq-2/.

13. Friedrich Klett to Schultheißenamt Stetten am Heuchelberg, Dec. 18, 1848, Nachlassteilung, StALB; "Local Items Reported for the Inquirer: County Board," *Philadelphia Inquirer*, Nov. 13, 1849; "Death of Captain Binder," *Philadelphia Inquirer*, Jan. 24, 1876.

14. "Serious Melee," *North American*, Oct. 23, 1850; "Affray," *Trenton State Gazette*, Oct. 23, 1850; "The Case of Capt. Binder and Others," *Public Ledger*, Nov. 7, 1850; "The Murder of George Emory," *New York Daily Tribune*, Feb. 13, 1851.

15. Report of medical examination by Ja. H. Oliver, June 2, 1865, in Soldier's Certificate No. 7739 (File No. 2995), Frederick W. Binder, NA; Binder, *Eighth Census of the United States*, 1860, NA; Binder, U.S. IRS Tax Assessment Lists, NA; "Local Affairs: Collection of Taxes for 1858," *Public Ledger*, Jan. 6, 1859; *McElroy's Philadelphia City Directory* (1858), s.v. "Binder, Fred W"; "Death of Captain Binder," *Philadelphia Inquirer*, Jan. 24, 1876; *Ordinances and Joint Resolutions*, 433–34.

16. "Probable Homicide," *Philadelphia Inquirer*, Apr. 4, 1865; "Brutal Assault on an Old Man: Probable Homicide," *Age*, Apr. 4, 1865.

17. Report of medical examination by Ja. H. Oliver, June 2, 1865, in Soldier's Certificate No. 7739 (File No. 2995), Frederick W. Binder, NA; "Death of Captain Binder," *Philadelphia Inquirer*, Jan. 24, 1876; see ch. 16 for a discussion of Binder's childhood orthopedic disability.

18. Hackenburg, *Pennsylvania in the War*, 133; Taylor, *Philadelphia in the Civil War*, 36–37, 116–17, 293; "Ein geschichtlicher Rückblick," *Philadelphia Volksblatt*, Mar. 9, 1885.

19. "Ninety-Eighth Regiment," in Bates, *History of Pennsylvania Volunteers*, 464–505; "Ein geschichtlicher Rückblick," *Philadelphia Volksblatt*, Mar. 9, 1885 [Ballier wrote the chapter in Bates's book].

20. "Vermischtes," clipping from an unidentified German newspaper from St. Louis, [Aug. 29?] 1885, in JFBP, JHML.

21. Hackenburg, *Pennsylvania in the War*, 137; Waskie, *Philadelphia*, Kindle version, ch. 3 (1st Philadelphia Volunteers).

22. Hackenburg, *Pennsylvania in the War*, 137.

23. Ibid., 136.

24. Ibid., 133.

25. Ibid., 137, 141.

Bibliography

In order to shorten the endnotes, I used a number of abbreviations listed below. Archival sources follow with separate sections for the United States and Germany. I listed the sources under the holding institutions. For published sources, the names of newspapers, both German and American, are listed in a separate section first. I conclude with a small section for the sources I consulted for converting currency and units of measurement in the former Kingdom of Württemberg into modern equivalents. Those sources do not appear in the endnotes.

ABBREVIATIONS

AEKB: Archiv der evangelischen Kirche Bönnigheim, Germany
AEKSaH: Archiv der evangelischen Kirche, Stetten am Heuchelberg
BMCOC: Bryn Mawr College Online Collections
BRBML: Beinecke Rare Book and Manuscript Library, Yale University
BUDL: Brown University Digital Library
CCC: *Constitutio Criminalis Carolina*
ER: *Eheregister* [marriage register]
FR: *Familienregister* [family register]
HGB: Historische Gesellschaft Bönnigheim, Germany
HSP: Historical Society of Pennsylvania, Philadelphia
HStAS: Landesarchiv Baden-Württemberg, Germany, Branch Depository Hauptstaatsarchiv Stuttgart
Investigative file: Kreisgerichtshof Esslingen: Kriminalsenat (1817–70), Verfahren gegen: Täter nicht ermittelt; Tatzeit: 21.10.1835; Tatort: Bönnigheim/Oberamt Besigheim; Tat: Stadtschultheiß Rieber wird vor seinem Haus erschossen; Erledigung: Verfahren gegen verschiedene Verdächtige am 17.02.1836 eingestellt, E319 Bü 146, Landesarchiv Baden-Württemberg, Germany, Branch Depository Staatsarchiv Ludwigsburg
JFBP: John F. Ballier papers (1831–92), German Amer. Col., Ms. Coll. 11, Joseph Horner Memorial Library, German Society of Pennsylvania, Philadelphia

JHML: Joseph Horner Memorial Library, German Society of Pennsylvania, Philadelphia
LOC: Library of Congress
MAK: Museum Arzney-Küche, Bönnigheim, Germany
NA: National Archives and Records Administration, Washington, D.C.
PB: Protokollbuch (part of the investigative file)
PSA: Pennsylvania State Archives
RG: Record group
SAB: Stadtarchiv Bönnigheim, Germany
SAS-SAH:Stadtarchiv Schwaigern, Germany, Branch Depository Gemeindearchiv Stetten am Heuchelberg, Germany
SBPC: Susanne Behling, Private Collection
SHC: Southern Historical Collection, Louis Round Wilson Special Collections Library, University of North Carolina at Chapel Hill
SR: *Sterberegister* [death register]
StALB: Landesarchiv Baden-Württemberg, Germany, Branch Depository Staatsarchiv Ludwigsburg
UTASC: University of Texas Arlington Special Collections
VHS: Virginia Historical Society
WLB: Württembergische Landesbibliothek, Stuttgart, Germany
WS: witness statement(s)

Unpublished Sources and Archival Material in Germany

Archiv der evangelischen Kirche, Bönnigheim
    Familienregister
    Eheregister
    Sterberegister
Archiv der evangelischen Kirche, Stetten am Heuchelberg
    Familienblätter 1638–1807, Band 2 [transcription of Familienregister Stetten, Band 1]
Historische Gesellschaft Bönnigheim
    Stock, C. A., "Auszüge aus dem Lebensbericht von Carl Adolf Stock, Forstdirektor i.R. mit Bezug zu Bönnigheim 1867–1881" [transcription].
Landesarchiv Baden-Württemberg, Hauptstaatsarchiv Stuttgart
    Konsulat Philadelphia: Bewerbungen und Ernennungen zum Konsul: Friedrich Klett, Wilhelm Ludwig Kiderlin/1842–65; E50/60 Bü 189.
Landesarchiv Baden-Württemberg, Staatsarchiv Ludwigsburg
    Aufnahme von Staatspfleglingen in orthpädische Heilanstalt Paulinenhilfe in Stuttgart (vor 1850 Armenabteilung des Paulineninstituts), E 163 Bü 931.
    Auswandererverzeichnisse (1815, 1817–60); F154 I Bü 167.
    Auswanderungen in verschiedenen Gemeinden/1832; F154 I Bü 170.
    Auswanderungen in verschiedenen Gemeinden/1836; F154 I Bü 174.
    Auswanderungen, Stetten Bd. 1 (1807–1850), Oberamt Brackenheim, F 158 I, Bü 173.
    Auswanderungsverzeichnis, Oberamt Brackenheim (1830–63, 1865–72, 1880–81), F158I Bü176a.

Criminalsenat Ulm: Strafsache gegen Philipp Jakob Speidel wegen Raubmordes (1845), E 350 Bü 52.

Fabrikation und Verkauf von Abschraubgewehren/1820–1821, E 245 I; Bü 1499.

Forstamt Bönnigheim (1818–1886) Findbuch, F105II.

Kreisgerichtshof/Landgericht Ellwangen: Kriminalsenat bzw. Strafkammer (1813–1949), Findbuch, E 341 I.

Kreisgerichtshof Esslingen: Kriminalsenat (1817–70), Findbuch, E 319.

Kreisgerichtshof Esslingen: Kriminalsenat (1817–70), Verfahren gegen: Friedrich Preiffer aus Ruit wegen Mord (1822–23) E 319 Bü 135a.

Kreisgerichtshof Esslingen: Kriminalsenat (1817–70), Verfahren gegen: Täter nicht ermittelt; Tatzeit: 21.10.1835; Tatort: Bönnigheim/Oberamt Besigheim; Tat: Stadtschultheiß Rieber wird vor seinem Haus erschossen; Erledigung: Verfahren gegen verschiedene Verdächtige am 17.02.1836 eingestellt; E319 Bü 146 [investigative file].

Kreisgerichtshof Tübingen: Kriminalsenat (1818–69), Findbuch, E331.

Kreisgerichtshof Ulm: Kriminalsenat (1819–68), Findbuch, E 350.

Kriminalsenat Tübingen: Strafsache gegen Johann Georg Fischer wegen Mordes (1824), Findbuch, E331 Bü 69.

Kriminalsenat Ulm: Strafsache gegen Philipp Jakob Speidel wegen Raubmordes (1845), E 350 Bü 52.

Nachlassteilung des in Amerika umgekommenen Gottlieb Friedrich Rüb von Stetten, Amstgericht Brackenheim; F258 Bü 370.

Oberjustizkollegium 1. Senats, ab 1811 Kriminaltribunal Esslingen Inquisitionen und Prozesse, Findbuch, D 70.

Personalakten der Forstamtassistenten des Forstamts Bönnigheim/1822–86; F 105 I Bü 243.

Personalakten der Forstmeister des Forstamts Bönnigheim; F105 I Bü 242.

Reißende und wütende Tiere (Wölfe, wütende Füchse und Hunde); deren Auftreten und Bekämpfung/1822–64; F105 I Bü 9.

Stetten Bd. 1/1807–50; F158 I Bü 173.

Museum Arzney-Küche, Bönnigheim
Wilhelm Vogel correspondence, in Apotheker-Briefe [transcription by Otfried Kies].

Stadtarchiv Bönnigheim
Bau von Dohlen und Wasserleitungen zu dem Brunnen im Schlossgarten und Garten des Forstamtes; Bau der Hauptwasserleitung und des Pumpwerkes in der Taubstummenanstalt (Kostenanschlag) F 40 Bü 135 0 (Flurkarten und Stadtplan Bönnigheim 1832).

Bauplan, Waschküchengebäude, K4812C.

Güter-Buch, Theil 3, B919.

Nachlass Elisabeth Zipperlen, Ordner "Berühmte Söhne," Abteilung "Stadtschultheiß Heinrich Rieber."

Nachlass Karl Friedrich Rieber, A2663b.

Nachlass von Georg Michael Rupp, Kammacher (1833), A7240.

Privat-Inventarium über die Hinterlassenschaft des Heinrich Rieber, Schultheiß in Bönnigheim [Private Inventory of the Estate of Heinrich Rieber, Mayor of Bönnigheim], A2664 (1835).

Stadtarchiv Schwaigern, Gemeindearchiv Stetten am Heuchelberg
Bürgerrechtsverzichts-Urkunden, 1800–50. A 429.
Gerichts- und Gemeinderatsprotokolle 1807–16 B 264; 1816–1819 B 265; 1827–33 B 267; 1819–27 B 261; 1834–38 B 268.
Register über die Steuer und Güterbücher, 1839. B 349.
Ruggerichtsprotokoll 1821–1912. B 318.
Schuldklagprotokoll, B 301, September 20, 1834 (unpaginated).
Schultheissenamtsprotokoll 1833–43. B 251.
Steuerbuch VIII. Theil. B 335.
Untersuchungs-Sache gegen den Forstwart Gottlob Friedrich Rüb von Stetten (K. Oberamts-gericht Heilbronn, 1829, A 55a (Mitteilung gerichtlicher Strafen) (June 6, 1829).
Verzeichnis der aktiven Gemeinde-Bürger, 1828. B 513.

UNPUBLISHED SOURCES AND ARCHIVAL MATERIAL IN THE UNITED STATES

Susanne Behling, Private Collection
Hiney, Elias F. Mexican American War Diary. Private collection of Susanne Behling. http://homepages.rootsweb.ancestry.com/~sam/elias.html.
Beinecke Rare Book and Manuscript Library, Yale University
Mexican War Articles, Western Americana Collection, Mss WA MSS S-561.
Brown University Digital Library
Nagle, James. Diary of Capt. James Nagle, Co. B, 1st Regiment, Pennsylvania Volunteers. Brown Olio series. https://repository.library.brown.edu/viewers/readers/set/bdr:40635#page/2/mode/2up.
Bryn Mawr College Online Collections
Erwin, Joseph Warner. Journal (1839–54). Transcribed by S. Hamill Horne. Places in Time collection, Textual Documents. http://www.brynmawr.edu/iconog/jwe/jweint.html.
College of William and Mary Digital Archive
Burdsall, Anna. Diary (1840–41). Transcribed. Charles Campbell papers, Mss. 65 C17, Series 3, MsV. 7. https://digitalarchive.wm.edu/handle/10288/13758.
Historical Society of Pennsylvania, Philadelphia
Kreitzer, John. Journal. John Kreitzer papers, collection no. Am.68835.
Joseph Horner Memorial Library, German Society of Pennsylvania, Philadelphia
John F. Ballier papers (1831–92), German Amer. Col., Ms. Coll. 11.
Library of Congress
DeButts-Ely collection of Lee family papers, MSS2911.
Louis McLane Correspondence, 1795–1894, MMC-3116.
Henry Eld papers, 1831–49, MMC-0404.
National Archives and Records Administration, Washington, D.C.
Binder, Fred W.: 3 [handwritten], line 3, District 1, Monthly and Special Lists, September 1862–August 1863, Pennsylvania, U.S. IRS Tax Assessment Lists, 1862–1918 (NA Microfilm Publication M787, Roll 1); RG 58.
Binder, F. W.: 432B [stamped], line 22, Walnut Ward, Philadelphia County, Pa., *Seventh Census of the United States*, 1850 (NA Microfilm Publication M432, Roll 813); RG 29.

Binder, F. W.: 102A [stamped], line 1, 1st Div., 12th Ward, Philadelphia County, Pa., *Eighth Census of the United States,* 1860 (NA Microfilm Publication M653, Roll 1162); RG 29.

Bounty Land Files: Act of 47–160 W.T. 67401, Gottlob [*sic*] Rueb or Rieb, 1847, Grade: Priv., Co. E, 1st Regiment, Pa. Vols., Can. no. 2335, Bundle 19.

Compiled Service Records of Volunteer Soldiers Who Served During the Mexican War (1846–48): Pennsylvania, 1st Regiment, Company E (NA Microfilm Publication M1028, Catalog ID 654520, Roll 0005); RG 94.

Fiatkowsky family: 261B [stamped], lines 10–19, Philipsburg, Beaver County, Pa., *Seventh Census of the United States,* 1850 (NA Microfilm Publication M432, Roll 750); RG 29.

Hospital Tickets and Cast papers, compiled 1825–89: Department of the Navy, Records of the Bureau of Medicine and Surgery (ID: 2694723); RG 52.

Kimmerle, John G.: 404A [stamped], line 26, Montgomery Township, Franklin County, Ohio, Seventh Census of the United States Census, 1850 (NA Microfilm Publication M432, Roll 697); RG 29; https://familysearch.org/ark:/61903/1:1:MXQM-HXF.

Letters Received by the Office of the Adjutant General Main Series, 1822–60: (NA Microfilm Publication M567); RG 94.

Logs of U.S. Naval Ships, 1801–1915: Logs of Ships and Stations, 1801–1946, Records of the Bureau of Naval Personnel; RG 24.

Old War Invalid Pension Application File No. 2995, Pension Certificate No. 7739: Frederick W. Binder, Captain, Company E, 1st Pennsylvania Regiment.

Records of the Adjutant General's Office, 1780sÐ1917: 4th Regiment, Roll 25, 1831–40, Roll 26, 1840–50); RG 94.

Records Regarding Enlisted Men Who Served in the Navy, 1842–85: Bureau of Navigation, Records of the Bureau of Naval Personnel; RG 24.

Rub, Gottlob, 182 [handwritten], line 33 (February 4, 1840): Descriptive and Historical Register of Enlistments in the U.S. Army, 1798–1914, Records of the Adjutant General's Office, 1780s–1917, (NA Microfilm Publication M233); RG 94.

Rupp family: 294A [stamped], lines 13–18, Lancaster North West Ward, Lancaster County, Pa., *Seventh Census of the United States,* 1850 (NA Microfilm Publication M432, Roll 788); RG 29.

Rupp family: 144 [handwritten], lines 36–40, 145, line 1, Washington Ward 7, District of Columbia, *Eighth Census of the United States,* 1860 (NA Microfilm Publication M653, Roll 102); RG 29.

Rupp family: *Petronella* Passenger Manifest, November 15, 1836; 1041B [stamped on reverse side], lines 13–18, 46; Passenger Lists of Vessels Arriving at New York, 1820–97 (NA Microfilm Publication M237, Roll 32), Records of the U.S. Customs Service; RG 36.

Soldier's Certificate No. 7739 (File No. 2995): Frederick W. Binder, Captain, Company E, 1st Pennsylvania Volunteers, Mexican War; Case Files of Pension Applications Based on Death or Disability Incurred in the Mexican War ("Old Wars"), 1847–1930; Case Files of Pension Applications Based on Death or Disability Incurred in Service Between 1783 and 1861 ("Old Wars"), Records of the Department of Veterans Affairs, Record Group 15.

Pennsylvania State Archives, Harrisburg
    Schultz, John R. Journal (December 9, 1846–January 8, 1848). Diaries and Jour-
        nals Collection, MG-6.
Philadelphia Department of Records, City Archives
    Clerk of Criminal Sessions, Docket, RG 23.1
    Clerk of Criminal Sessions, Forfeited Recognizances, RG 23.3
    Clerk of Criminal Sessions, Minute Book, RG 23.2
    County Recorder's Court, RG 26.1 Equity Docket, RG 20.5
    Court Dockets 1836–40, 1845–46
    Mayor's Court Docket, RG 130.1
    Mayor's Grand Petit Juror's Docket, RG 130.4
    Mayor's Minute Books, RG 130.2
    Proceedings in Equity, RG 20.19
    Prothonotary of District Court, Appearance Docket, RG 22.1
    Prothonotary of District Court, Debits, Single Bill, RG 22.14
    Prothonotary of District Court, RG 22.18
    Quarter Sessions, Bills of Indictments, RG 21.46
    Quarter Sessions, Minute Book, RG 21.4
    Quarter Sessions, Oyer and Terminer Docket, RG 21.3
    Registration Commission, Insolvency Petitions, 1836–40, 1845–46, RG 20.30
University of North Carolina, Louis Round Wilson Special Collections Library, Southern
    Historical Collection
    D. H. Hill Diary, #00882.
University of Texas–Arlington Special Collections
    Brown, Alex, and Chauncey Brown. Mexican War letters, 1846–48. U.S.-Mexico
        War Collections, GA51. http://library.uta.edu/usmexicowar/item.php?content
        _id=294.
Virginia Historical Society, Richmond, Virginia
    George Bolling Lee papers, 1841–68, Mss1 L5114.
    DeButts-Ely family papers, Mss1 L51c.
    Talcott family papers, Mss1 T1434.

NEWSPAPERS

Age (Philadelphia)
Allgemeine Forst-und Jagdzeitung (Germany)
Allgemeiner Zeitung von und für Bayern (Bavaria)
Army and Navy Chronicle
Commercial Advertiser (New York, N.Y.)
Congressional Globe
Critic-Record (Washington, D.C.)
Evening Star (Washington, D.C.)
Heilbronner Intelligenz-Blatt (Heilbronn, Germany)
Ludwigsburger Tagblatt (Ludwigsburg, Germany)
Monroe Democrat (Rochester, N.Y.)
Newark Daily Advertiser

New Hampshire Gazette
New York Daily Tribune
Niles' National Register
North American (Philadelphia)
Oakland Tribune
Pennsylvanische Staats-Zeitung (Harrisburg, Pa., German newspaper)
Philadelphia Demokrat (German newspaper)
Philadelphia Inquirer
Philadelphia Volksblatt (German newspaper)
Public Ledger (Philadelphia)
Regensburger Zeitung (Regensburg, Germany)
Schwäbische Chronik (Stuttgart, Germany)
Trenton State Gazette
Vedette (Washington, D.C.)

PUBLISHED SOURCES

Adjutant General's Office. Regulations for the Uniform and Dress of the Army of the United States (June 1839). http://www.history.army.mil/reference/1839U.htm.
Anderson, Robert. *An Artillery Officer in the Mexican War 1846–7: Letters of Robert Anderson.* New York: G. P. Putnam's Sons, 1911.
Ballentine, George. *Autobiography of an English Soldier in the United States Army....* New York: String & Townsend, 1853.
Bates, Samuel H. *History of Pennsylvania Volunteers, 1861–5; Prepared in Compliance with Acts of the Legislature.* Vol. 3. Harrisburg: B. Singerly, 1870. http://www.pacivilwar.com/bates.html.
Bauer, K. Jack. *The Mexican War 1846–1848.* New York: Macmillan, 1974.
———. *Surfboats and Horse Marines: U.S. Naval Operations in the Mexican War, 1846–48.* Annapolis: United States Naval Institute, 1969.
Becker, Monika. *Kriminalität, Herrschaft und Gesellschaft im Königreich Württemberg.* Freiburg i. Br., Germany: edition iuscrim, 2001.
Blackwood, Emma Jerome, ed. *To Mexico with Scott: Letters of Captain E. Kirby Smith to His Wife.* Cambridge, Mass.: Harvard University Press, 1917.
Block, Eugene B. *Science vs Crime: The Evolution of the Police Lab.* San Francisco: Craigmont Publications, 1979.
Bösken, Clemens-Peter. *Das Ende der großen rheinischen Räuber- und Mörderbande.* Erfurt: Sutton Verlag, 2011.
Brandt, Hartwig. *Parlamentarismus in Württemberg, 1819–1870, Anatomie eines deutschen Landtags.* Düsseldorf: Droste, 1987.
Bronner, Johann Philipp. *Der Weinbau im Königreich Württemberg.* Zweite Abteilung. Heidelberg: Universitätshandlung von C. F. Winter, 1837.
Brunner, Bernd. *Nach Amerika: Die Geschichte der deutschen Auswanderung.* Munich: C. H. Beck, 2009.
Bullitt, Thomas W. "Lee and Scott." *Southern Historical Society Papers* 11 (1883): 443–54.
Campbell, Randolph B. *Gone to Texas: A History of the Lone Star State.* Oxford: Oxford University Press, 2003.

Cast, Friederich. *Historisches und genealogisches Adelsbuch des Königreiches Württemberg.* . . . Stuttgart: J. A. Gärtner, 1839.

Churchill, Winston. *The Great Democracies.* Vol. 4 of *A History of the English-Speaking Peoples.* London: Cassill and Company, 1958.

Clark, Donald A. *The Notorious "Bull" Nelson: Murdered Civil War General.* Carbondale: Southern Illinois University Press, 2011.

Clark, Paul C., Jr., and Edward H. Moseley. "D-Day Veracruz 1847—A Grand Design." *Joint Force Quarterly* 10 (Winter 1995–96): 102–15. http://www.dtic.mil/dtic/tr/fulltext/u2/a528542.pdf.

Clary, David A. *Eagles and Empire: The United States, Mexico, and the Struggle for a Continent.* New York: Bantam Books, 2009.

Clement, Werner, ed. *Schwaigern: Heimatbuch der Stadt Schwaigern mit den Teilorten Massenbach, Stetten a. H. und Niederhofen.* Schwaigern, Germany: Stadtverwaltung, 1994.

Complete History of the Late Mexican War. . . . New York: F. J. Dow, 1850.

Connelly, Thomas L. *The Marble Man: Robert E. Lee and His Image in American Society.* New York: Alfred A. Knopf, 1977.

Conner, Philip Syng Physick. *The Home Squadron under Commodore Conner in the Mexican War.* N.p.: N.p., 1896.

Conway, James, and David F. Jamroz. *Detroit's Historic Fort Wayne.* Charleston, S.C.: Arcadia Publishing, 2007. Google Books version. https://books.google.de/books?id=_sanOKkhcoUC&pg=PA6&lpg=PA6&dq=Detroit%E2%80%99s+Historic+Fort+Wayne+Jamroz&source=bl&ots=8BYXqO_d9N&sig=05IXIicIfv9safDGvBwP3aFBKH4&hl=de&sa=X&ved=oahUKEwjf692cpsLKAhUBgBoKHbzYB5sQ6AEIMjAD#v=onepage&q=Detroit%E2%80%99s%20Historic%20Fort%20Wayne%20Jamroz&f=false.

Crocker, H. W., III. *Robert E. Lee on Leadership: Executive Lessons in Character, Courage, and Vision.* New York: Three Rivers Press, 1999.

Cuthbert, Norma B. "To Molly: Five Early Letters from Robert E. Lee to His Wife 1832–1835." *Huntington Library Quarterly* 15, no. 3 (May 1952): 257–76. http://www.jstor.org/stable/3816356?seq=1#page_scan_tab_contents.

Dalkowski, Sebastian. "Die Retter des Abendbrots." *Der Tagesspiegel,* November 2, 2012. http://www.tagesspiegel.de/weltspiegel/essen-trinken/essen-und-trinken-die-retter-des-abendbrots/7339700.html.

Dana, Napoleon Jackson Tecumseh. *Monterrey Is Ours! The Mexican War Letters of Lieutenant Dana 1845–1847.* Edited by Robert H. Ferrell. Lexington: University Press of Kentucky, 1990. https://books.google.de/books?id=nLEfBgAAQBAJ&pg=PA198&lpg=PA198&dq=#v=onepage&q&f=false.

Dyer, Alexander B. "Fourth Regiment of Artillery." *Journal of the Military Service Institution* 11 (1890): 843–68.

Ehrensperger, Vera. *Besigheimer Häuserbuch.* Besigheim: Stadt Besigheim, 1993.

Eppenauer. *Ueber den Kometen Halley und seine bisherigen Erscheinungen.* Bamberg, Germany: Literarisch-Artistische Institut, 1846.

An Eye-Witness. "The Capture of Vera Cruz." *The Knickerbocker* 30 (July 1847): 1–8.

Feuerbach, Paul Johann Anselm von. *Aktenmäßige Darstellung merkwürdiger Verbrechen,* 3rd ed. 1811. Aalen, Germany: Scientia, 1984.

Fischer, Hermann Eberhard. *Behandlung der Schusswunden.* Vol. 2 of *Handbuch der Kriegschirurgie.* Vol. 17b of *Deutsche Chirurgie.* Stuttgart: Ferdinand Enke, 1882.

————. *Uebersicht der Gesamtliteratur der Kriegschirurgie.* Vol. 1 of *Handbuch der Kriegschirurgie.* Vol. 17a of *Deutsche Chirurgie.* Stuttgart: Ferdinand Enke, 1882.

Foos, Paul. *A Short, Offhand, Killing Affair: Soldiers and Social Conflict during the Mexican-American War.* Chapel Hill: University of North Carolina Press, 2002.

Forry, Samuel. *The Climate of the United States and Its Endemic Influences.* . . . New-York: J. & H. G. Langley, 1842.

Franck, Salamo. "Auf meinen Jesum will ich sterben." Lyrics in *Württembergisches Gesangbuch zum Gebrauch für Kirchen und Schulen.* Stuttgart: Hof- und Kanzleidrücker Cottas Erben, 1819.

Freeman, Douglas Southall. *R. E. Lee: A Biography.* Vol. 1. New York: Charles Scribner's Sons, 1942.

Frevert, Ute. *Die kasernierte Nation: Militärdienst und Zivilgesellschaft in Deutschland.* Munich: C. H. Beck, 2001.

Frost, J. *The Mexican War and Its Warriors.* . . . New Haven, Conn.: H. Mansfield, 1850.

Furber, George C. *The Twelve Months Volunteer; or, Journal of a Private in the Tennessee Regiment of Cavalry, in the Campaign, in Mexico, 1846–7.* . . . Cincinnati: J. A. & U. P. James, 1850.

Gammel, H. P. N. *The Laws of Texas, 1822–1897.* Vol. 1. Austin: Gammel Book, 1898.

Glaser, J., and R. Nowak, eds. "Strafsache: Mord oder Totschlag?" *Allgemeine österreichische Gerichts-Zeitung* 18, no. 74 (September 13, 1867): 300–302. http://anno .onb.ac.at/cgi-content/anno?aid=aog&datum=18670913&zoom=33.

Goltdammer, Theodor, ed. *Archiv für Preußisches Strafrecht.* Vol. 8. Berlin: Verlag der königlichen Geheimen Ober-Hofbuchdrückerei R. Decker, 1860.

Goodman, David. *Spanish Naval Power, 1589–1665: Reconstruction and Defeat.* Cambridge: Cambridge University Press, 1997.

Grant, Ulysses S. *Personal Memoirs of U. S. Grant.* New York: Charles L. Webster & Company, 1885–86.

Greenberg, Amy S. *A Wicked War: Polk, Clay, Lincoln, and the 1846 U.S. Invasion of Mexico.* New York: Alfred A. Knopf, 2012.

Grone, Carl von, and A. C. E. Grone. *Brief über Nord-Amerika und Mexiko und den zwischen beiden geführten Krieg.* Braunschweig, Germany: George Westermann, 1850. Reprint, British Library Historical Print Editions.

Groß, Dominik. *Die Entwicklung der innerlichen und äusseren Leichenschau in historischer und ethischer Sicht.* Würzburg: Königshausen & Neumann, 2002.

Gross, Hanns. *Handbuch der Untersuchungsrichter als System der Kriminalistik.* Dritte Vermehrte Auflage, Graz, Austria: Leuschner & Lubensky's Universitäts-Buchhandlung, 1899.

Gundert. *Rede am Grabe des Herrn Eduard von Hammer.* Esslingen, Germany: A. Mann, 1850.

Gürth, Peter. *Alte Heimat, Neue Welt: Nordamerika-Auswanderer aus Baden-Württemberg.* Tübingen, Germany: Silberburg Verlag, 2012.

Gwinner, Wilhelm Heinrich. *Die Königlich Württembergische Forstdienst-Prüfungen von 1818 bis 1830.* . . . Stuttgart: Metzler, 1830.

Gwynne, S. C. *Empire of the Summer Moon.* New York: Scribner, 2010.

Hackenburg, Randy W. *Pennsylvania in the War with Mexico: The Volunteer Regiments.* Shippensburg, Pa.: White Mane Publishing Company, 1992.

Hahn, Christoph Ulrich. *Beschreibung des Kantons Appenzell mit besonderen Rücksicht auf seine Kuranstalten.* Heilbronn, Germany: J. D. Claß, 1827.

———. *Rede nach der Beerdigung des durch Mörderhand den Seinigen entrissenen Stadtschultheissen J. H. Rieber.* Nürtingen, Germany: J. S. Senner, 1835.

Hammer, Eduard. "Ueber den Zustand der Rechtspflege bei den Ortsobrigkeiten in Württemberg." *Jahrbücher der Gesetzgebung und Rechtspflege* 2, no. 3 (1826): 311–28.

Hartman, G. W. *A Private's Own Journal.* . . . Greencastle, Pa.: E. Robinson, 1849.

Hartmann, Carl Friedrich Alexander. *Populäres Handbuch über die allgemeine Technologie.* Vol. 1. Berlin: Verlag der Buchhandlung Carl Friedrich Amelang, 1841.

Hatch, Alden. *Heroes of Annapolis.* New York: Julian Messner, 1943.

Haumer, Stefanie. "1863: The Creation of the First National Society and the Beginning of the Movement's History." *International Review of the Red Cross* 94, no. 888 (Winter 2012): 1–9. doi:10.1017/S1816383113000386.

Heard, Brian J. *Handbook of Firearms and Ballistics: Examining and Interpreting Forensic Evidence.* 2nd ed. Chichester, West Sussex: Wiley & Sons, 2008.

Helbich, Wolfgang. "German Immigrants in the American Civil War." In *The German Presence in the U.S.A.*, edited by Josef Raab and Jan Wirrer, 165–88. Berlin: Lit Verlag, 2008.

Henderson, Thomas. *Hints on the Medical Examination of Recruits for the Army and on the Discharge of Soldiers from the Service on Surgeon's Certificate.* 1840. Rev. ed. Philadelphia: J. B. Lippincott, 1856.

Herschel, John F. W. *Results of Astronomical Observations Made During the Years 1834,5,6,7,8, at the Cape of Good Hope.* London: Smith, Elder & Co., Cornhill: 1847.

Hitchcock, Ethan Allen. *Fifty Years in Camp and Field: Diary of Major-General Ethan Allen Hitchcock.* Edited by W. A. Croffut. New York: G. P. Putnam's Sons, 1909.

Hitzig, Julius Eduard, ed. *Annalen der deutschen und ausländischen Criminal-Rechtspflege.* 73 vols. Berlin: Dümmler, 1818–35; Altenburg, Germany: Pierer 1837–40; Leipzig: Hermann Theodor Schletter, 1840–55.

Hitzig, Julius Eduard, and W. Alexis Häring, eds. *Der neue Pitaval: eine Sammlung der interessantesten Criminalgeschichten aller Länder aus älterer und neuerer Zeit.* 36 vols. Leipzig: Brockhaus, 1842–90.

Horn, Ernst, Friedrich Nasse, and Wilhelm Wagner, *Vollständiges Universal-Register des Archives für Medizinische Erfahrung.* Berlin: G. Riemer, 1832.

Hughes, Nathaniel Cheairs, Jr., and Timothy D. Johnson, eds. *A Fighter from Way Back: The Mexican War Diary of Lt. Daniel Harvey Hill, 4th Artillery.* Kent, Ohio: Kent State University Press, 2002.

Jones, J. William. *Life and Letters of Robert Edward Lee, Soldier and Man.* 1906. Reprint, Big Byte Books: 2014.

Kappler, Friedrich. *Handbuch der Literatur des Criminalrechts und dessen philosophischer und medizinischer Hülfwissenschaften.* Stuttgart: J. Scheible's Buchhandlung, 1838.

Kemp, L. W. "Battle of San Jacinto." Texas State Historical Association, Handbook of Texas. Last modified December 4, 2015. https://tshaonline.org/handbook/online/articles/qes04.

Kendall, George Wilkins. *Dispatches from the Mexican War.* Edited by Lawrence Delbert Cress. Norman: University of Oklahoma Press, 1999.

Kesper-Biermann, Sylvia. *Einheit und Recht: Strafgesetzgebung und Kriminalrechtsexperten in Deutschland vom Beginn des 19. Jahrhunderts bis zum Reichsstrafgesetzbuch 1871.* Frankfurt a.M.: Vittorio Klostermann, 2009.

Kies, Otfried. "Der Wolf ist tot! Die Erlegung des letzten Wolfs in Württemberg." *Ganerbenblätter der Historischen Gesellschaft Bönnigheim* 20 (1997): 46–57.

Kitchen, D. C. *Record of the Wyoming Artillerists.* Tunkhannock, Pa.: Alvin Day, 1874.

Königlich-Württembergisches Hof- und Staatshandbuch. Stuttgart: Joh. Friedr. Steinkopf, 1831, 1835, and 1843.

Königliches Finanz-Ministerium. *Instruktionen für die königlichen Forstwarthe und Waldschützen.* Stuttgart: N.p., 1822.

Königliches statistisch-topographisches Bureau. *Beschreibung des Oberamts Besigheim.* 1853. Reprint, Stuttgart: Verlag für Kultur und Wissenschaft Bissinger, 1962.

———. *Beschreibung des Oberamts Brackenheim.* 1873. Reprint, Stuttgart: Verlag für Kultur und Wissenschaft Bissinger, 1976.

Korda, Michael. *Clouds of Glory: The Life and Legend of Robert E. Lee.* New York: Success Research Corporation, Harper Collins, 2014. Kindle edition.

Kraft, B. "Kritisches zur gerichtlichen Schußuntersuchung." *Archiv für Kriminologie* 87 (1930): 133–77.

Kurz, Josef, Kurt Sartorius, Werner Holbein, and Dieter Gerlinger. *Die wechselvolle Geschichte einer Ganerbenstadt Bönnigheim.* Bönnigheim, Germany: Stadt Bönnigheim, 1984.

Lacassagne, Alexandre. "De la déformation des balles de revolver, soit dans l'arme, soit sur le squelette." *Archives de l'anthropologie criminelle* 4, no. 19 (1889): 70–79. https://criminocorpus.org/fr/ref/114/1987/.

Laennec, R. T. H. *Treatise on the Diseases of the Chest and on Mediate Auscultation.* 3rd rev. ed. Translated by John Forbes. London: Thomas & George Underwood, 1829.

Langbein, John H. *Prosecuting Crime in the Renaissance: England, Germany, France.* Cambridge, Mass.: Harvard University Press, 1974.

———. *Torture and the Law of Proof.* Chicago: University of Chicago Press, 1977.

La Roche, Sophie von. *"Ich bin mehr Herz als Kopf": Ein Lebensbild in Briefen.* Edited by Michael Maurer. Munich: Verlag C. H. Beck, 1983.

Linck, Otto. "Der Wolf von Cleebronn." *Zeitschrift des Zabergäuvereins* 2 (1955): 17–20.

Lloyd, J. A. "An Account of an Observatory Constructed at the Mauritius: Communicated by Sir J. Herschel." *Monthly Notices of the Royal Astronomical Society* 3, no. 22 (April 8, 1836): 187–90.

Long, A. L. *Memoirs of Robert E. Lee.* New York: J. M. Stoddart, 1887.

Mansfeld, Edward Deering. *The Mexican War: A History of Its Origin.* 10th ed. New York: A. S. Barnes, 1849.

Mayer, Brantz. *Mexico as It Was and as It Is.* Philadelphia, Pa.: G. B. Zieber, 1847.

McCaffrey, James M. *Army of Manifest Destiny: The American Soldier in the Mexican War 1846–1847.* New York: New York University Press, 1992.

McCrery, Nigel. *Silent Witnesses: A History of Forensic Science.* London: Random House, 2013.

McElroy's Philadelphia City Directory. Philadelphia, Pa.: E. C. & J. Biddle, 1845, 1847, and 1858.

McLaughlin, Shaun J. *The Patriot War Along the New York-Canada Border: Raiders and Rebels.* Charleston: History Press, 2012.

McWilliams, Joseph. "A Westmoreland Guard in Mexico, 1847–1848: The Journal of William Joseph McWilliams." Edited by John William Larner Jr. *Western Pennsylvania Historical Magazine* 52, no. 3 (July 1969): 213–40.

Meade, George Gordon: *The Life and Letters of George Gordon Meade, Major-General of the United States Army*. New York: Charles Scribner's Sons, 1913.

Meighörner, Jeannine. *"Was ich als Frau dafür halte": Sophie von La Roche; Deutschlands erste Bestsellerautorin*. Erfurt: Sutton Verlag, 2006.

Mims, Forrest. "Weather Records from the Siege of the Alamo." San Antonio's home page. Last modified February 28, 2012. http://www.mysanantonio.com/life/article/Weather-records-from-the-siege-of-the-Alamo-3365437.php.

Mittermaier, C. J. A. *Die Lehre vom Beweise im deutschen Strafprozesse*. Darmstadt: Hohann Wilhelm Heyer's Verlagshandlung, 1834.

Montero, Pablo. "Guerra, Navagación y Piratería." In *San Juan de Ulúa: Puerta de la Historia*. Vol. 1. Veracruz [?]: Instituto Nacional de Antropología e Historia/Internacional de Contendedores Asociados de Veracruz, 1996.

Montgomery, Thomas Lynch, ed. *Pennsylvania Archives: Sixth Series*. Vol. 10. Harrisburg, Pa.: Harrisburg Publishing, State Printer, 1907.

Moody, John A., Robert H. Meade, and David R. Jones. *Lewis and Clark's Observations and Measurements of Geomorphology and Hydrology, and Changes of Time*. Circular 1246. Reston, Va.: U.S. Department of the Interior, U.S. Geological Survey, 2003.

Moore, H. Judge. *Scott's Campaign in Mexico*. Charleston: J. B. Nixon, 1849.

Müller, Corinna. *Um Kopf und Kragen: Historische Kriminalfälle der frühen Neuzeit im heutigen Württemberg*. Heidelberg: verlag regionalkultur, 2011.

———. *Verurteilt: Historische Kriminalfälle aus Alt-Württemberg*. Erfurt: Sutton Verlag, 2014.

Norris, Walter Biscoe. *Westmoreland County, Virginia, 1653–1983*. Westmoreland County, Va.: Westmoreland County Board of Supervisors, 1983.

Ordinances and Joint Resolutions of the Select and Common Councils of the Consolidated City of Philadelphia as Passed by Them and Approved by the Mayor, from January First to December Thirty-First, 1858. Philadelphia, Pa.: Bicking & Guilbert, 1858.

Orr, William J., and Robert Ryal Miller. "Introduction." In *An Immigrant Soldier in the Mexican War* by Frederick Zeh. Translated by William J. Orr. College Station: Texas A&M University Press, 1995.

Oswandel, J. Jacob. *Notes of the Mexican War 1846–47–48*. Rev. ed. Philadelphia, Pa.: N.p., 1885.

Parker, William Harwar. *Recollections of a Naval Officer*. 1883. Reprint, Annapolis: Naval Institute Press, 1985.

Payne-James, Jason, and Margaret Stark. "Clinical Forensic Medicine: History and Development." In *Clinical Forensic Medicine: A Physician's Guide*, 3rd ed., edited by Margaret Stark, 1–44. New York: Humana Press, 2011.

Peña, José Enrique de la. *With Santa Anna in Texas: A Personal Narrative*. Translated and edited by Carmen Perry. Expanded ed. College Station: Texas A&M University Press, 1999.

Pérez-Mallaína, Pablo E. *Spain's Men of the Sea: Daily Life in the Indies Fleets in the Sixteenth Century*. Translated by Carla Rahn Phillips. Baltimore: Johns Hopkins University Press, 1998. https://books.google.de/books?id=Cn-htZjQm8oC&p

g=PA228&lpg=PA228&dq=Spain%E2%80%99s+Men+of+the+Sea&source=b
l&ots=-QM9PGRwTT&sig=qdWbmfEyGdFeEVjFtnizj2LtTS4&hl=de&sa=
X&ved=0ahUKEwjrv6GU78TKAhVBmw4KHXwzAuoQ6AEIaDAO#v=onep
age&q=Spain%E2%80%99s%20Men%20of%20the%20Sea&f=false.

Peskin, Allan. *Winfield Scott and the Profession of Arms*. Kent, Ohio: Kent State University Press, 2003.

Peskin, Allan, ed. *Volunteers: The Mexican War Journals of Private Richard Coulter and Sergeant Thomas Barclay, Company E, Second Pennsylvania Infantry*. Kent, Ohio: Kent State University Press, 1991.

Peters, Edward. *Folter: Geschichte der Peinlichen Befragung*. 1985. Translated by Jobst German. Hamburg: Europäische Verlagsanstalt, 2003.

Pflieger, Klaus, ed. *Die Geschichte(n) der württembergischen Staatsanwaltschaften*. Vaihingen/Enz, Germany: IPa Verlag, 2009.

Pierer, Heinrich August. *Universal-Lexikon*. Altenburg: Literatur Comptoir, 1835.

Pryor, Elizabeth Brown. *Reading the Man: A Portrait of Robert E. Lee Through His Private Letters*. New York: Penguin Books, 2007.

Quellmalz, Alfred. "D. Dr. Christoph Ulrich Hahn." In *Lebensbild aus Schwaben und Franken*. Vol. 8, 176–211. Stuttgart: W. Kohlhammer, 1962.

Rattermann, Heinrich Armin. "General August Moor, Part IV Mexico." *Der deutsche Pionier* 16 (1884–85): 482–512.

Reilly, Tom. *War with Mexico! America's Reporters Cover the Battlefront*. Edited by Manley Witten. Lawrence: University Press of Kansas, 2010.

Richardson, R. S. "An Attempt to Determine the Mass of Pluto from Its Disturbing Effect on Halley's Comet." *Publications of the Astronomical Society of the Pacific* 54, no. 31 (1942): 19–23. http://adsabs.harvard.edu/full/1942PASP...54...19R.

Rollwagen, Christoph. "Halley (1986): Begleiter der Jahrhunderte." Astro Corner. Last modified June 9, 2010. http://www.astrocorner.de/index/02_wissen/01_kosmologie/01_sonnensystem/06_kometen/1p.php.

Rosengarten, J. G. *The German Soldier in the Wars of the United States*. 2nd ed. Philadelphia, Pa.: Lippincott, 1890.

Sargent, Chauncey Forward. *Gathering Laurels in Mexico: The Diary of an American Soldier in the Mexican American War*. Edited by Ann Brown Janes. Lincoln, Mass.: Cottage Press, 1990.

Sauer, Paul. *Im Namen des Königs: Strafgesetzgebung und Strafvollzug im Königreich Württemberg von 1806 bis 1871*. Stuttgart: Konrad Theiss Verlag, 1984.

Schaaf, Fred. *Comet of the Century: From Halley to Hale-Bopp*. New York: Springer, 1997.

Schäffer, M., ed. *Archiv für practische Rechtswissenschaft*. Vol. 1. Regensburg, Germany: G. Jospeh Manz, 1852.

Scharf, Thomas. *History of Philadelphia: 1609–1884*. Vol. 1. Philadelphia: L. H. Everts, 1884.

Schild, Wolfgang. "Geschichte des Verfahrens." In *Justiz in alter Zeit*, edited by Ch. Hickeldey, 129–224. Rotherburg o.d.T.: Mittelalterliches Kriminalmuseum, 1984.

———. *"Von peinlicher Frag": Die Folter als rechtliches Beweisverfahren*. Rothenburg o.d.T.: Schriftenreihe des Mittelalterlichen Kriminalmuseums Nr. 4, [1999?].

Schmal, Helmut. "Verpflanzt, aber nicht entwurzelt: Die Auswanderung aus Hessen-Darmstadt (Provinz Rheinhessen) nach Wisconsin im 19. Jahrhundert."

Vol. 1 of *Meinzer Studien zur Neueren Geschichte*. Frankfurt a.M.: Peter Lang, Europäischer Verlag der Wissenschaften, 2000.

Schmidlin, Johann Gottlieb. *Handbuch der württembergischen Forst-Gesetzgebung, oder systematische Zusammenstellung aller über das Jagd-, Fischerey- und Holz-Wesen.* Vol. 1. Stuttgart: Metzler, 1822.

Schrag, Zachary M. "Nativist Riots of 1844." *Encyclopedia of Greater Philadelphia*. Dated 2013. http://philadelphiaencyclopedia.org/archive/nativist-riots-of-1844/.

Schuler, Hans-Karl, Jürgern Häußermann, and Joachim Winter. *Zur Geschichte des Forstberufs und der forstlichen Ausbildung.* Vol. 18 of *Schriftenreiher der Fachhochschule Rottenburg*. Rottenburg a.N., Germany: Fachhochschule Rottenburg, Hochschule für Forstwirtschaft, 2004.

Schultz, Ronald, and Eugen Heck. *Ensinger Bilderbogen.* Ensingen, Germany: Gemeinde Ensingen, 1971.

Schulz, Thomas. "Aus der Geschichte des Oberamts Besigheim." *Ludwigsburger Geschichtsblätter* 64 (2010): 151–80.

Scott, Winfield. *Memoirs of Lieut.-General Scott, LL.D., Written by Himself.* New York: Sheldon, 1864.

Semmes, Raphael. *The Campaign of General Scott in the Valley of Mexico.* Cincinnati: Moore & Anderson, 1852. https://play.google.com/books/reader?id=rAsTAAA AYAAJ&printsec=frontcover&output=reader&hl=en_GB&pg=GBS.PA25.

———. *Service Afloat and Ashore During the Mexican War.* Cincinnati: Wm. H. Moore, 1851.

Singer, Samuel. *Lexikon der Sprichwörter des romanisch-germanischen Mittelalters.* Vol. 11. Berlin: Walter de Gruyter, 2001.

Smith, Gustavus W. *Company "A," Corps of Engineers, U.S.A., 1846–1848 in the Mexican War.* N.p.: Battalion Press, 1896.

Smith, Justin H. *The War with Mexico.* Vol. II. New York: Macmillan Company, 1919.

Stadler, Hans, and Udo Wilken. *Pädagogik bei Körperbehinderung.* Vol. 4 of *Studientext zur Geschichte der Behindertenpädagogik.* Weinheim, Germany: Beltz Verlag, 2004.

Starr, Douglas. *The Killer of Little Shepherds: A True Story and the Birth of Forensic Science.* New York: Alfred A. Knopf, 2010.

Steele, Lisa. "Ballistics." In *Science for Lawyers,* edited by Eric Yorke Drogin, 1–20. Chicago: American Bar Association, 2008.

Stierle, Herman. "Die Auswanderer aus Bönnigheim seit dem 18. Jahrhundert." *Ganerbenblätter* 23/24 (2000/2001): 40–68.

Taylor, Frank H. *Philadelphia in the Civil War: 1861–1865.* Philadelphia: City of Philadelphia, 1913.

Texas Declaration of Independence. Republic of Texas, 1836. Texas State Library and Archives Commission. https://www.tsl.texas.gov/treasures/republic/declare-01.html.

Thomas, Emory M. *Robert E. Lee: A Biography.* New York: W. W. Norton & Co., 1995.

Thomas, Hugh. *Rivers of Gold: The Rise of the Spanish Empire.* London: Weidenfeld & Nicolson, 2003.

Thorwald, Jürgen. *Das Jahrhundert der Detektive: Weg und Abenteuer der Kriminalistik.* Zurich: Droemer, 1964.

Tortora, Gerard J. *Principles of Human Anatomy.* 4th ed. New York: Harper & Row, 1986.

"Treaties of Velasco." Texas State Historical Association, Handbook of Texas. Uploaded June 15, 2010. http://www.tshaonline.org/handbook/online/articles/mgt05.

Treaty of Velasco (Public and Private). Republic of Texas-Mexico, May 14, 1836. Texas Independence: The Treaties of Velasco. http://www.upa.pdx.edu/IMS/currentprojects/TAHv3/Content/PDFs/Velasco_Texas_Treaties.pdf.

Tucker, Spencer D., James Arnold, Roberta Wiener, Paul G. Pierpaoli, Thomas W. Cutrer, and Pedro Santoni, eds. *The Encyclopedia of the Mexican-American War: A Political, Social, and Military History.* Santa Barbara, Calif.: ABC-CLIO, 2013.

Urwin, Gregory J. W. *The United States Infantry: An Illustrated History; 1775–1918.* 1988. Reprint, Norman: University of Oklahoma Press, 2000.

U.S. Department of State, Office of the Historian, "A Guide to the United States' History of Recognition, Diplomatic, and Consular Relations, by Country, since 1776: Württemberg." http://history.state.gov/countries/wurttemberg.

Verhandlung in der Versammlung der Landstände des Königreichs Württemberg. Vol. 8. Stuttgart [?]: N.p., 1815.

Viereck, J. C. *Captain F. W. Binder's Quick Step, Arranged for the Piano Forte.* No. 6, op. 77. Philadelphia, Pa.: A Fiot, 1848.

Wagner, E. J. *The Science of Sherlock Holmes: From Baskerville Hall to the Valley of Fear, the Real Forensics Behind the Great Detective's Greatest Cases.* Hoboken, N.J.: John Wiley & Sons, 2006.

Waskie, Anthony. *Philadelphia and the Civil War: Arsenal of the Union.* Charleston: History Press, 2011. Kindle version.

Watson, A. D. "Halley's Comet and Its Approaching Return." *Journal of the Royal Canadian Astronomy Society* 3 (1909): 210–19. http://adsabs.harvard.edu/full/1909JRASC . . . 3..210W.

Weigley, Russell F. *History of the United States Army.* New York: Macmillan Company, 1967.

Winders, Richard Bruce. *Mr. Polk's Army: The American Military Experience in the Mexican War.* College Station: Texas A&M University Press, 1997.

Yates, Bernice-Marie. *The Perfect Gentleman: The Life and Letters and George Washington Custis Lee.* Vol. 1. N.p.: Xulon Press, 2003.

Young, John Russell, ed. *Memorial History of the City of Philadelphia.* Vol. 2. New York: New York History Company, 1898.

Zeh, Frederick. "Erinnerungen eines alten Artilleristen aus dem mexikanischen Kriege vom 1846–1848." *Der Deutsche Pioneer* 13, no. 2 (1881): 56–63. http://www.nausa.uni-oldenburg.de/pionier/j13/ho2/009.html.

———. *An Immigrant Soldier in the Mexican War.* Translated by William J. Orr. College Station: Texas A&M University Press, 1995.

Zweiter Jahres-Bericht über die Armen-Anstalt für Verkrümmte im Paulinen-Institute zu Stuttgart. Stuttgart: Königliche Hofbuchdruckerei, 1847.

CONVERSIONS

MONETARY CONVERSIONS ARE BASED ON
Deutsche Bundesbank Eurosystem, "Kaufkraftäquivalente historischer Beträge in deutschen Währungen." http://www.bundesbank.de/Redaktion/DE/Downloads

/Statistiken/Unternehmen_Und_Private_Haushalte/Preise/kaufkraftaequiv
alente_historischer_betraege_in_deutschen_waehrungen.pdf?__blob=publi
cationFile.

Internal Revenue Service. "Yearly Average Currency Exchange Rates Translating Foreign Currency into U.S. Dollars." http://www.irs.gov/Individuals/International
-Taxpayers/Yearly-Average-Currency-Exchange-Rates.

CONVERSIONS OF LENGTH, VOLUME, AND WEIGHT ARE BASED ON

von Hippel, Wolfgang. *Maß und Gewicht im Gebiet des Königreichs Württemberg und
der Fürstentümer Hollenzollern am Ende des 18. Jahrhunderts.* Stuttgart: W. Kohlhammer Verlag, 2000.

Index